The Story of Investment Companies

ROBERT FLEMING

The Story of Investment Companies

By HUGH BULLOCK

Columbia University Press New York

First printing 1959

Second printing 1960

Library of Congress Catalog Card Number: 59-13778

Published in Great Britain, India, and Pakistan
by the Oxford University Press
London, Bombay, and Karachi

Manufactured in the United States of America

To Pretty Marie

Preface

THIS IS THE STORY of investment companies. Since it is written primarily for American readers and treats extensively of the American scene, it might well be termed the story of American investment companies—from the genuine initiation of the movement in the early 1920s, over the subsequent period of almost four decades. Appropriate space, however, is devoted to an understanding of our British ancestors, the famous English and Scottish investment trust companies, as well as mention of comparable entities in certain other countries.

It is hoped that the following pages will be useful to those who are already familiar with investment companies but are not too conversant with their history. The book presupposes that the reader has some knowledge of investment company terminology; it is by no means an exposition for beginners. Yet it is not a legal treatise, nor is it written for accountants. It is a narrative, a history in a way, a story.

And every effort has been made to tell the story with accuracy and perspective: commendable objectives which should scarcely prevent the book from being readable. Contributing to readability is mention of various personalities which have been identified with the institution known as an investment company. For institutions are dead things without people; institutions are built by men of flesh and blood.

The author has known these men, many of them intimately. He has known, indeed, virtually all of the important personalities connected with the development of investment companies in America, as well as many key figures abroad. Most have been men of high integrity and distinct ability; some have been men who used poor judgment. As in any business or profession there have also been a small handful of outright rogues.

Moreover, the author has read over the years every book on investment companies that, to his knowledge, has been written in the English language, besides hundreds of newspaper and magazine articles and thousands of investment company reports. This reminds him of a question he is often asked, namely what reading should one do to acquire a thorough understanding of investment companies? By all odds the most important book to read is the latest edition of *Investment Companies,* written and published by Arthur Wiesenberger & Co.; these manuals, produced each year since 1940, are the best books that have been written on the subject. Then the student will read the monumental reports obtainable from the Government Printing Office covering the Securities and Exchange Commission's recommendations to Congress. This should be followed by a careful reading of the ensuing legislation itself, the Investment Company Act of 1940. For an understanding of the Act, an article by Alfred Jaretzki, Jr., in the April, 1941, issue of the Washington University *Law Quarterly* is invaluable. If one desires to read the best book of the 1920s, Leland Rex Robinson's two editions of *Investment Trust Organization and Management,* published by the Ronald Press Company, are recommended. And the late George Glasgow's three books of the 1930s, *The English Investment Trust Companies, The Scottish Investment Trust Companies,* and *Glasgow's Guide to Investment Trust Companies,* have long been standard reading on

British investment trust companies. To the late Mr. Glasgow the author owes grateful acknowledgment for review and suggestions respecting two chapters of the present book.

But this book is not the product of reading. It could scarcely be written by anyone—unless, like the author, he had experienced the things he tells about. For considerably over a generation the author has been closely identified with the investment company movement. He has lived the story of investment companies.

Is he prejudiced in favor of investment companies? Is a man apt to choose as a profession something in which he does not believe? This need not mean that he is unconscious of or condones honest mistakes of judgment or deliberate malpractices that occurred during the evolution of the investment company movement. Indeed his duty is to tell what happened as he saw it. For this is the story of investment companies, an objective story. It should be of value to present and future investors by alerting them to pitfalls of the past and problems of the future. Nor should it fail to detail constructive features of one of the most dynamic industries the financial world has ever seen.

We trust that you, Reader, will like his telling of the story.

H. B.

New York City
July, 1959

Contents

Illustrations

Charts

The Story of
Investment Companies

1

Our British Ancestors

ONE IMPORTANT ANCESTOR was not British. In 1822 William I, first king of the Netherlands, established at Brussels the oldest Belgian banking corporation, the "Société Générale des Pays-Bas pour favoriser l'industrie nationale"—entitled to act as banker for the government, issue currency, and develop agriculture, commerce, and industry in the "Southern Provinces."

As the century progressed and Belgium separated from Holland the company was the major factor in the financing of Belgium's basic industries. A financial crisis in 1848 divorced the company from its government banking functions; in 1904 its name was changed to the Société Générale de Belgique and, in 1936, it further divested itself of commercial banking activities. While it always would have been viewed as a banking institution and, later, as a finance or holding company rather than an investment company, today it has several of the characteristics of a true investment company. Its interests are world-wide and embrace some eighty companies in a score of major industries. It was and is the major factor in the Belgian Congo. Net worth is difficult to determine, but on December 31, 1958, the company's assets appeared to approximate the equivalent at book value of $125 million, which is a figure undoubtedly far below their actual worth.

THE FOREIGN AND COLONIAL GOVERNMENT TRUST

While the International Financial Society of London was organized in 1863 with the financial assistance of the Crédit Mobilier of Paris—itself performing some functions analogous to those of an investment company—the company, like the Société Générale, could not be compared with an investment trust until many years later. A similar reservation must be applied to the Continental Union—formerly the Continental Union Gas Co., registered in 1864. The London Financial Association, formed in 1863, could be said, by stretching the imagination, to have had some characteristics of an investment trust, but it was unsuccessful.

Meanwhile, in 1868, the Foreign and Colonial Government Trust was founded in London. Since its purpose from the very start, according to its prospectus, was to provide "the investor of moderate means the same advantages as the large capitalist, in diminishing the risk of investing in Foreign and Colonial Government Stocks, by spreading the investment over a number of different stocks," [1] and since it engaged in no financing or banking operations, it can be said—in so far as research enables us to tell—that this investment trust was the pioneer of them all.

And this pioneer initially resembled in some respects what we would call today a fixed or unit trust, although there were certain elements of flexibility and discretion allowed.[2] Against the deposit with the private banking house of Glyn, Mills, Currie & Co. of eighteen different issues of bonds of fifteen foreign governments, there were issued a specified number of certifi-

[1] *The Times* (London), March 20, 1868.

[2] For a description of this trust see Arthur Scratchley, *On Average Investment Trusts* (London, 1875), Part I, chapter I. See also Charles H. Walker's article in *Economic History,* a supplement of *The Economic Journal of London,* February, 1940; also *Investors' Chronicle, London,* issue of April 24, 1954.

cates of £100 each "bearing 6 percent interest" and issued at 85—to yield 7 percent. The sales charge was almost 3 percent, and "expenses of management" were limited to £2,500 or one-fourth of 1 percent per annum of the proposed issue of £1,000,-000. There was apparently no substitution of securities originally chosen for the portfolio permitted, although it was stated that "a power of sale under special circumstances, will be vested in the Trustees and a Committee of Certificateholders." Unlike a fixed or unit trust, there was no self-liquidating feature, but there was a sinking fund derived from any income accruing to the trust after payment of £6 interest on each £100 certificate and after expenses. Proceeds from any portfolio security that might be called also swelled the sinking fund. And the fund was used to call by lot at par and retire as many outstanding £100 certificates as possible. The original prospectus estimated that all certificates would be retired in not more than 24 years. Attached to each certificate, however, in addition to the semi-annual interest coupons, was a coupon which would entitle the holder, even if his certificate was called, to his pro rata share of whatever assets were available when the trust was terminated.

The eighteen portfolio securities were placed in the names of five well-known trustees: Lord Westbury, formerly Lord Chancellor of England, Lord Eustace Cecil, M.P., B. M. W. Sandford, M.P., George Woodhouse Currie, and Philip Rose.

Not more than £100,000 was permitted to be invested in the securities of any one government. The government loans making up the original portfolio were:

Argentina 6%, 1868
Austria 5%, 1859
Brazil 5%, 1865
Chile 6%, 1867
Chile 7%, 1866
Danube 8%, 1867
Egypt 7%, 1864
Egyptian 7% Railway Loan
Italy 5%, 1861
New South Wales 5%, 1866
Nova Scotia 6%, 1864
Peru 5%, 1865

Portugal 3%, 1867	Turkey 5%, 1865
Russian Anglo Dutch 5%, 1866 (Fl. 1,070,000)	Turkey 6%, 1865
Spain New 3%, 1867	United States, 5%, 1864

All these securities were dealt in on the London Stock Exchange and their average yield was over 8 percent.

The trust only issued £588,300 in certificates and, subsequently, four additional series, for a total of £3,438,300. Management expenses on the total amount were restricted to £12,500 per year. And the spread to the sponsors between the par value of portfolio securities purchased and the price to the public ranged on the different series from 1½ to 2½ percent—probably 2 to 3 percent of the actual market value.

Spanish and other bonds defaulted, holdings fluctuated severely in value, but this pioneer trust appears to have had a satisfactory record until and after its transformation into modern form in 1879. Today its assets at cost are somewhat over $30 million.

EARLY 1870s

Two factors accounted for the advent of British investment trust companies. The Joint Stock Companies Acts of 1862 and 1867 for the first time permitted shareholders to share in the profits of an enterprise, with their liability limited to the amount of capital individually subscribed, and specifically included companies dealing in general market securities. Moreover British government securities—"consols"—had risen in price to yield little more than 3 percent.

The financial writers of that period welcomed the creation of a vehicle whereby a man with either large or small sums to invest could avoid the risk inherent in a single security by purchasing certificates of a trust which would itself purchase a selected list of securities offering greater safety through diversification than an individual security and more generous returns than were available from British government bonds.

Before 1875, eighteen trusts had been formed, with a paid in capital of over £6,500,000. Until 1873 all the trusts were started in London—some under the legal form of trusts, others as limited liability corporations. The general pattern was the same as that of the Foreign and Colonial Government Trust. They were apt to specialize in particular fields as most of their names suggest; e.g., the Submarines Cables Trust, the Government Stock Investment Company (Limited), the Share Investment Trust, the Governments and Guaranteed Securities Permanent Trust, the Mortgage Debenture and Government Securities Trust, the American Investment Trust, the Anglo-American Railroad Mortgage Trust, the Railway Debenture Trust Company (Limited), the Railway Share Trust Company (Limited), the Globe Telegraph and Trust, the Gas and Water Debenture Trust Company (Limited), the Municipal Trust.[3]

The year 1873, however, is significant as the birth date of the first of the famous Scottish investment trusts: The Scottish American Investment Trust.

THE FATHER OF INVESTMENT TRUSTS

Robert Fleming,[4] pioneer of the investment company movement and, later, the universally acknowledged dean of the industry, was born in Dundee in 1845. A bookkeeper in the important textile firm of Edward Baxter & Son, he was private clerk to the head of the firm. Mr. Baxter had American busi-

[3] Samples taken from Scratchley, *On Average Investment Trusts.*

[4] For background on Mr. Fleming and his early trusts the author is primarily indebted to Mr. A. K. Aitkenhead, secretary of the First Scottish American Trust Company, Limited; to J. C. Gilbert's *A History of Investment Trusts in Dundee* (London, 1939); to *The Times* edition of August 2, 1933; to *The Bankers' Magazine* (London) issue of September, 1933; to discussions over thirty years with various partners of Robert Fleming & Co.—and with Mr. Fleming himself.

ness interests and substantial sums invested in American securities and, in 1870, sent Fleming, at the age of 25, to the United States in his behalf.

The young man returned, enthusiastic over the investment opportunities afforded by this country, which was just recovering from the effects of the Civil War. The pound sterling stood at a large premium over the dollar. U. S. government bonds and railroad mortgage bonds yielded double the return available on comparable securities in Great Britain and considerably more than other "foreign" securities. The jute merchants of Dundee were exceptionally prosperous and were attracted by this field for investment.

Robert Fleming's enthusiasm resulted in the formation on February 1, 1873, of "the first Association in Scotland for investment in American railroad bonds, carefully selected and widely distributed, and where the investments would not exceed one-tenth of the capital in any one security." On the fiftieth anniversary of the Scottish American Investment Trust, Fleming, in a speech, described the launching of this initial Scottish trust:

> Dundee had not, up to that time, in any sense been a financial centre, and we went to the printer in grave doubt of success with a proposed issue of £150,000. But such was the confidence in the Board, which consisted of four of the best men in the town—John Guild, John Sharp, Thomas Cox, and Thomas Smith—that the first day the British Linen Company Bank was flooded with applications to such an extent that, to meet in some measure the demand for shares, it was decided to withdraw the prospectus and print a new one with a capital issue of £300,000. This also was largely oversubscribed. At the start it took the form of a Trust with a trust deed, the terms of which were printed on the back of bearer certificates of £100 each.

The trust was to terminate in 10 years and pay 6 percent per annum; annual expenses were limited to £1,000. Surplus income after the first two years was to be used to redeem bearer certificates offered by tender at £110 until 1878 and £115 thereafter. Surplus income not so employed, if any, was to be invested in securities of the same character as the original securities. At the termination of the trust all securities were to be sold and proceeds distributed pro rata to remaining certificate holders. Meanwhile trustees could sell any security held by the trust and reinvest proceeds in securities of the same character if they deemed it in the best interests of certificate holders. No list of holdings was published but, at the first annual meeting, the chairman indicated that some thirty American railway mortgage bond issues had been purchased, yielding, after expenses of the trust, an average of fully 7 percent. A second issue of £400,000 of certificates was floated in the fall of 1873 and a third of £400,000 in 1875. These latter issues of certificates, however, while still paying 6 percent and having similar provisions to the first issue, were to have a life of 20 years and were based on somewhat broader holdings of American railroad mortgage bonds.

Mr. Fleming's first trust is not to be confused with the Scottish American Investment Company Limited, which was founded, interestingly enough, just two months later on March 29, 1873, in Edinburgh, by a lawyer, William J. Menzies, and which invested some £500,000 in the United States and Canada in land mortgages and railroad and government bonds, investment in any one security being limited to 10 percent of the trust's assets. Perhaps, to avoid confusion as to which was the pioneer trust in Scotland, as well as for legal reasons explained later, the name of the Fleming trust was changed, in 1879, to the First Scottish American Trust Company Limited.

Robert Fleming was nominally secretary to the Scottish American Investment Trust, but his shrewd investment judgment largely guided its affairs. After he opened an office in London in 1900, he continued as correspondent of the successors of this original Scottish trust. Meanwhile in London, in

1888, he had organized the Investment Trust Corporation, Ltd. In 1909 he actually moved his headquarters to London and formed the famous firm of Robert Fleming & Co. to carry on a general financial business. For a considerable period the firm was identified with the issuance of American railroad securities. The Atchison, Topeka, and Santa Fe and Denver and Rio Grande railroads were reconstructed under his advice; he likewise helped to complete the Cuba Railroad and to form the Anglo-Persian Oil Company.

But his principal activities became more and more identified with investment trust companies and his firm represented numerous Scottish trusts as well as acting as secretary to important British companies. Although never a director himself of more than half a dozen trusts, his reputation for sound judgment was such and his contacts so broad that his influence was immense. The success of many underwritings depended on his evaluation of their terms. One financial historian [5] estimates that, because of interlocking directorships or more direct relationship, Robert Fleming & Co. exerted an influence on the investment policies of some fifty-six trusts with aggregate resources of £114 million.

Robert Fleming was an unassuming man to meet—quiet, conservative, wise, and deeply respected. His integrity, pertinacious courage, and shrewdness matched his modesty. He was active until two years before his death at the age of 88. And his monument is the stamp of character and methods he left, more than any other man, on the important industry of which he will always be called the father.

GROWTH OF MOVEMENT

Over the years there were instances on the continent of Europe where certain institutions appeared analogous to investment trusts, but Great Britain, for a century before the First World

[5] Hanns Linhardt, *Die Britischen Investment Trusts* (Berlin, 1935).

War the world's leading creditor nation, was their original home and fostered by far their greatest early development. Three cities were involved in particular: London, Edinburgh,

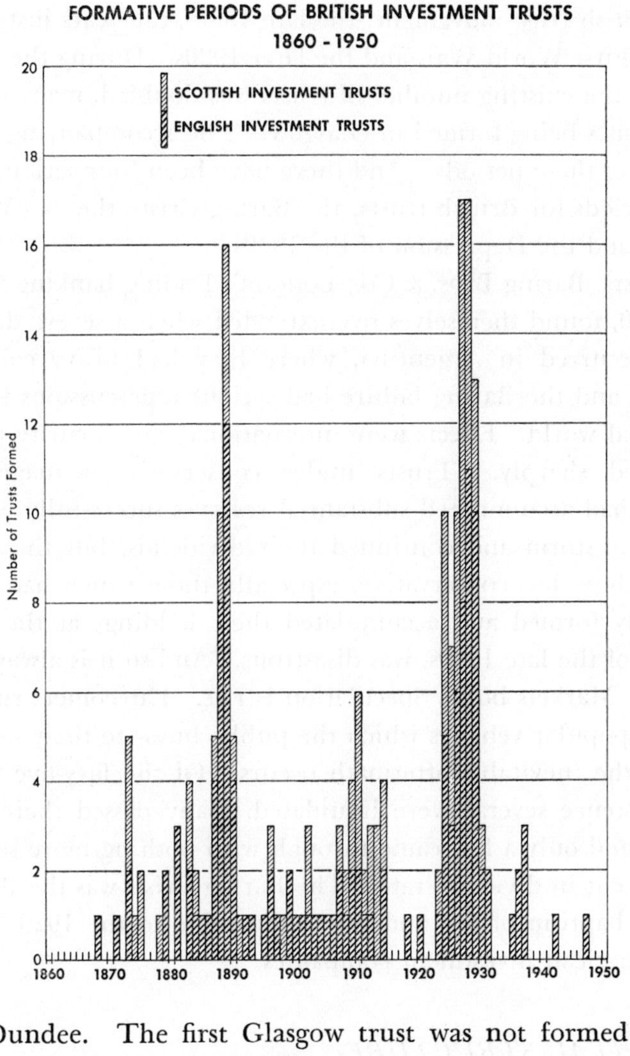

and Dundee. The first Glasgow trust was not formed until 1907. Almost two-thirds of the trusts have always been located in London, but the Scottish third is a very potent fraction, representing almost 40 percent of the industry's assets. Moreover, many an English trust is managed by a Scotsman resident in London. Indeed, one of the largest trusts in the world is the Alliance Trust Company, Ltd., formed in 1888 in Dundee.

There have been three distinct major formative periods for the British trust movement: the late 1880s, the years just prior to the First World War, and the later 1920s. During the latter period the existing number of trusts was doubled, many of the new trusts being formed in Glasgow. The accompanying chart indicates these periods. And there have been four serious testing periods for British trusts: the Baring Crisis, the two World Wars, and the Depression of the 1930s.

Messrs. Baring Bros. & Co., London's leading banking house in 1890, found themselves overextended when a severe depression occurred in Argentina, where they had heavy commitments; and the Baring failure had serious repercussions in the financial world. Effects were international, and security prices declined sharply. Trusts under conservative management which had accumulated substantial reserves successfully weathered the storm and continued their dividends, but the effect upon those less conservative, especially those which had been recently formed and accumulated their holdings at the high prices of the late 1880s, was disastrous. And so it is always apt to be. Markets boil. Speculation is rife. Latecomers rush to create popular vehicles which the public buys—to their sorrow, when the inevitable aftermath occurs. Of the fifty-five trusts in existence several were liquidated, many passed their dividend, and only a few came through with nothing more serious than a cut in dividend rate. The Baring Crisis was the British trusts' baptism of fire and was comparable to the 1929 lesson for American investment companies.

CAPITAL STRUCTURE

Almost all of the early British trusts had at the start a simple capital structure. Participating certificates were issued against securities held in trust or, if the "trust" was in corporate form, the corporation issued only common stock—the British term is "ordinary shares." Some trusts in corporate form later borrowed money from the banks or issued terminable debentures (debentures with a maturity date, usually short-term, 3 to 10 years). Other trusts issued debenture stock (a debenture with no maturity). Scottish trusts preferred terminable debentures and English trusts, debenture stock. At a still later date the capital stock of many trusts was split into preference and ordinary shares. Debentures or preference shares gave the trusts what we call leverage—the British call it "gearing." In the course of time most British trusts had a high degree of leverage. Of two hundred trusts recently listed by Laing & Cruickshank all had gearing and none were of simple capital structure.

Until the 1930s all British trusts were closed-end trusts. In other words, they did not continuously issue stock, had no self-liquidating feature, and only raised new capital by infrequent underwritings. Moreover, when new capital was raised it was often accomplished by organizing a second trust of the same name under identical management, e.g., the Second Guardian Investment Company.

INCOME

The emphasis of British investment trust companies was on income. The very first trusts organized were for the purpose of paying to participants an income of 6 percent, with the safety that accrued from having such income derived from a broad list of securities yielding considerably more. Earnings, above dividend requirements and expenses, were allocated to a reserve to protect the participant's income against a rainy day. Capital profits were never paid out. On occasion they might be capitalized in the form of a stock dividend, but this was the great exception rather than the rule. Rather such profits were used to write down the original costs of specific securities; such securities were always carried at cost or less—never written up if the market price advanced. In short, the most conservative accounting practices were followed.

THE NAME "INVESTMENT TRUST"

The very earliest English and Scottish trusts were true common law trusts, hence the name "investment trust." In 1879 they were declared illegal on the grounds that they were "associations of more than 20 persons for the acquisition of gain" and had not registered under the Joint Stock Companies Acts of 1862 and 1867. Even though the decision was later reversed on appeal, all the trusts except one (the Submarine Cables Trust, which kept its original status and terminated in 1926) converted into corporate form or were liquidated. Henceforth they were called "investment trust companies," the common British term in use today. In the United States the term "investment trust" was used until 1940, when the Securities and Exchange Commission preferred that such vehicles be called "investment companies."

STATUS AFTER THE FIRST WORLD WAR

British investment trust companies, no different from other business ventures for generations, were organized or issued additional capital primarily during periods of prosperity—when investors had money to invest and optimism was the order of the day. The obvious sequel was that they usually paid relatively high prices for the securities in which they invested and were severely tested when the level of securities prices inevitably declined. During the first fifty years of their existence there were numerous fluctuations in the economic cycle and frequent changes in the level of world markets. We have noted that the first severe test of management was the Baring Crisis; the next was the First World War.

When this grim four-year period commenced in 1914, a shudder went through the civilized world. The London and New York Stock Exchanges were closed for some months, the British government mobilized American securities held by British nationals as security for American loans and British investment trust company portfolios lost most of their American holdings in exchange for British government bonds. But managements, especially of the trusts that had not been formed immediately before the war, generally passed this second major test with flying colors. Of approximately a hundred trusts in existence George Glasgow [6] tells us that fourteen did not even reduce their dividends on their ordinary stock and a few actually increased their dividends.

So this was the picture of British investment trust companies when the decade of the 1920s began—the decade that saw the genuine initiation of the investment company movement on the North American continent.

Debentures of the older British trusts had a credit rating second only to British consols; preference and ordinary shares could virtually always find a buyer, but because their owners were loath to part with them, they were seldom available on the market. The soundness of the principle of a diversified list of holdings, watched over by professional investment management, first ventured by Lord Westbury in 1868 and later developed, refined, and proved by Robert Fleming and other distinguished British financial figures, attracted pioneer investment men on this side of the Atlantic. Simultaneously the young giant of the West, the United States of America, was emerging from the First World War as a leading creditor nation of the world.

[6] George Glasgow, *The English Investment Trust Companies* (London, 1930), p. 3.

2

Early American

WHICH WAS THE FIRST American investment company? The Massachusetts Hospital Life Insurance Company had an arrangement with clients resembling a common trust fund as early as 1823. Building and loan associations and farm mortgage companies during the nineteenth century employed the principle of diversification as protection for their obligations and the public's participation. American insurance companies, with their extensive investment portfolios, were early compared by the British financial community to their own investment trust companies. Public utility and other holding companies long had characteristics analogous to investment companies, except that their primary objective was control or influence of corporations whose securities they held.

There was supposed to be a New York Stock Trust, organized in 1889, which stated in a circular "The New York Stock Trust is the first American Investment Trust ever organized."[1] It is not illogical that various small ventures such as this have been lost in the haze of the years.

[1] Leland Rex Robinson, *Investment Trust Organization and Management* (rev. ed., New York, 1929), p. 501.

BOSTON PERSONAL PROPERTY TRUST

The oldest investment company still in existence in this country, however, is the Boston Personal Property Trust, created by a declaration of trust under Massachusetts common law in 1893. It started with capital of approximately $100,000 and has never until the last year or two exceeded $10,000,000 in its long and successful history, with an unbroken dividend record for over sixty years.

Whether the original trustees consciously formed an investment company or were merely placing some family holdings in a type of legal vehicle that had been previously created in Massachusetts to avoid restrictions on the holding of real estate by corporations is open to question. In any event, as years went on the company's portfolio became characterized by a diversified list of conservative securities with real estate in the minority and it met every definition of a closed-end, general management investment company. It has a simple capitalization of no-par capital shares. Individuals identified with the trust throughout its history have been well-known Boston trustees.

RAILWAY AND LIGHT SECURITIES COMPANY

Incorporated originally in Maine in 1904, but managed in Boston, this company for a generation limited its investments to street railway and public utility securities. It always had senior securities outstanding and was unquestionably our oldest closed-end investment company with leverage. In only three years out of the last forty-six has it failed to pay dividends on its common stock; during this period no dividend was ever omitted on its preferred stock up to the latter's retirement in 1950.

Although its size until recently has been relatively small, the company has had excellent sponsorship and a conservative management record. In 1952 its name was changed to the more descriptive Colonial Fund, Inc., in view of its holdings of many industrial as well as utility securities. In 1954 it was converted into an open-end investment company.

ALEXANDER FUND

The Alexander Fund was started in 1907 in Philadelphia by W. Wallace Alexander. It was neither a corporation nor an association nor a trust. Mr. Alexander merely acted as his clients' agent in investing their money for them, a receipt being given them at the time of each deposit. The first year there were four clients who deposited a total of $1,200; two decades later there were over 1,700 participants in a fund of over $4,000,000.

This unincorporated agency was registered with the Pennsylvania State Banking Department and operated somewhat along the lines of the well-known building and loan associations. It had definite characteristics of the unit trusts of the 1920s and even greater similarities to the mutual funds of today.

Hundred-dollar units of participation in the Fund were issued semi-annually, in various series. No further units would be issued in any series where units had an asset value of less than their $100 parity; but newcomers in an old series which had gone to a premium would have to pay the higher asset value for units they purchased; units had maturity but could be redeemed at any time by the holder at their current asset value.

Quarterly distributions at an annual rate of 6 percent were made on each new series. If the units in a series attained an asset value of $115, 7 percent would be paid, with the rate increasing as the value increased. There was a management fee of 10 percent of all income and profits; rent, clerical salaries, printing, and postage were charged to the Fund.

As the Fund grew, the securities Mr. Alexander purchased were deposited in a bank. As many as two hundred and fifty general market securities—bonds and stocks of a diversified list of well-known industrial and financial corporations—were held by the bank, with not more than 2 percent of the assets of the Fund invested in any one security; the Fund, indeed, was always fully invested. Investments were made in accordance with a set of printed rules. Five participants called "overseers" were kept in touch with all operations. In 1928 Mr. Alexander incorporated his agency to provide continuity of operations. In 1941, after more than 40 years of operation, dissolution of the Fund began.

AMERICAN INTERNATIONAL

American International Corporation was incorporated under the laws of New York in November, 1915, under the original sponsorship of President Frank A. Vanderlip and other officials of the National City Bank of New York, including a board of directors of exceptional prominence in the business world. Formed when Europe was at war, it used its $50 million of capital to finance foreign trade and development. After the postwar deflation the company was recapitalized. Certainly a finance or trading company at first, in due course it became an investment company with 1929 assets of over $60 million for the most part invested in domestic securities. In more recent years it has been closely affiliated with the Adams Express Company.

Adams Express is another example of a company in 1929 classified as an important closed-end investment and holding company which was formed over a century ago for entirely different and obvious purposes. In 1945 it acquired control of American International Corporation, and the two companies use the same management facilities and have an almost identical directorate.

Two small ventures, the American Investment Company, organized in Wisconsin in 1914, and the First Investment Company of Concord, New Hampshire, incorporated in 1916, are no longer in existence. The Overseas Securities Corporation, incorporated in New Hampshire in 1920, was also short-lived, but its New York successor since 1923 has been well sponsored and of some importance. Then there were four public utility holding companies and two finance companies, the earliest formed in 1910, certain of which in later years were defined by some authorities as investment trusts.

But in April, 1921, there was incorporated a trust which was not formed to hold real estate, could not be confused with a public utility holding company, was not designed to finance international trade, and did not stretch one's imagination to be exactly what it purported to be. With no ifs, ands, or buts, history will doubtless call it the first important pioneer of the investment company movement in the United States.

THE FOUNDERS GROUP

The first of the Founders group of companies was a Massachusetts trust organized in 1921 (although actual capital was not contributed until the following year), called International Securities Trust of America, which really initiated the vigorous growth of American investment companies during the 1920s. After a slow start the trust became for some years the largest single company and the Founders group the dominant investment company venture until the Panic of 1929.

William R. Bull, a Bridgeport, Connecticut, securities dealer, was the trust's president. In 1922, with Christopher F. Coombs, a Boston investment dealer, Bull formed a second Massachusetts trust—subsequently known as American Founders Trust—to raise capital for International Securities and furnish its research facilities. The bulk of the capital was raised in New England through day-by-day selling.

International Securities Trust of America was patterned after the successful British investment trust companies. It had a multiple capital structure of debentures, preferred stock and two classes of common. Its elaborate restrictions relative to the investment of its portfolio were somewhat more complicated than usual British practice. Its portfolio included more than five hundred different holdings, primarily senior securities and, to a lesser extent, equities, and was world-wide in composition. It did not publish its portfolio, but gave a breakdown of classes of securities held, as well as geographical distribution.

Subsequently a Second International Securities Corporation was formed (and the two previous trusts changed to corporations) as well as United States and British International Company, Ltd. Founders General Corporation was next incorporated to take over American Founders' function of raising capital. This was the picture of the group early in 1928.

The original concept of International Securities Trust, with its management affiliate of American Founders Trust, was sound, and certain distinguished economists, as well as Dr. Leland Rex Robinson, the best-known American authority on the British Investment Trust Company movement, were identified with Founders' activities. Moreover, the elaborate research organization that the group developed has never—certainly in number of personnel—been equaled.

UNITED STATES & FOREIGN SECURITIES CORPORATION

By far the most eminent of the trusts of the early 1920s was the United States & Foreign Securities Corporation, organized and syndicated in October, 1924, by the then most active investment banking house in the country, Dillon, Read & Co. It was the first time an important private banker had identified himself with a trust (American International when formed was not a true investment trust and International Securities Trust was organized by relatively little known individuals and, at the start, grew rather slowly). The brilliance of Clarence Dillon was something of a legend in Wall Street, and the saying went that "this was an opportunity to let the public in on Dillon's investment brains."

The new trust issued 250,000 shares of $6 first preferred, 50,-000 shares of $6 second preferred and 1,000,000 shares of common for a total of approximately $30,000,000. The entire issue of second preferred was bought by the organizers for $5,000,000, and they retained 750,000 shares of common, one share of common going to each purchaser of first preferred, full payment for which was not asked for some time.

Like International Securities Trust and other closed-end trusts, no portfolio was published, but substantial investments were early made in Central Europe. Today, holdings are almost entirely domestic. After consolidation with a successor trust, today's assets are substantially over $100,000,000, and the long term record of Dillon, Read investment companies is among the best in the industry.

FIXED TRUSTS

Another kind of development in the trust field was meanwhile taking place.

William J. Thorold, an Englishman, organized in November, 1923, a fixed trust called United Bankers Oil Company, Inc., which deposited shares of ten Standard Oil companies in units of 144 shares with the Empire Trust Company of New York as trustee. Seven hundred "bankers shares" were issued against each unit. The British & General Debenture Trust, Ltd., in London and a New York investment dealer—a prominent tennis player, Harold Throckmorton—then publicly offered the shares.

In 1924 the Empire Trust Company likewise acted as trustee for three similar fixed trusts, United American Railways, United American Electric Companies, and United American Chain Stores, with the same London sponsor and Bonner Brooks & Company as New York distributor. All these trusts were liquidated by 1926.

The best known of the fixed trusts, however, for a few years after its initiation, was Diversified Trustee Shares, sponsored by the same Throckmorton & Company in 1925. The American Trustee Share Corporation deposited with the Chatham Phenix National Bank & Trust Co. 24 well-known railroad, public utility, oil, and other industrial stocks in units totaling 214 shares, against which were issued 1,000 shares of beneficial interest in bearer form in different convenient denominations. No substitutions were permitted in the portfolio except in case of merger, or the like. No management fee was charged, the sponsors adding a premium, presumably of 10 percent or so, to the actual value of the shares to establish the public offering price, out of which premium trustee fees, cost of certificates, merchandising expense, and profit were paid. A holder of 1,000 shares could demand from the trustee the underlying shares comprising his unit, a provision which established a bid price within a reasonable range of the actual value of the listed stocks comprising the unit.

The redemption privilege of the fixed trusts of 1923 and 1924, however clumsy, forecast provisions of that general nature in vehicles to come.

FAMOUS BOSTON TRUSTS

The years 1924 and 1925 saw the beginnings of three famous Boston investment companies, which, as years went on, became major and highly constructive factors in the industry.

In March, 1924, Massachusetts Investors Trust—destined

later to be for a quarter century the largest of all investment companies—was born. Learoyd, Foster & Co. of Boston formed this Massachusetts common law trust; original Trustees were Edward G. Leffler, Hatherly Foster, Jr., and Charles H. Learoyd —Leffler and Foster being replaced in June and July of the same year by L. Sherman Adams and Ashton L. Carr, respectively. With its simple capital structure, self-liquidating feature, publication of portfolio, and sound investment restrictions and policies, indisputably it was the first of what later were termed open-end investment companies—and it has been a credit to its kind.

In August of that same year the State Street Investment Corporation had its initial capital subscribed by the company's officers, President Richard C. Paine, Vice-President Richard Saltonstall, and Treasurer Paul C. Cabot; these men, for a year or two, ran the company privately.

Then, in November of 1925, another corporation, Incorporated Investors was, like State Street, organized under Massachusetts law, with George Putman as president, Edward G. Leffler as vice-president, and William A. Parker as treasurer. Though of different legal status, these two companies had a single share capitalization like Massachusetts Investors. Incorporated Investors from the start had a self-liquidating feature and, until the early 1930s, was the most prominent of the Boston open-enders.

Not an open-end investment company but an interesting Massachusetts common law trust was also formed as early as 1923 by the well-known Boston banking house of Harris, Forbes & Co., namely the Bond Investment Trust. Certificates of beneficial interest were issued by Harris, Forbes against deposit with them of a broad selection of domestic and some foreign bonds. A second and slightly larger bond trust was formed three years later by the same firm, which exists today as an open-end investment company.

New York made its contribution in 1924 by the formation of a New York Joint Stock Association—the Investment Managers Co., headed by the economist Edgar Lawrence Smith and sponsored by the high-grade firms of Roosevelt & Son and Wood, Low & Company. A "Trust Fund A" was established (and later another fund) against which were issued certificates having a specified face value and certifying that the holder had a stated number of shares in the investment fund, paying 5 percent, plus an additional 12½ percent of a holder's proportionate part of the fund's income after the 5 percent annual payment. Certificates were redeemable at the holder's option, but were non-transferable. Compensation to the company was 1 percent when a holder purchased certificates, one-half of 1 percent a year and 1 percent, if a holder redeemed, of the value of his shares. No affiliated persons could deal as principals in making purchases or sales for the fund. Later the company became affiliated with the Irving Trust Co., and it should be viewed less as a type of open-end investment company than as a forerunner of the common trust funds of banks that were to follow.

CALVIN BULLOCK

In 1924 there appeared on the scene an individual who, for a generation, was to have a decided influence on the development of the investment company movement on the North American continent.

A Massachusetts man who established in Denver, in 1894, what is today the oldest investment firm in the Mountain States, Calvin Bullock early became interested in the soundness of the theory underlying the successful British investment trust companies, and he studied them at first hand in England and Scotland.

His initial venture, a unit trust called Nation-Wide Securities Company, in December, 1924, was a far cry from the typical

British trust, and the dean of the profession in London, the famous Robert Fleming, said to him: "Don't tie yourself with too many restrictions. Restrictions you put in today that you think are for the protection of your shareholders, will rise up some day to plague you."

Nevertheless this first trust and its successor, with headquarters in New York, three years later, were defined as semi-fixed trusts until Mr. Bullock was willing to move into the closed-end, general management field in 1928. His trusts reflected the severe market declines of 1929 and after, but, with his aversion to borrowed money, even though amounts fluctuated, no trust under his sponsorship ever failed to pay a cash dividend on a regular dividend date. In the United States and Canada he was the major factor in the open-end field in the early 1930s, and his mutual funds were studied and widely purchased in the British Isles.

Throughout his long career Calvin Bullock was the dominant figure in all his companies, insisting on principles and practices in the interest of stockholders that are now taken for granted. His outstanding characteristic was his stern integrity. Because of reputation, continuity, innovations, and the position his companies have occupied, financial historians will doubtless refer to him as much as or more than any man as a pioneer of the American investment company movement.

From a painting by Frank O. Salisbury

CALVIN BULLOCK

3

The Roaring Twenties

THE EARLY 1920s were drab enough. To be sure 1920–21 witnessed a severe collapse of commodity prices from the extravagant levels created by the war. For example, lead, steel, wheat, and wool declined more than 60 percent, cotton and tin more than 70 percent, rubber, sugar, zinc, and coffee more than 80 percent, while Dow-Jones Industrial Averages of common stocks declined from 119 to 63. Liberty 4¼'s sold at 82; the Goodyear Tire and Rubber Co. was compelled to float at par a first mortgage issue carrying an 8 percent coupon; and a large billboard in the vicinity of Forty-Second Street and Broadway in New York read "When people will start looking up and thinking up—then business will pick up." This gloomy period coincided with the genesis of our genuine investment company movement in this country.

But the United States could not be held down. The war-to-end-war had just been fought and won. The country emerged as the first industrial and, in due course, the largest creditor nation of the world. And several million investors who had not heretofore known the difference between a stock and a bond had become familiar with securities through the extensive war-time Liberty Bond drives.

A few dozen investment companies were formed in the early and middle twenties, the most important of which have been mentioned. It was not until 1927, however, that the pace accelerated, and in 1928 and, especially, 1929 new investment companies came in a veritable flood.

From the last half of the nineteenth century until after the First World War the securities business in this country was primarily concerned with the financing of railroads, but in the 1920s utilities, especially those pertaining to electric light and power, took first place. Gigantic utility holding company systems were created; in fact, holding companies embracing numerous industries became the order of the day. So many holding and financing companies were formed that some were difficult to distinguish from true investment companies, and, because a certain magic began to attach itself to the name "investment trust," numerous ventures were launched which called themselves "trusts" but never should have been so categorized.

As the end of the decade neared optimism was rampant, speculation was frenzied, fortunes on paper were made in a few months. Bootblacks and millionaires played the stock market; one utility financier ran his modest fortune up to an estimated billion dollars on paper within ten years.

Those were the speakeasy days, the easy money days, the Chicago gangster days, the days of the dapper Mayor Jimmy Walker of New York. People could buy stocks by putting up 25 percent margin or usually considerably less; the federal income tax on corporations was only 11 percent; the highest rate on personal incomes was 24 percent; the federal budget was $4 billion; the total federal debt was $18 billion. They were the days of laissez faire, the less government the better, Coolidge prosperity.

To be sure there were warnings. On March 14, 1929, Secretary of the Treasury Andrew W. Mellon said of stocks: "Some . . . are too high in price to be good buys. For prudent investors I would say, if making a suggestion, that now is the time to buy good bonds." But usual statements were to the effect that we were living in "a new era," that stocks were on "a permanently high plateau." Stocks it was that had caught the public imagination, even when they sold at twenty, thirty, forty times their per share earnings—and yielded less than good grade bonds.

Heretofore government bonds, first mortgages on real estate, prime railroad bonds, and, later, utility bonds were considered appropriate investments for conservative accounts. Stocks were labeled distinctly speculative. But an economic treatise by Edgar Lawrence Smith, entitled *Common Stocks as Long Term Investments,* appeared in 1924 and was reprinted frequently until 1928. It became the bible of a new school of thinking for investors. To quote from some of the book's interesting pages:

> These studies are the record of a failure—the failure of facts to sustain a preconceived theory. This preconceived theory might be stated as follows:
>
> While a diversity of common stocks has, without doubt proved a more profitable investment than high-grade bonds in the period from 1897 to 1923, during which dollars were depreciating, yet with the upturn in the dollar, bonds may be relied upon to show better results than common stocks, as they did in the period from the close of the Civil War to 1896, during which the dollar was constantly increasing in purchasing power.

There followed various historical data and tabulations which disproved the preconceived theory. The book continued:

> If our tests have been of any significance, they have shown that even in periods of appreciating currency, such as the periods from 1865 to 1885 and 1880 to 1900, well diversified lists of common stocks in the largest and most important industries of the country have shown, on the whole, favorable results in comparison with bonds during the same periods. In periods when the dollar was depreciating, they have shown results so far superior to those obtained from high grade bonds, that there is really no comparison to be made between them.
>
> There would, therefore, seem to be ample justification for including as a part of the investment of any large private fortune a relatively large proportion of sound, well diversified common stocks,

selected not for their immediate market possibilities, but rather with their long-term investment prospects in mind.

The book was sound and made no extravagant statements, but stock promoters and investment company sponsors used it to a fare-thee-well. And, the portfolios of American investment trusts contained a far greater proportion of common stocks than their counterparts in Great Britain. And trusts came thick and fast.

Investment trusts were formed by investment bankers, by brokers (broker after broker seemed to want his own trust), by industrialists, by banks and trust companies. The Securities and Exchange Commission (SEC), in its monumental study of the investment company industry some years later, said:

> In particular, houses of issue, brokers, and security dealers sponsored and undertook the distribution of the securities of investment company after investment company, these types of sponsorship accounting, on the basis of assets, for over 60% of management investment companies proper in 1929.[1]

Trusts were formed not only in financial centers, but in many of the country's smaller cities. They were formed by promoters of many types who saw an opportunity to ride the wave of popularity, but some of whom had very few qualifications to provide appropriate management.

Every conceivable type of trust was formed: orthodox corporations with or without a pyramided capital structure; Massachusetts common law trusts with one class of share outstanding, and others with leverage; fixed and semi-fixed trusts with certificates of beneficial interest issued against identical units of securities; common stock trusts and trusts owning senior as well as junior securities; trusts with restrictions regarding what management could do and others with few or no restrictions; trusts that published their portfolio and others that never revealed

[1] Report of the Securities and Exchange Commission, *Investment Trusts and Investment Companies*, Part Three, chap. I, p. 4.

their investments; trusts with self-liquidating features and trusts that listed their shares on some exchange; trusts that invested in foreign securities and trusts that confined themselves almost entirely to the domestic field. But most of them were corporations, most of them owned more common stocks than bonds, most of them confined themselves to domestic investments, most of them possessed great flexibility of management, most of them had a complicated capital structure. Today the vast bulk of the "trusts" of the 1920s would be classified as pyramided, closed-end investment companies and holding companies. The SEC Report states:

The development in the investment company movement prior to the end of 1929 was heavily concentrated in certain types of companies. New capital in the investment field from 1927 through 1929 was raised largely by the sale of securities of closed-end companies, that is, by closed-end management investment companies proper and management investment-holding companies.[2]

Bonus stock and stock options frequently went to promoters, cost of raising capital was often high, hidden profits were occasionally present, capital structures were unduly complicated, inter-company holdings were apt to be like a Chinese puzzle. One large "trust" had 45 directors. In the speculative atmosphere common shares often would sell at a high premium above their asset value. Sponsors would not always use the pool of money under their aegis in the best interests of stockholders; sometimes it would prove a convenient resting place for unmarketable securities or a source of too-frequent stock exchange commissions. Of course, as in everything in life, there were men of high integrity and genuine talent connected with investment companies, but there were also those of doubtful ethics and ability—and some outright crooks. The latter were the small minority, but it is always these who are primarily publicized.

[2] *Ibid.*

The New York Stock Exchange, the National Association of Securities Commissioners, the Attorney General of New York state and the Investment Bankers Association of America had taken a position that the investment company industry might be going too far too fast. But an investment company official himself, Paul C. Cabot of the State Street Investment Corporation of Boston, in an article in the March, 1929, issue of the *Atlantic Monthly,* used stronger words than almost anyone else. Having sketched the history of British investment trusts, some of their excesses before the Baring Crisis of 1890, and the aftermath, he wrote:

I strongly believe that unless we avoid these and other errors and false principles we shall inevitably go through a similar period of disaster and disgrace. If such a period should come, the well-run trusts will suffer with the bad as they did in England forty years ago.

He said:

In my opinion there is today in this country a large and well-known investment trust whose shares are selling for far more than their intrinsic or liquidating value, which has continually managed its portfolio so that it can show the greatest possible profits and thereby obtain the greatest market value for its shares, regardless of their real worth. Generally speaking, in this trust during the past year the good securities that have appreciated in value have been sold and the poorer ones retained or increased, simply to show profits.

Further:

Some months ago, in testifying before a committee of the New York Stock Exchange, I was asked to state briefly what were, in my opinion, the present abuses in the investment-trust movement. My reply was: (1) dishonesty; (2) inattention and inability; (3) greed.

He speaks of

Two common abuses to which the investment trust is now being put. First, that of being run for ulterior motives and not primarily for the best interests of the shareholders; second, that of being used as a depository for securities that might otherwise be unmarketable.

. . . The practice by which a house of issue sells a part of its own underwriting to its own trust, although not necessarily unethical or unusual, is extremely dangerous. Those trusts run by banks and brokers are particularly subject to this temptation.

He criticizes undue profits to promoters, and "investment-trust prospectuses in which it takes literally hours to figure out just how profits are to be divided," and "a very large funded or floating debt or an excessive market price to which, in my opinion, the shares of certain trusts have been bid." His cure for abuses? "Publicity and education." He wants complete financial information, dividends "clearly separated from profits from sales," salaries revealed. "If the investment trusts of the country pursue this policy of complete information, bad practices, simply by revelation, will be eliminated."

But the flood of trusts continued. And, amid the sound and fury, those that followed unsound policies rode the wave along with the sounder ones. For the later 1920s was a period of great prosperity; there were to be two chickens in every pot, and stock market levels reflected the measure of the universal optimism. The optimism was scarcely dampened by a statement of the President of the United States in December, 1928:

No Congress of the United States ever assembled, on surveying the State of the Union, has met with a more pleasing prospect than that which appears at the present time.[3]

—or of the Secretary of the Treasury, the previous September:

There is no cause for worry. The high tide of prosperity will continue.[4]

—or of the chairman of a famous steel company on October 25, 1929:

In my long association with the steel industry I have never known it to enjoy a greater stability or more promising outlook than it does today.[5]

[3] Edward Angly, *Oh Yeah?* (New York, 1931).
[4] *Ibid.*, p. 22. [5] *Ibid.*, p. 27.

—or of Colonel Leonard P. Ayers, vice-president of the Cleveland Trust Company, whose monthly economic bulletin was standard reading throughout the financial world, on August 15, 1929:

This is truly a new era in which formerly well established standards of value for securities no longer retain their old significance.[6]

—or of the chairman of one of our largest banks, on September 20, 1929:

There is nothing to worry about in the financial situation in the United States.[7]

To be sure, Roger W. Babson, head of a well-known investment service, made the following surprising and unpopular statement on September 5, 1929:

I repeat what I said at this time last year and the year before . . . that sooner or later a crash is coming which will take in the leading stocks and cause a decline of from 60 to 80 points in the Dow-Jones barometer.

Fair weather cannot always continue. The economic cycle is in progress today, as it was in the past. The Federal Reserve System has put the banks in a strong position, but it has not changed human nature. More people are borrowing and speculating today than ever in our history. Sooner or later a crash is coming and it may be terrific. . . . [8]

But he was immediately answered on the same day by Professor Irving Fisher of Yale, an eminent economist who had gained a wide reputation through his authoritative cost of living indices:

There may be a recession in stock prices, but not anything in the nature of a crash. Dividend returns on stocks are moving higher. This is not due to receding prices for stocks, and will not be hastened by any anticipated crash, the possibility of which I fail to see.[9]

Then, on October 16, 1929, Dr. Fisher went on to say:

[6] New York *Times*, Aug. 16, 1929.
[7] Angly, *Oh Yeah?*, p. 50.
[8] New York *Times*, Sept. 6, 1929.
[9] Angly, *Oh Yeah?*, p. 37.

Stock prices have reached what looks like a permanently high plateau. I do not feel that there will soon, if ever be a fifty or sixty point break below present levels, such as Mr. Babson has predicted. I expect to see the stock market a good deal higher than it is today within a few months.[10]

No wonder optimism was the order of the day, that the stock market boiled, that U. S. Steel common advanced 60 percent from its low of the year. No wonder that investment trusts were organized.

THE GOLDMAN SACHS TRADING CORPORATION

Perhaps the most spectacular investment trust of the 1920s was the Goldman Sachs Trading Corporation, incorporated on December 4, 1928, and syndicated by the well-known private banking firm of Goldman, Sachs & Co., securities underwriters and specialists in commercial paper and foreign exchange since 1869. $100,000,000 was paid into the company's treasury by the underwriters, who marketed 900,000 shares at 104 and kept 100,000 shares as their own investment. Shares on a "when issued" basis immediately went to a substantial premium and the issue was the talk of Wall Street. Shortly thereafter the corporation issued an additional 125,000 shares.

Then came a merger with the Financial and Industrial Securities Corporation, bringing total assets of the Trading Corporation to $235,000,000. In mid-1929 the corporation joined forces with the Central States Electric Corporation, a public utility holding company, in sponsoring a new investment company, the Shenandoah Corporation, exchanging some of its capital stock for preferred stock of Shenandoah. Shenandoah then sponsored the Blue Ridge Corporation with the same board of directors. (Something new to financial lore was added by the

10 *Ibid.*, p. 38.

Blue Ridge offer to investors of a unit of one share of its preference and common stock in exchange for a share of common stock, at a specified price, of any one of twenty-one well-known corporations—over the protests of several of such corporations' officers.) Additional Goldman Sachs Trading Corporation stock was exchanged for control of the American Company, which owned virtually all the stock of the American Trust Company in San Francisco. By this time, by direct issue to the public and otherwise through exchange of its stock for stock or assets of these other corporations, the Trading Corporation had 5,537,892 shares of capital stock outstanding with a market value on September 16, 1929, of over $650 million. In less than a year it had been born and grown to a company actually capitalized at $326,000,000. The three Goldman Sachs issues had been heavily oversubscribed, and public enthusiasm had carried their common stocks to high premiums over asset values.

The senior partner of Goldman Sachs Trading Corporation was Waddill Catchings, a prominent economist, who wrote in 1928 an idealistic book called *The Road to Plenty*. Curiously the book, ahead of its time, advocated vigorous governmental action, typical of the as yet unborn New Deal, to endeavor to cure any substantial unemployment whenever it might occur.

UNITED FOUNDERS

Meanwhile the Founders' group moved on apace. Mr. Bull became relatively inactive and Louis H. Seagrave, formerly sales manager of the First National Corporation of Boston, seems to have played a dominant part. Finally, the large and conservative investment banking house of Harris, Forbes & Co. became interested in Founders' senior financing. A holding company, The United Founders Corporation, came into being at the top of the pyramid, organized by Mr. Seagrave, Christopher F. Coombs, and Frank B. Erwin—Seagrave and Erwin having been major factors in the Founders' group since 1925.[11] By the end of 1929 thirteen companies comprised the group:

United Founders Corporation
American Founders Corporation
International Securities Corporation of America
Second International Securities Corporation
United States & British International Company, Ltd.
American & General Securities Corporation
American and Continental Corporation
Investment Trust Associates
Founders Associates
Founders General Corporation
Public Utility Holding Corporation of America
United States Electric Power Corporation
United States & Overseas Corporation

The Founders' group, above all others, was the hallmark of the Roaring Twenties. Organized in 1921, the first actual capital of $500 was contributed the following year. By 1929 it had developed into a pyramided system of investment trusts and investment holding companies with paid in capital of over $686 million, some $503 being contributed by the public and some $182 million being subscribed by various companies within the group. No other investment trust or group had ever raised this amount of capital.[12] Nor, in retrospect, was all of it soundly raised. A few skeptics of the day suggested that the method had some similarity to bootstraps. By this they meant that, with leverage existing in a given company in the group and the common stock of such company selling at a premium above its asset value, a second Founders' company, again with leverage would purchase some of the first company's stock. When the public purchased common stock of the second company, which of course was sold above its asset value, such asset

[11] Report of the SEC, *Investment Trusts and Investment Companies,* Part Three, chap. VI, p. 2112.
[12] *Ibid.*, p. 2220.

value was partially based on inter-company holdings which themselves were leverage stocks selling at premiums. And so it went. And it went well because of strenuous selling efforts and advancing stock prices generally.

The SEC in its report of September 10, 1940, says:

The 13 companies of the United Founders Corporation group had numerous other companies loosely affiliated with them largely through stock ownership, and the group was by far the largest group of investment enterprises in the United States. In all, there were affiliated with the United Founders Corporation 22 investment companies including hybrids of investment company and holding company and hybrids of investment company and intermediate credit company. Of these, 14 were organized under the exclusive or joint sponsorship of the United Founders Corporation group as constituted at the time. These investment companies in turn at one time or another effectively dominated seven security distributing enterprises and at least 16 other companies, including nine utility holding companies, the largest of which, United States Electric Power Corporation, held joint control of the billion dollar Standard Gas and Electric Company utility empire. The resources so dominated by the United Founders Corporation group were at one time in excess of $2,100,000,000.[13]

TRI-CONTINENTAL CORPORATION

The genesis of what is now the largest closed-end investment company occurred in January, 1929, when J. & W. Seligman & Co., a prominent New York underwriting and brokerage house, organized the Tri-Continental Corporation. It sold 900,000 shares of common stock and 250,000 shares of 6 percent preferred to the public and 100,000 shares of common to the sponsors. Each share of preferred carried an option warrant to purchase a share of common. The investment company started with $50,000,000. A second $50,000,000 company, Tri-Continental Allied Company, Inc., was launched in August, 1929. On Decem-

[13] *Ibid.*, p. 2108.

ber 27 the two companies were consolidated, the new company being still known as the Tri-Continental Corporation.

THE LEHMAN CORPORATION

The last large trust to be formed before the Panic was the Lehman Corporation, organized by the private banking firm of Lehman Brothers in September, 1929. The $100,000,000 that the company received was largely invested at lower prices than prevailed before the holocaust, which was one factor—another being the simple capital structure, with a third factor to be mentioned later—in the company's excellent record since organization.

Lehman Brothers had previously been associated with Lazard Frères in forming General American and Second General American Investors Company, Inc., leverage investment companies. The resulting consolidated company has likewise been known for good management.

OTHER COMPANIES

Over 700 investment trusts and investment holding companies were formed from 1927 to 1930.[14] But 1929 was a year to remember. By this time the pace was frantic. Companies were being formed at the rate of almost one every business day; 265 new companies were organized in the single year of 1929, over $3 billion being subscribed.[15]

New York was active headquarters of the most important "trusts" of the 1920s, but other cities were also prominent. In Chicago Samuel Insull, the utility magnate, formed, in late 1928, Insull Utility Investments, Inc., and, in October, 1929, Corporation Securities Co. of Chicago, each holding substantial amounts of the other's securities as well as of Insull operating

[14] *Ibid.*, Part Two, chap. II, p. 29.

[15] *Ibid.*, Part Three, chap. I, p. 3.

and public utility holding companies. Assets at the end of 1929 were $157 million and $72 million respectively. Field, Glore & Company in February of 1929 syndicated $59 million of securities of the Chicago Corporation and, in September, participated with Continental Illinois Co. in organizing and raising almost $64 million for the Continental Chicago Corporation. The two companies had interlocking directors and somewhat the same interests in intermediate banking, and, in December, they were merged under the latter name. (In 1932 the name came full circle for, after merger with Chicago Investors, another Chicago Corporation came back into being.)

In Detroit, back in 1926, Johnathan B. Lovelace, a member of E. E. MacCrone & Co., had originated with others the $13-million Investment Company of America and, elsewhere, three other companies: the $13-million Pacific Investing Corporation in 1927, the $15-million American Capital Corporation in 1928, and a small Birmingham company. A former associate of MacCrone, Fred Y. Presley, with the support of the Guardian Detroit Company of Detroit and with the participation of the Shawmut Corporation of Boston, sponsored four investment companies: National Investors Corporation in 1927, and the Second, Third, and Fourth National Investors in 1928 and 1929, with total net capital of some $48 million.[16] Cleveland, in 1926, saw Cyrus S. Eaton of Otis & Co. form Continental Shares, Inc., with $6 million initial capital; its assets, by the end of 1929, were reported at approximately $140 million. This, together with another Eaton company, the $30-million Commonwealth Securities, Inc., had such broad charter provisions that there were practically no limitations upon the kind of business they could conduct. However, the original prospectus offering Continental Shares common stock stated: "The stock of this company is, therefore, not recommended for investors who cannot afford to incur losses nor to those without business experience." [17]

[16] *Ibid.*, p. 11.

[17] *Ibid.*, Part Four, chap. I, pp. 206–7.

Continental Shares as well as the $110-million Petroleum Corporation of America, syndicated by Blair & Co. of New York in January, 1929, were accepted by the public as "investment trusts." New York companies like the $70-million Selected Industries, Inc., floated by C. D. Barney & Co. and Stone & Webster and Blodget, Inc., and others at the end of 1928, did come within the definition of investment trusts—as did Dillon Read's $60-million U. S. and International Securities Co. in 1928, a subsidiary of their first investment trust. But finance and holding companies were all mixed up with investment trusts. A borderline case was the $50-million Chatham Phenix Allied Corporation, organized in late September, 1929, by the security affiliate of the Chatham Phenix National Bank & Trust Company of New York. Then there was an outstanding public utility holding company, the United Corporation, which was organized in January, 1929, by the country's leading private banking house, J. P. Morgan & Co., together with Bonbright & Co., Inc., and Drexel & Co., of Philadelphia, the assets of which, by the year's end, substantially exceeded $300 million. This company is typical of those holding companies which, in later years having divested themselves of control of various subsidiaries, are now classified as investment companies. "At the end of 1929," the SEC Report reads, "there were five management investment companies proper and nine investment-holding companies, with assets of more than $100,000,000 each." [18]

The five management investment companies with 1929 year-end assets in excess of $100 million, according to the SEC, were:

	Assets (in millions of dollars)
The Goldman Sachs Trading Corporation	251
United Founders Corporation	208
American Founders Corporation	171
Blue Ridge Corporation	133
Shenandoah Corporation	104

[18] *Ibid.,* Part Three, chap. VII, p. 2500.

The nine investment-holding companies were:

	Assets (in millions of dollars)
Christiana Securities Co.	361
The United Corporation	332
Alleghany Corporation	263
American Superpower Corporation	225
The Chesapeake Corporation	169
Solvay American Investment Corporation	165
Central States Electric Corporation	161
Continental Shares, Inc.	140
Insull Utility Investments, Inc. (a so-called unclassified management investment company)	157

Two of the investment-holding companies, Christiana Securities and Solvay American, were essentially chemical holding companies, the first, for example, consisting of stocks of companies controlled by the duPont interests; outside interest was comparatively small. With respect to the other companies in which the public broadly participated, ten years later four of the five management investment companies had disappeared as independent entities through merger, and two of the seven investment-holding companies were in receivership.[19]

The SEC study, therefore, encompassed management investment-holding companies as well as strictly investment companies. A company classified as a management investment-holding company such as Christiana Securities Co. or the United Corporation or Alleghany Corporation we would term simply a "holding company," usually concerned with controlling or influencing the management of certain companies whose securities it owned, rather than being formed primarily with the objective of investing in a broad list of securities (almost never representing a controlling interest in any issuer) and distributing the investment income therefrom to the investment company's stockholders.

[19] *Ibid.*

The SEC Report estimates that, at December 31, 1929, there were 675 investment companies of all types in the United States with total assets of $7,157,000,000. Of these 193 were management investment companies with assets of $2,782,000,000—all closed-end companies except for 19 open-end companies with assets of a mere $140,000,000.

The remainder consisted of 45 management investment-holding companies (which we should call holding companies) with assets of $2,738,000,000 and $1,400,000,000 of assets of 376 unclassified companies. Then there were 52 fixed and semi-fixed trusts with $163,000,000 of assets, plus $74,000,000 of assets of common trust funds and installment certificate companies.[20]

The $7 billion total assets of all companies considered at the year's-end, at the peak of the 1929 market the SEC estimates may well have been at least $8 billion. But remember that this book is the story of investment companies—what we call true investment companies—the assets of which would only represent something more than half of this figure. Specifically the assets of the types of companies we are studying, at the end of 1929, are estimated by the SEC Report to have been $3,019,-000,000. Perhaps half or more of the assets of the "unclassified companies" should be added to this figure.

Keane's Manual of Investment Trusts for 1930 gives an interesting table of all "Investment Trust Financing" for the years 1924 through 1929. Their total figure is $2,841,367,639, and they feel that untraceable fixed trust sales would bring the figure to "over $3,000,000,000." They include several Canadian companies and one or two American companies such as Electric Power Associates, Inc., which we should term holding companies. Their tabulation of course reflects the price the public paid for investment company securities at time of issue rather than the market value of the assets of investment companies at the 1929 year-end.

The Appendix includes a tabulation of all American com-

[20] *Ibid.*, Part Two, chap. II, p. 27.

panies existing at the end of 1929, with date of organization and assets where available. This is followed by tabulations from the SEC study of the larger closed-end investment companies, management investment-holding companies, unclassified management investment companies, and unit trusts.

From all sources our best estimate is that true investment company assets at December 31, 1929, were about $4 billion and, at the peak of the 1929 market, perhaps as much as $4½ billion.

4

"After Me the Deluge"

KING LOUIS XV of France had said, "apres moi le deluge." The speculative excesses of 1929 brought the era of what New Dealers called "Economic Royalists" to an end. The confusion that followed the Panic in a very minor way was reminiscent of the political and economic turbulence of the French Revolution. And indeed the 1930s ushered in a group of political figures and economic innovators whose New Deal philosophies and legislation achieved a bloodless but nevertheless a genuine political and economic revolution in the United States.

The fall of 1929 started serenely so far as business was concerned. But the stock market topped off in early September and registered some nervous declines and lesser recoveries over several weeks. Then, on October 24, the Panic struck. This twelve-million-share day, Black Thursday, for a while saw the market utterly demoralized. On Monday, October 28, as nine million shares changed hands, Dow-Jones Industrial Averages declined 13 percent; American Telephone broke 34 points, and the most active stock on the Curb Exchange closed without a bid. The next day, Tuesday, was the worst of all—sixteen million shares, more money lost than on the previous day, the Industrial Averages off another 12 percent. From the highest prices of 1929 to the year-end there was a decline in the value of shares listed on the Exchange of $25 billion or 28 percent. And, carrying on such figures to the depth of the Depression—when a quarter of our working force was unemployed in 1932—

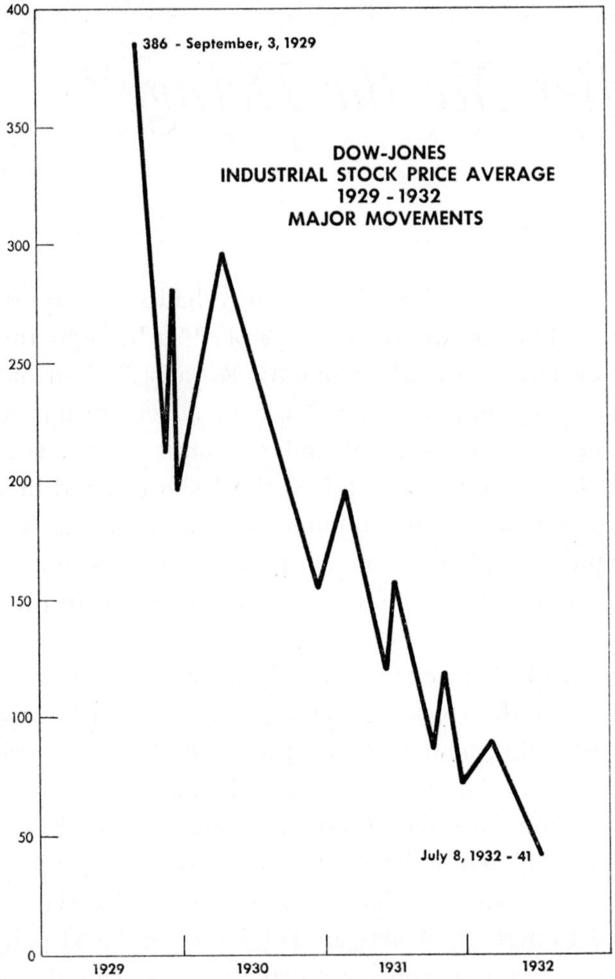

values at the nadir had declined $73 billion, or more than 80 percent.

Tens of thousands of speculators were wiped out; hundreds of thousands of investors suffered tragic losses. Numerous banks, investment bankers, brokers, railroads, utility and industrial companies went into receivership, perhaps the hardest hit of all being the highly pyramided holding companies that controlled even some of our most fundamental industries. Suicides were not infrequent and the most popular story concerned the hotel clerk who queried the man standing before his desk requesting a room with "For sleeping or jumping?"

Obviously, investment company portfolios reflected the drastic deflation in security prices. The deflation was world-wide. As the chairman of the Alliance Trust Company, Ltd., of Dundee said at an annual meeting of his shareholders:

> Trust Companies . . . have reckoned that by a wide spreading of their investment risk, a stable revenue position could be maintained, as it was not to be expected that all the world would go wrong at the same time. But the unexpected has happened, and every part of the civilized world is in trouble . . . .[1]

And the prices of investment company securities themselves declined sharply. Inevitably the common stocks of companies with leverage showed substantially greater decline than those of companies with simple capital structure. Leverage was working in reverse. Common stocks of companies with leverage had registered spectacular rises in advancing markets. But what went up with accelerated speed declined precipitously. The SEC Report, referring to the years from 1929 through 1937, reads:

> Over the period as a whole, the market experience of the common stocks of closed-end leverage investment companies was much worse than that of the common stocks of non-leverage companies. By the end of 1937, the average dollar which had been invested in July 1929 in the index of leverage investment company common stocks was worth 5¢, while the non-leverage dollar was worth 48¢.[2]

[1] George Glasgow, *Glasgow's Guide to Investment Trust Companies* (London, 1935).

[2] Report of the Securities and Exchange Commission, *Investment Trusts and Investment Companies,* Part Two, chap. IV, p. 276.

Remember that, at the end of 1929, of the public's investment of over $7 billion in the companies studied by the SEC, the vast bulk was in closed-end companies, about evenly divided between true investment companies and what should strictly be called holding companies, most with multiple capital structure. There was a mere $140 million in open-end companies, $163 million in fixed trusts and very minor amounts in other types.

By the middle of 1932 the SEC Report estimated that these $7 billion of assets had probably shrunk to below $2 billion or approximately a quarter of the $8 billion that they may have been worth at the peak of 1929. (It will be seen, however, that investment companies repurchased and retired several hundred million of their own securities—which would modify the implications of this figure.) Dow-Jones Industrial Averages, however, had shrunk over the same period to 11 percent of their 1929 highs.

Why did investment companies lose billions for their shareholders? The outstanding reason is that they themselves were holders of securities which showed a tremendous depreciation. But there were other reasons.

One reason was that, although most companies had issued senior capital themselves in the form of preferred stock and/or debentures—the average for the closed-end investment companies was a ratio of 40 percent in senior capital to 60 percent in common stock—nevertheless the bulk of the securities they owned were common stocks of other corporations. (The SEC gives only figures for 1936 for all the companies included in their study, embracing investment holding companies as well; but, at that time, 88 percent of portfolio investment was in commons, 6 percent in preferreds, and 6 percent in bonds.) [3] Therefore, when prices declined, and with the leverage that the pyramided capital structure gave the common shareholders of investment companies working in reverse, the asset value of

[3] *Ibid.*, chap. VIII, p. 527.

their common shares declined not only much faster than the decline in value of the investment company's portfolio, but obviously faster than it would have if the portfolio had not been so largely comprised of common stocks.

Another reason for investors' losses in the common stocks of investment companies was that virtually all such shares had sold at premiums, sometimes very substantial, above their asset value during the speculative era before the Panic. After the Crash many sold at considerable discounts, although there were instances where the common shareholder's equity had been completely wiped out and, in pyramided companies, when the shares had a negative asset value, even a nominal quotation for such shares represented a premium above their asset value. The SEC Report states: "The aggregate market values of shares in investment companies following the close of 1929 was approximately 35% less than the actual value of the assets of these companies." [4]

Finally, of course, many companies had departed from conservative principles of investment company management—although in some instances this is what the purchaser of their securities apparently wanted. According to the SEC Report:

> Investment Companies employed their publicly contributed funds in a wide variety of ways: participation in underwritings of securities; trading in securities and commodities; dealing in puts and calls, foreign exchange, bankers' acceptances and commercial paper, and oil and gas royalties; short selling; loans to brokers, dealers, and others on securities; granting of options on securities issued by others; dealing in real estate; reorganization of industrial companies, and rendering investment advisory service.[5]

The months following the Panic found the word "investment trust"—the term in use in those days—in high disfavor. The magic had disappeared. Not only were common stocks of

[4] *Ibid.*, Part Three, chap. IV, p. 1021.
[5] *Ibid.*, chap. VII, p. 2501.

investment companies selling at discounts below their asset value, but preferred shares and bonds of trusts were selling substantially below the price to which they were entitled in case of liquidation. Moreover, many were a drug on the market. So managements began repurchasing their own securities at discounts and retiring them. This provided a better market for their own securities and was to the benefit of their remaining security holders. One of the largest companies for instance, one without leverage, was able to repurchase its shares at from 25 percent to a 50 percent discount and retire them; it actually retired a third of its outstanding capitalization. It is estimated that investment companies spent over half a billion dollars in similar operations.

The wreckage in the securities markets after the Panic was bad enough, but as the Depression deepened in 1932, pessimism not only among investors, but among sponsors of the prevailing investment companies of the 1920s began to equal their previous exuberant optimism. In this connection, the SEC Report declares:

> . . . the majority of investment companies had been formed by investment bankers and securities brokers. With the collapse in the market value of securities, their interest in their companies had to a large extent, diminished. The utility of their investment companies as a source of underwriting and brokerage commissions had substantially decreased. Their security interest in their investment companies had lost all, or almost all, asset value and had diminished substantially in market value. The value of option warrants to purchase stock of their investment companies which they had received as management or underwriting compensation had also become worthless.[6]

Throughout the investment trust industry many sponsors were in a frame of mind to have their companies consolidated or turn over management functions to new hands. Certain hands were ready and waiting. The ablest belonged to Floyd B. Odlum.

[6] *Ibid.*, chap. IV, p. 1018.

Photograph by Underwood and Underwood

FLOYD B. ODLUM

ATLAS CORPORATION

Mr. Odlum was a lawyer who had become a vice-president of the Electric Bond & Share Company, a giant public utility holding and servicing company, and had played the major part in building up one of Electric Bond & Share's most important subsidiaries, the American & Foreign Power Corporation, of which he was vice-chairman.

In 1923 he and George Howard, then a partner of the law firm of Simson, Thacher & Bartlett, put up $10,000 apiece, as did their respective wives, and incorporated a small company, the United States Company, primarily as a hobby "to see what could be done" [7] to make their stake increase. Odlum's brother-in-law, L. Boyd Hatch, joined the venture the following year; other friends joined them later. By 1928 the contributed capital of some $300,000 had doubled in value.

The group formed a Canadian company which absorbed the original company, raised more capital, and then, in July, 1929, formed in Delaware the Atlas Corporation, to which was transferred the Odlum's, the Howard's, and Hatch's Canadian company stock plus some $3,000,000 worth of securities in exchange for Atlas stock and option warrants. In the spring of 1930 Atlas had assets of about $17,000,000. From this base Odlum launched Atlas on its interesting career of acquisition and absorption until 1936. In the course of its program Atlas Corporation acquired control of 21 investment companies. Of these 21 companies, control of two was sold by Atlas at a profit, 16 were dissolved, and three were consolidated with Atlas in October, 1936.

During 1930, Odlum's investigation of investment companies indicated that the market value of their securities was at least 35 percent less than the actual value of the assets owned by the holders of such securities. The opportunity was presented to acquire the portfolios of diversified securities of other invest-

[7] *Ibid.*, p. 1053.

ment companies at a total price less than their actual value. This was the fundamental purpose of the Atlas Corporation's campaign to buy control of, and to amalgamate with itself, the assets of other investment companies. To the extent of the differential between the cost of the securities of investment companies acquired by Atlas Corporation and its actual value, Atlas had a "cushion" [8] against further depreciation in the market value of securities. And through the medium of its exchange offers Atlas was enabled to distribute its own securities for the securities of other companies having asset values in excess of the asset value of its own securities.

The preferred stocks of other investment companies that Atlas bought always had an asset value greatly in excess of their market value. Common stocks of such investment companies, however, usually had no asset value—or even a negative asset value. So, whatever price Atlas paid in purchasing the latter represented a premium above their asset value. Those commons with voting power obviously had to be acquired to assure control of a company, but Atlas was careful to purchase preferreds and commons in a ratio that would end up by giving Atlas a net gain in asset value.

Atlas Corporation fished in many waters. It purchased for cash securities of other investment companies in the open market. It made offers of exchange of its own securities to a broad list of the security holders of other trusts. In this connection, Atlas addressed letters to hundreds of commercial banks, investment bankers, and brokers, offering to compensate them for their services in helping to effect the exchanges. Since its own common had a market value substantially in excess of its asset value, and since the market value of its own preferred provided less asset value than other preferreds it might be acquiring, the operations obviously benefited Atlas shareholders. Finally, Atlas dealt directly with the management of trusts it wanted

[8] *Ibid.*, p. 1056.

to acquire. It purchased common and preferred stocks of other investment companies from sponsors, directors, and others affiliated with such companies' managements for a total consideration of $20,651,457. This was $7,044,544 in excess of the market value of the securities on the date they were acquired. In addition Atlas paid out $732,895 for option warrants held by such persons, even though the warrants had no apparent value.[9] But it had to—to get control. And when Atlas was in the saddle and could liquidate or consolidate such companies with itself, the arithmetic worked out very well for its own shareholders. With respect to the companies that were dissolved, all shareholders were given the opportunity to obtain their distributive share of corporate assets either in cash or in kind. Atlas always chose to take its share in kind and thereby acquired a portfolio of securities whose asset value exceeded its market value. Minority shareholders could have done the same, but the majority of these chose cash.

The best known of the acquisitions of the Atlas Corporation were the Goldman Sachs Trading Corporation (whose name was changed to the Pacific Eastern Corporation in 1933), the Shenandoah Corporation, and the Blue Ridge Corporation. Blue Ridge again became independent of Atlas in 1935.

Besides these, Atlas acquired control of Widlor, Inc., All America General Corporation, Exide Securities Corporation, Power & Light Securities Trust, Selected Stocks, Inc., Ungerleider Financial Corporation, Iroquois Share Corporation, Federated Capital Corporation, General Empire Corporation, Jackson & Curtis Investment Associates, Sterling Securities Corporation, Chatham Phenix Allied Corporation, Chain Store Stocks, Inc., National Securities Investment Co., Aviation Securities Corporation, American, British & Continental Corporation (later sold to the Equity Corp.), Atlantic Securities Corporation, and American Investors, Inc.

9 *Ibid.*, p. 1066.

All America General Corporation was the first investment company to be acquired by Atlas, in June, 1930. The former had raised $5,025,000 in 1929, but was worth $3,149,555 when Atlas took it over. The acquisition took place despite the strong efforts of the company's president to block it. But Atlas was not always successful in the consummation of its intended acquisitions. It failed to acquire the National Investors group, valued at the end of 1931 at about $25 million. Again the president of these four companies was opposed to the deal and Atlas withdrew from the effort and sold its holdings back to the respective companies.

A typical case history of the method employed by Atlas in acquiring an investment company is the Sterling Securities Corporation story, Sterling being one of Atlas' larger acquisitions. This company was incorporated early in 1928 and, after its final financing in September, 1929, had issued 297,465 shares of $50 first convertible 6 percent preferred, 500,000 shares of $20 par value 6 percent preference, 603,802 shares of no-par Class A common, and 298,297 shares of Class B common—the latter designed to receive 25 percent of corporate earnings after payment of 6 percent per annum on all senior securities. Classes A and B common had one vote per share. All but 50,000 shares of the Class B stock were acquired at 50 cents per share by directors, officers, and managers. The company received a total of $32,475,898 from its financing, most of which was invested in common stocks. On July 31, 1931, when Atlas acquired working control, the company's net worth was $16,764,854.

Although the Class B stock had no asset value and no quoted market, it was important that Atlas acquire it for control; this it proceeded to do, in large measure from those who had been identified with the corporation, paying as high as $4 a share and accumulating 71 percent. The Class A shares had no asset value either, but they likewise carried voting power and Atlas paid $2 above their market price. By the end of December,

1931, even though Atlas possessed only a third of the voting shares of Sterling, it took over management of its portfolio and four Atlas men became directors. But it was still necessary for Atlas to acquire enough additional shares of A and B stocks to be able to consolidate or liquidate the corporation. It was equally important that Atlas purchase more than enough preferred stock below its asset value—the preference by now had no asset value—to more than offset the premium it was forced to pay for the A and B stocks and for some of the preference stock. So two exchange offers ensued.

The first was made in June, 1932. For each share of Sterling Securities first preferred Atlas offered a unit of one-third of Atlas preference, a share of common, and one option warrant. For each share of Sterling preference it offered one-tenth of a share of Atlas common and four-tenths of an option warrant. For each share of Sterling Class A it offered one-fifth of an Atlas warrant. For each share of Sterling Class B it offered one-tenth of an Atlas warrant. Atlas warrants had of course no asset value, and in the offer to Sterling preference shareholders Atlas sacrificed asset value of only 27 cents per share. Sterling first preferred, however, had an asset value of $37.35, and the package that Atlas offered had an asset value of $19.64. The holders of the first preferred were attracted because their market value was $14.50 and the market value of the Atlas package $17.46. As a result of the shares of all classes exchanged through this offer Atlas had a gain in asset values of $421,072.

Atlas paid a Chicago and a New York brokerage house commissions to solicit Sterling Securities stockholders, and when Atlas made a second exchange offer, somewhat comparable to the first offer, it also employed a well-known Buffalo firm. In addition, Atlas continued to accumulate Sterling stock of all classes by direct purchases on the general market. By the end of December, 1935, Atlas had accumulated 75 percent of Sterling preferred, 62 percent of Sterling preference, 46 percent of

Class A, and 88 percent of Class B stocks. Cost to Atlas was $7,546,338. Sterling paid dividends and arrearages of $2,121,-012. Asset value of all Sterling stocks held by Atlas was $14,-583,003. Atlas's profit from the Sterling venture by October 31, 1936, was therefore $9,157,676. While much of it was as a result of appreciation of Sterling's assets under Atlas Corporation's management, nevertheless a substantial enough portion of such profit was derived from the differential in asset values resulting from Atlas exchange offers to justify the thesis upon which Atlas based its operations.[10]

Atlas did not do the job alone. It made use of its subsidiaries to help finance its expansion program. A substantial part of the assets of almost all the investment companies acquired prior to 1933 were, like the assets of Atlas itself, employed in the purchase of securities of other investment companies. After Atlas acquired control in August, 1931, of Chatham Phenix Allied Corporation—a company incorporated in late 1929 by Chatham Phenix Corporation, an affiliate of the Chatham Phenix National Bank & Trust Company—whose assets at the time of acquisition were over $31 million, Atlas caused this company, subsequently renamed Securities Allied Corporation, to purchase from Atlas and its existing affiliates substantial blocks of other Atlas-controlled companies. Thereafter, it became the principal agent through which the other companies were held. When it was eventually dissolved over three quarters of its portfolio consisted of securities of other Atlas companies. It was therefore an intermediate holding company. The other investment trust of comparable size at the time that Atlas took over its management, in April of 1933, as the holder of the largest single block of stock (approximately 40 percent), namely the Goldman Sachs Trading Corporation, with assets of approximately $32 million, was not dissolved but was consolidated with Atlas.[11]

10 *Ibid.*, pp. 1162 ff.

11 *Ibid.*, chap. V, p. 1922.

Atlas dissolved a total of sixteen companies. At time of dissolution it usually held over 90 percent of the dissolved companies' securities. The aggregate assets of the dissolved companies, at the dates of their dissolution, totaled $69,880,271, of which over 95 percent was distributed to Atlas and less than 5 percent to minority stockholders. But the interest of minority stockholders in the assets of Pacific Eastern Corporation (the subsequent name for Goldman Sachs), Shenandoah Corporation and Sterling Securities Corporation, the three companies consolidated with Atlas, totaled approximately $20 million. Atlas would obviously have lost control of this sum if it had dissolved rather than consolidated these three companies.[12] Finally, the two companies which Atlas sold at a profit in 1935 were the American, British & Continental Corporation and the Blue Ridge Corporation.

The investment trusts acquired by the Atlas Corporation were all formed between 1926 and 1929. Approximately $783 million was contributed by the public and by sponsors; $24 million, or 3 percent went to sponsors as selling commissions; and $159 million was returned to stockholders because of repurchase by the various companies of their own securities or by payment of dividends and interest. Of the roughly $600 million remaining capital originally contributed, $420 million represented realized and unrealized losses prior to acquisition by Atlas. This loss was about 70 percent of the net capital investment in the companies, after payment of underwriting commissions, repurchases of their own securities, and payment of dividends and interest.[13]

Atlas started its acquisition program with $17,000,000. Its assets increased to $106,000,000 by early 1937. The program was actually concluded before the end of 1936 by the consolidation of Atlas with its then existing investment company sub-

[12] *Ibid.*, chap. IV, p. 1429.
[13] *Ibid.*, p. 1066.

sidiaries: Pacific Eastern, Shenandoah, and Sterling Securities Corporation.

Atlas did a good job. The SEC Report confirms that

The record indicates that the experience of the stockholders of the companies acquired by Atlas Corporation after they joined with the Atlas Corporation as "partners" in the acquisition program, was comparatively better than would have been the case had the original portfolios of the acquired companies been retained or if their assets had been reinvested in the securities which form the basis for the calculation of the commonly known stock market averages.[14]

THE EQUITY CORPORATION

It is obvious that the heavily pyramided United Founders group would have had an unhappy sequel. According to the SEC:

Between November 30, 1929, and November 23, 1935, the public's investment in the group, measured in terms of market price, declined from $545,181,000. to $41,151,000., only $41,571,000. of the $504,-030,000. decline being accountable by reason of disbursements or reacquisition of securities by companies in the group.[15]

The Founder's venture, starting as a well conceived series of investment companies, had almost completely changed its character by 1929. Far different from the British trusts it was organized to emulate, trading profits were paid out as income and a large proportion of these profits were from inter-company transactions in each other's securities. Finally the Founders group departed from conservative investment principles and became essentially a pyramided holding company structure with entirely different objectives.

The United Founders' group of companies became the core of the other important company which, like Atlas, embarked

14 *Ibid.*, p. 1063.
15 *Ibid.*, chap. VI, p. 2116.

upon an acquisition program, namely the Equity Corporation. The SEC Report reads:

In 1935, when the surviving companies of the Founders Group, after having come under the control of The Equity Corporation, were consolidated into American General Corporation, they had total assets of about $50,000,000.[16]

The Equity Corporation was organized in December, 1932, by Wallace Groves and his associates, with initial assets of $300,-000. It immediately acquired control of Allied General Corporation and the Yosemite Holding Corporation. The latter controlled Chain & General Equities, Inc., which controlled Interstate Equities Corporation. Six months later control of the Equity Corporation itself changed.

For approximately $1,000,000 Groves sold control to interests headed by two partners of the well-known New York law firm of Satterlee and Canfield, David M. Milton and Ellery C. Huntington, Jr.

Under the management of Mr. Milton the corporation underwent a period of rapid growth, its gross assets increasing within three years from $311,926.35 to $24,710,048.27. Similarly, the gross assets subject to its control mounted from $6,225,789.66 to $205,000,000. This growth represented for the most part the absorption of the bulk of the assets of seventeen publicly held companies, in addition to the four investment companies under the control of The Equity Corporation at the time of its organization.[17]

The four investment companies which the Equity Corporation controlled when it embarked on its acquisition program have already been named. Of the additional seventeen publicly held companies the bulk of the assets of which Equity absorbed, eleven were the following investment companies: American, British & Continental Corporation, American and Continental Corporation, American Founders Corporation, American & General Securities Corporation, Eastern Shares

[16] *Ibid.*, p. 2222. [17] *Ibid.*, chap. IV, p. 1046.

Corporation, International Securities Corporation of America, Reliance International Corporation, Reliance Management Corporation, Second International Securities Corporation, United Founders Corporation, and United States & British International Company, Ltd. In addition there were the following six insurance companies: American Colony Insurance Company, American Merchant Marine Insurance Company, Colonial States Fire Insurance Company, General Alliance Corporation, Majestic Fire Insurance Company, and North Star Insurance Company.

The Equity Corporation made approximately fifty exchange offers to the security holders of thirteen of these twenty-one companies. Mergers accounted for the absorption by Equity or by its controlled subsidiaries of the assets of nine of the twenty-one. Four companies were dissolved, eight others were consolidated into a subsidiary of The Equity Corporation.[18] This subsidiary was the American General Corporation. The end of the story is that in 1950 American General and Equity were merged, keeping the Equity name. In 1952 the Equity Corporation absorbed a later acquired subsidiary, the First York Corporation. Wall Street wags of the day termed the Equity story a lawyer's dream.

Of all the Equity Corporation's acquisitions, however, the companies comprising the Founders' system were the most noteworthy. The key to this operation was the United Founders Corporation, the net assets of which, in June, 1933, were approximately $15 million. United Founders capitalization consisted of 1,000,000 shares of Class A stock and 9,000,000 shares of common. Class A stock had a voting power equal to one-half the voting power of any amount of common that might be outstanding. The sole holders of the Class A, in equal amounts, were Messrs. Seagrave, Coombs, and Erwin, the total asset value of the Class A stock being then about $48,000. Equity purchased from the two latter their Class A stock, namely 666,-

[18] *Ibid.,* p. 1047.

666⅔ shares plus 635,000 shares of common, Messrs. Coombs and Erwin receiving $954,000 cash and 260,150 shares of Equity common stock. The premium paid by Equity gave it effective working control of the Founders system. For United Founders owned 78 percent of American Founders voting stock, and the latter controlled First and Second International Securities Corporations, United States & British International, American & General, and American and Continental. The next step was for Equity to make exchange offers to shareholders of United Founders and its subsidiaries. By July, 1933, it had acquired 39 percent of the voting control of United Founders. In May of 1935 Equity made an offer to United Founders common stockholders to exchange their shares for three-tenths of a share of Equity. In November of 1935 the Equity Corporation caused all of these companies to be consolidated into a new company, American General Corporation.

The technique of the acquisitions by the Equity Corporation followed a fairly constant pattern. First it was necessary to acquire actual or at least working control of a company. In all instances the original block of stock was purchased from the management of the company to be acquired or from some large institutional holder, never on the general market. Premiums above asset and market value were paid for such control. And, frequently, funds of the Equity Corporation's subsidiaries were used to finance the transaction. The second step was for Equity to make exchange offers of its own securities to the security holders of the companies of which it had actual or working control. The final step was to liquidate or merge such companies.

There were never more than a few individuals and organizations that actively went out for acquisitions and consolidations. Another, however, was the prominent Tri-Continental Corporation. The SEC Report says of this:

Tri-Continental Corporation, with assets of approximately $76,500,000. at January 1, 1930, and sponsored by J. & W. Seligman & Co., investment bankers, absorbed three other investment companies during the period 1931–1935. In addition, Tri-Continental Corporation acquired stock interests in or management contracts with four other investment companies and a fire insurance company. By December 31, 1936, Tri-Continental Corporation and the other companies in the group had gross assets of approximately $170,000,000.[19]

The three companies which Tri-Continental Corporation acquired control of and absorbed by 1935 were Wedgwood Investing Corporation, in January, 1931; Investors Equity Company, Inc., in May, 1932; and Graymur Corporation, in January, 1933. Total assets of these companies were somewhat over $12 million. In May, 1931, a far larger company came under Tri-Continental control: Selected Industries, Inc., with assets exceeding $53 million, previously under the control of C. D. Barney & Company. Tri-Continental purchased, for approximately $6½ million, 18 percent of the common and 37½ percent of Selected Industries' convertible preferred, concluding a contract to manage the latter's portfolio for an annual fee of one-half of 1 percent per annum. Throughout the active period of its acquisition of other companies, Tri-Continental's guiding motive was to acquire a constantly larger quantity of assets to manage and thus spread the costs of its extensive investment management organization.

In June of 1932 Tri-Continental purchased, for slightly over $300,000, 64 percent of the common stock of Broad Street Management Corporation, Ltd., which managed two investment companies, Capital Administration Company, Ltd., and Broad Street Investing Co., Inc., thus bringing another $6 million under its jurisdiction. In November of 1935 Tri-Continental paid somewhat over $6 million for a quarter interest in the then $39-million Blue Ridge Corporation and contracted to manage it for an annual fee of one-fifth of 1 percent of assets, dividing management responsibilities with the Northern Shares Co., a

[19] *Ibid.*, chap. I, p. 24.

company affiliated with Harrison Williams interests. Blue Ridge control, however, was later transferred to another Williams company, and control of the $17-million Electric Shareholdings Corporation came under Tri-Continental, Electric Shareholdings' name being changed to General Shareholdings. Another kind of company came within the Tri-Continental system in August, 1933, with Selected Industries owning a minority interest and Tri-Continental executing a service contract with the $13-million Globe-Rutgers Fire Insurance Co. Two small real estate properties completed the system. In due course the relationships were simplified by liquidation and consolidation, and Tri-Continental emerged as the largest of the closed-end investment companies. A unique feature is the Union Service Corporation, a non-profit management organization, owned at that time proportionately by and servicing Tri-Continental and the Broad Street Investment Corporation, the latter being the only investment company within the system that was not liquidated or consolidated.

The operations of Atlas, Equity, and others followed a familiar pattern. As we have seen, the absorbing company would acquire large blocks of the senior securities of the companies it intended to absorb at a price far below their value in case of liquidation. Previously it had acquired by purchase in the open market or by negotiation with original sponsors of such companies enough voting stock to give it an influence in the companies' affairs. Next would come an offer of its own stock at an attractive price in exchange for securities of the company it intended to absorb. Now it had control, and it would vote its stock to liquidate the company or force a consolidation with itself—at genuine profit to its own shareholders.

This "picking up of the pieces" was a natural aftermath of the debacle of 1929. It lasted for several years. Virtually no new capital was raised from the public during such operations. Meanwhile, what was the public buying?

5

Investor Reaction

DURING THE 1920s pyramided management investment companies had dominated the scene. And the SEC, viewing the entire securities field, estimates that in 1929 investment company issues totaled 30 percent of all corporate financing.[1]

After the Panic the pendulum swung to the other extreme. The word "investment trust" was anathema to the investing public. "Management" was at a discount; the public wanted no part of "management." Whatever trusts the public would even look at were of an entirely different type. The years 1930 and 1931 saw the heyday of so-called fixed trusts.

Fixed trusts were well named because of their rigidity. A block of specified stocks was deposited in "units" with a trustee. Shares of beneficial interest were issued against the unit of stocks. The sponsor then sold such shares to the public, adding a premium of perhaps 10 percent above their asset value to cover cost and profit. The stocks comprising a unit could never be changed unless an individual stock passed a dividend—then it must be sold. A few trusts, to be sure, were a bit more flexible, and in these management had some discretion.

The public, however, liked this absence of management; they

[1] Report of the Securities and Exchange Commission, *Investment Trusts and Investment Companies,* Part Two, chap. III, p. 186.

also liked the redemption feature, where the holders of shares representing a unit could demand either the underlying stocks deposited against the unit or the proceeds from their liquidation. Consequently, sponsors could more easily make a ready market. And it meant at least that the shares should have a market that bore some relationship to their true worth.

We have seen that fixed trusts had their genesis back in 1923, but, since they were not spectacular, the Roaring Twenties virtually passed them by. Now in 1930, they came into their own.

The SEC Report tells us:

> Up to January 1929, the fixed trust movement was of minor importance, comparatively few trusts being organized year by year and a few dissolutions taking place. In 1929, 23, and in 1930, 77 new fixed trusts were organized. One of the reasons for this increase was the reaction of investors to management investment companies. The market price of the shares of United Founders Corporation, one of the largest management investment companies, had dropped from a high of \$75½ in 1929 to \$6 in 1930 and a new low of \$1⅜ in 1931.[2]

The Report continues:

> At the end of 1929 only 52 fixed and semi-fixed trusts were known to be in existence as compared with 143 two years later. In 1930 total sales of their new certificates amounted to \$336,000,000. as compared with \$88,000,000. in 1929 and \$47,00,000. in 1928. Another year of large scale distribution followed in 1931 with \$266,000,000. of new sales, but sales dropped sharply to \$74,000,000. in 1932. Thereafter sales dwindled steadily until they virtually ceased. At the peak of the fixed trust boom in 1930 and 1931, \$600,000,000. of their certificates were sold . . . .[3]

The assets of fixed trusts amounted to almost 8 percent of the total assets of the industry at the end of 1931.

[2] Report of the Securities and Exchange Commission, *Fixed and Semifixed Investment Trusts,* chap. III, p. 24.
[3] *Ibid.,* p. 28.

NORTH AMERICAN TRUST SHARES

The largest of the fixed trusts during their short run of popularity was North American Trust Shares. It was typical of most of the others.

As of March 1, 1930, four shares each of twenty-eight well-known railroad, utility, oil, and other industrial stocks, together with a reserve fund of $1,200 in cash, plus an amount to cover accumulated dividends, comprised a unit which was deposited with the Guaranty Trust Co. as trustee; and 2,000 certificates of beneficial interest were issued against such unit in bearer form in different convenient denominations.

No change could be made in the composition of the unit, except that if a stock had not paid a dividend for 100 days after a customary date it had to be sold and the proceeds distributed to shareholders. Not only dividends received from the underlying stocks but all rights, stock dividends, split-ups, and the like were sold and distributed semiannually to certificate holders. Often a "dividend" represented an actual return of capital. An advertisement in *Keane's Manual* of 1930 reads in part: "A security valued today at more than the offering price of a year ago—having returned 11.2% in the meantime."

Holders of a quarter unit could demand their pro rata share of underlying stocks at any time from the trustee. The trust was to run to 1953. The daily price to the public was stated to be based upon the odd lot prices of the deposited stocks, plus brokerage fees, plus 18 cents per share for issue and deposit, plus the proportionate amount of accumulated cash and other property held by the trustee, with 5 percent added for cost of distribution and profit. This fixed trust was merchandised by a master salesman, Thomas F. Lee, some $184,891,572 worth being sold.

Lee's principal rival was Ross Beason, originally a Salt Lake City securities dealer, the major factor in Corporate Trust

Shares, who merchandised $144,995,823 worth of its shares. An advertising and selling campaign was carried on by Lee and Beason that exceeded anything heretofore known in the trust field.

But the pattern of investment companies was about to change. As the year 1931 drew to a close, public interest in fixed trusts began to wane. As early as January 4, 1932, an article captioned "New Investment Trust Form Held Need of Financial Life" appeared in the New York Evening *Post* and was repeated almost verbatim, with slight amplification, in the March, 1932, issue of *Keane's Investment Trust Monthly* under the title "The Future of the Investment Trust." Some years later, in 1938, at the preliminary hearings of the SEC's investigation of the investment company industry, one of the investigators held up the article and said to the author "Did you write that? It might well have been written by the SEC." The article to which the investigator referred follows.

The Future of the Investment Trust

By HUGH BULLOCK

What accounts for the popularity over the last two years of so-called fixed trusts?

The fact that people saw what they were buying. They could open a circular and see what actual securities their money was being put into. They could even see the relative amount that was invested in each security. And they knew that such securities and amounts could not be materially changed.

The second point of great appeal was the fact that the market action of fixed trust shares could be no better or no worse than that of the weighted average of the securities contained in their portfolios. This was made certain because of their familiar liquidation feature.

Why were fixed trust shares saleable at a premium when management trust shares had no appeal at a discount? The word discount gives us the answer. Investors were tired of having the price of management trust shares fluctuate with no regard to asset value.

They demanded something that would bear a fixed relationship to such value.

What accounts for the unpopularity during the last two years of so-called management trusts?

Primarily this disgraceful market action of their shares. The action of management trust shares has been far worse than justified by results of management. Originally they were marketed at various premiums over their asset value. Speculative enthusiasm subsequently carried them up occasionally to several times their asset value. Conversely, the crash of 1929 and the following period of unfavorable markets not only erased any premium, but depressed some shares to a discount of twenty to forty per cent below their asset value.

The second major factor that contributed to the unpopularity of management trusts is the fact that people were often greatly concerned when they finally ascertained what use had been made of their money. They sometimes found the bulk of it invested in shares of other investment companies. Sometimes a large portion was used to secure control of a utility, or commercial bank or investment banking house. Sometimes a large investment was made in some promotional project. Oftentimes, a list of little known domestic or foreign securities made the investor uneasy. Occasionally, the investor would be puzzled to find the portfolio of his company contained almost an entirely different list of securities from that shown by its previous report.

Occasionally, such investments proved most lucrative. The point is not that they were good or bad. The point is that such vehicles should never have been termed investment trusts. In reality, they were holding companies or finance companies or trading pools.

To be sure there have been severe critics of fixed trusts.

The extremely rigid provisions of some will work very much to their disadvantage as time goes on. I always remember hearing Robert Fleming's remark to my father—"Don't tie yourself with too many restrictions. Restrictions you put in today that you think are for the protection of your shareholders, will rise up some day to plague you."

The provisions of other trusts forcing the elimination of stocks at depressed prices are, on the face of them, wrong. That may be the very time a trust should be buying such stocks.

The irresponsible sponsorship of some finally gave the fixed trust field the name of being virtually a "racket." At one time they were coming so fast that you couldn't even find a name for a new trust.

Another point for criticism was the merchandising methods of some sponsors. The Stock Exchange quite correctly put a stop to all this. Fixed trust merchandising has since been on a much higher plane.

And to be sure, one can find in the management trust field commendable examples of conscientious trusteeship, of sound judgment, of excellent results. Measured by the infallible yardstick of comparing asset values of various trusts (adjusting for intermediate change in capitalization) with the trend of security averages several trusts have done better than the averages. That is the reason for being of any trust—to secure better than average results.

But the fact remains that for the past two years fixed trusts have been the more popular of the two types. Today, however, the public appear to be wavering. They are confused. I wonder whether we can blame them?

Ten years ago, an investor did not know what an investment trust was. Little by little, he learned to attach some vague magic to the name. But not until '28 and 9 did so-called trusts come with a rush. Billions of the public's money were poured into them. When the panic hit us there were over 500 management trusts in this country with assets sometimes estimated as high as 5 billion dollars. In ten years we had raised almost 5 times the amount of money for our trusts that it took the British 5 times as long to raise. But "after us, the deluge." Investors saw a terrific shrinkage in their portfolios. By last summer as accurate an estimate of the assets of all our management trusts as can be made showed that they had shrunk to about 3 billion dollars. As of today, I should conservatively take another billion from that. But the magic disappeared immediately after the panic. The swing of the pendulum made investors turn to fixed trusts.

Some 150 of these were organized in the two years subsequent to the panic. At no time have their assets totaled more than 1/10 of those of management trusts. But they had certain points of great appeal. The beginning of last year saw the fixed trust in its heyday. If one thing more than another has caused its popularity to waver, it has been the type of sponsorship connected with these trusts.

We have already spoken of some of the merchandising methods used. The financial responsibility of some sponsors has been proved to be insufficient. And competition between various sponsors would be highly amusing if it did not act to the detriment of the field as a whole.

In all this confusion—if the investor wants a touchstone by which to orient himself, let him remember the following undisputable fact. The most important consideration with respect to any trust—management or fixed—is sponsorship. The integrity, judgment and financial responsibility of the sponsors outweigh all other considerations.

Investment trusts attained their most successful development in Great Britain. Except for two unimportant examples, all are of the management type. Their principal theory of operation is based on the time tested method of distribution of risk by industry, location and type of security. The individuals who manage them are engaged in a profession. Their accounting methods are standardized. They frown on payment of dividends from trading profits. They aim at security of principal and stability of income. Their average record is infinitely superior to the average of American trusts.

We can borrow much from the British. We have initiated certain sound practices ourselves. The investment ideal would be a vehicle that contained the best features, and excluded the doubtful features, of management trusts and fixed trusts.

Specifically, what would be the provisions of such a trust?

It would be a "management trust," if you will. It might have a restriction that not more than a certain percentage could be invested in the securities of any one issuer. Its holdings would be broadly diversified—by industry, by location, by type of security. After all, diversity is the cardinal principle of a true investment trust. The principle is derived from the law of averages and the premise that industries as a whole over a period of time will progress rather than retrogress.

But unlike British and many American management trusts, investors should know how their money was being invested. They should have access to the list of securities comprising the portfolio at all times. For convenience, periodic statements should be mailed to all participants.

The managers should correspond to the class of men in Great Britain who devote their careers to managing funds. Investment management in Great Britain is a profession. There are approximately 200,000 seasoned, marketable securities in the world. It takes specialists to find the best. We in America are somewhat new at this business. But I believe you will see a class of men grow up who are as honest and able as those in Britain. I believe you will see men who look upon themselves as much as public trustees as the presidents of savings banks and life insurance companies. A Board of fifty directors stretching from coast to coast has lost its magic. Everyone knows they can't actively manage a company. And as to the accuracy of judgment of many prominent men whose names have graced trust boards of the new era, I refer you to the little red book, *Oh Yeah?* I believe we are through with all that. We prefer a small board composed of men who will devote all the time necessary to doing their job well. They needn't be in the *Social Register* or *Who's Who.* Their records will speak for themselves.

What should be the mechanics of managing a trust? We believe substantially as follows:

The most comprehensive information should be compiled and kept continually up-to-date on every subject that bears an influence on security prices. Such subjects are for example world and domestic politics; social and labor movements; legislation; trade, banking; commodity indices; railroad statistics, crop reports, figures relating to each industry of consequence, relative positions of companies in each industry. So much for statistics. The most perfect statistics represent only half the story. Because they only give us the past.

Of equal importance with statistics, we believe, are contacts. From this source only can we hope to ascertain what statistics later will tell us. Two or three hundred men ought to be talked to periodically—men who are authorities on particular subjects. Every well run trust must have access to opinion in London. London has a world outlook that we lack here. Often their perspective is better than ours regarding even our domestic situation. Trust executives ought to check with British bankers, trust managers, industrialists, statesmen. They should have access to German, French, Swiss, Dutch men of affairs. In this country, they should constantly check the judgment of men in public life, bankers, railroad, utility, industrial executives, economists—practical men and theorists. Very few trusts indeed have even attempted to do this. None has done it thoroughly. But it is interesting to note that those who have at least made some attempt at this method of management are by and large those with the best records.

If they are justified, stockholders should be able to vote out the management. Participants in the trust should have a voice in its operation corresponding to the size of their interest.

Compensation of management and expenses of operation should be reasonable. Too often the public has come out the short end in the past. Our deductions from income have been double or treble what they are in the case of the British trusts. Our cost of raising capital has been high. And our organizers have received too large a share of the theoretical profits in option stock or otherwise. As fair and feasible a method as any to compensate management would be a modest periodic fee based on the assets of a trust.

Such a trust should be operated in the most conservative possible fashion. It should be prohibited from borrowing money, buying on margin or selling short. Such provision would prohibit much of the undesirable speculation noticeable in the past. No firm of which any officer or director was a member should be permitted to act as principal in purchasing or selling securities for the account of the trust. This would put a legal barrier in the way of the frequent human desire, born of enthusiasm or necessity, of placing too much of a good or any part of a bad investment in the portfolio.

Distributions to participants should represent only income received from securities or moneys held—never trading profits. This is a point of fundamental difference between British and American trusts. In British the older trusts have piled up comfortable reserves from realized profits that have stood them in good stead in times like these. Unfortunately, most of our trusts paid such profits out in dividends.

Finally, to take a leaf from our fixed trusts, our theoretical trust should have a self liquidating feature. The primary object in this is to make certain the price paid or obtainable by the participants for their interest would always bear a definite relationship to the asset value of such interest. This liquidating feature would necessarily prohibit issuance of any senior securities. British trusts and many American trusts customarily have senior securities. Additional benefits thereby accrue to ordinary shareholders if operations are successful. The pyramid, however, puts a much more speculative aspect on the common stock. In the interests of conservatism, and to assure reliability of market action, we suggest that our trust be limited to issuing but one type of security and contain a liquidating feature.

The future will see trusts of this type. It will of course see trusts with customary British capital structure. And there will be a great growth in the uniform trust funds of banks. Genuine investment companies are here to stay. They will become an ever increasingly important factor in our financial life. Because a true investment trust is the best medium for investment of any vehicle yet devised.

THE MUTUAL FUNDS

The year 1932, scarcely a quarter of a century ago, marked the beginning of broad public acceptance of what we now know as mutual funds.

To be sure, a few pre-dated 1932. The three famous Boston trusts, Massachusetts Investors Trust, State Street Investment Corporation, and Incorporated Investors, were formed in 1924 and 1925. But their public shareholders had no vote, two of them borrowed money, one had no investment restrictions and multiple capitalization, and one of them was not required to determine its liquidating value oftener than once a month.

Investment Trust Fund A of Investment Managers Company was set up in 1924 and in many ways resembled a mutual fund, except that its shares were non-transferable; actually, it was equally comparable to a common trust fund of a bank and, indeed, in effect it became such when the company was affiliated with the Irving Trust Company of New York, being reincorporated in 1929 and changing its name to Irving Investors Management Co., Inc.

Wellington Fund's predecessor, Industrial and Power Securities Company, was incorporated in 1928 and many of its personnel were the same as those identified with it today, including President Walter L. Morgan. In those earlier years it is described by *Keane's Manual* as "an investment corporation of the general management type." Certain stock options were held by management but, in other respects, like today's mutual funds, the company appears to have been ready to purchase and retire common shares (preferred was authorized but not issued) at only slightly less than liquidating value.

A very few other funds, such as those formed by the well-known investment counsel firms of Scudder, Stevens & Clark and Loomis-Sayles & Company, as well as Century Shares Trust of Brown Brothers & Co. and Spencer Trask Fund, Inc., operated essentially as mutual funds before the year 1932, but 1932 can be marked as the year during and after which almost all newly organized investment companies for the next quarter of a century took the form of a mutual fund.

Calvin Bullock, who since 1924 had sponsored four limited management or semi-fixed trusts of the unit type and two management investment companies, formed four mutual funds in the year 1932. Bullock Fund, Ltd., appearing in January, more closely resembled the pattern of today's mutual funds than any investment company previously organized. Another was the first mutual fund in Canada. Another, Dividend Shares, Inc., shortly became, for a period, the most widely sold of its type in the United States.

Numerous other new funds began to appear. Ross Beason of Corporate Trust Share fame organized Quarterly Income Shares, Inc., and again showed himself an able merchandiser. Then the Boston trusts once more took over the lead.

The story of the growth of Massachusetts Investors Trust—for the next quarter of a century the largest of all the open-end or mutual funds—during the 1930s is partially the story of a popular and rugged Westerner, Mahlon E. Traylor, who came to Boston and was able to transmit to investors throughout the United States an understanding of the atmosphere and traditions of conservative Boston trusteeship identified with that cultured and distinguished city. Traylor had been a Denver securities dealer who took over the presidency of Massachusetts Distributors, which heretofore had distributed a fixed trust and now merchandised Massachusetts Investors Trust, and his monumental work was a major factor for the remaining ten years of his life in the spectacular building of the assets of this best known of all mutual funds. The two other trusts of the Boston triumvirate, Incorporated Investors and the State Street Investment Corporation, began to be widely purchased by investors, this being the first occasion on which the second named company had actively merchandised its shares.

Thus, by the 1930s we had run the gamut of all major forms of investment companies. The twenties belonged to the closed-end, customarily pyramided, management investment companies—which were occasionally referred to as "British type" investment trusts, but which usually were managed in far different fashion from their British ancestors. There was a spate of fixed trusts in the first two years following the Panic. The thirties, however, and succeeding decades, saw the genuine development of what we now term mutual funds. When did that term acquire common usage?

The term "investment trust" was current until the passage of the Investment Company Act. Thereafter "trusts" were referred to as "investment companies." The first time the word "mutual" ever crept into official language was in the Revenue Act of 1936, which permitted "mutual investment companies" that distributed their taxable income to their shareholders to be themselves relieved of federal taxes on such income. But it was not until the 1940s that management investment companies, divided by the SEC into "open-end" and "closed-end," gradually began to refer to the "open-end" variety as mutual investment companies and, in due course, as mutual funds.

6

Political Reaction

ECONOMIC FORCES ARE stronger than political forces. While political actions can have vast influence on economic trends, and while there is intricate interrelationship between these two major social sciences, nevertheless it is economic prosperity or adversity, a full larder or hunger and want that fundamentally determines the composition of any subsequent political scene.

Logically, therefore, after the worst economic collapse in the memory of living Americans and, even though, in retrospect, it is evident that the Great Depression bottomed out in mid-1932, when November of that year came the voting public decisively threw the "ins" out and placed the opposition in power. And, understandably, many things the "ins" had stood for were scorned by a new administration and Congress. Laissez faire? Government will do the job. Business? It had been tried and found wanting.

In contrast to the carefree, slap-happy days of the twenties we entered a crusading, investigational, punitive, government regulatory period. With all the attendant unpleasantness, many pieces of constructive legislation were passed. In the securities industry, the Securities Act of 1933 and the Securities Exchange Act of 1934 unquestionably gave the general public a generous measure of the protection that they had long deserved. There was banking legislation, labor legislation, public utility legislation, all varieties of legislation, and, in due course, investment company legislation.

The Public Utility Holding Company Act of 1936 contained a provision directing the SEC to make a study of investment companies and report its findings back to the Congress. The study was exhaustive. It consisted of a mountain of statistical compilations, supplemented by testimony from executives of all investment companies and so-called investment holding companies of any consequence. Preliminary hearings began in 1938; formal hearings followed.

From the investment company industry the small and the great trooped to Washington. Disreputable promoters, guilty of sharp practices, testified, as did outstandingly honorable and distinguished citizens like James V. Forrestal, subsequently Secretary of the Navy and our first Secretary of Defense. Doubtful ethics and outright dishonesty were uncovered, but mostly lack of judgment. In numerous instances, however, conduct was exemplary and investors' losses could scarcely be blamed on anything other than the economic holocaust.

Businessmen of course were on the defensive. Government investigators on the other hand were in the role of reformers and naturally emphasized any "abuses" they could find in the course of their labors. Some were not without prejudice, such as the important Government employee who stated that no man deserved to earn more than $25,000 a year and he was dedicated to see that no man did. Officials of the SEC were convinced that legislation was necessary to protect the investment company investor; their report to the Congress was designed to document the need for legislation. The current retort of investment company officials was "You can't legislate honesty." But government men were determined to make dishonesty carry such severe penalty to the perpetrator that he would think twice before committing any dishonest deeds. Their philosophy has unquestionably been vindicated.

The monumental SEC Report is a masterpiece of detail, documentation, and determination. It is prejudiced, yes. It features abuses and any negatives that could be found; commendatory statements are conspicuous by their absence. It drags in various "management investment-holding companies" that were not even first cousins to investment trusts. The period necessarily chosen for the study—generally 1927 to 1936—is unfortunate because, even though most trusts were formed in 1927, 1928, and 1929, the bulk of the capital was raised in 1929 and it took twenty-five years for Dow-Jones Industrial Averages of common stocks to again attain their 1929 peak; consequently investor losses were the order of the day. But the Report is economic history. It is brilliantly organized and splendidly written. And, even though a major investment company executive ably disputed the validity of the yardstick used, no objective person could conscientiously refute the Report's conclusion:

It can, then, be concluded with considerable assurance, that the entire group of management investment companies proper failed to perform better than an index of leading common stocks and probably performed somewhat worse than the index over the 1927–1935 period.[1]

Of the five commissioners of the SEC, one in particular was responsible for general supervision of the study and the Report. This was Judge Robert E. Healy, a tall, lean, quiet Vermonter, the essence of integrity and judicial bearing. The director of the study was Dr. Paul P. Gourrich, technical adviser to the Commission, whose previous assignment as economist in an eminent private banking house had earned him a highly re-

[1] Report of the Securities and Exchange Commission, *Investment Trusts and Investment Companies*, Part Two, Appendix J, p. 905.

spected reputation. Most colorful of all the SEC team, however, was husky, handsome David Schenker, who, as chief counsel, ably examined the most important of the witnesses.

The first draft of proposed regulatory legislation, a draft originating with the SEC, was so unacceptable to the investment company industry that it became apparent that the Congress would not pass it over the industry's protests. The sequel was a unique and constructive effort on the part of the SEC and investment company representatives to hammer out a bill which would give investors the protection the SEC demanded and give the investment companies a Magna Charta under which they felt they could operate.

Innumerable individuals from the industry and their respective counsels participated in these conversations. Conflicting interests within the industry itself had first to be settled; next the industry's ideas had to be resolved with those of the SEC. There is no doubt but that Arthur H. Bunker, executive vice-president of the Lehman Corporation, was, more than any individual, the spokesman for the investment company industry as a whole. But Cyril J. Quinn, a vice-president of Tri-Continental Corporation, had equal say respecting closed-end investment company matters. In the open-end field Merrill Griswold, chairman of Massachusetts Investors Trust, was a distinct leader, along with Paul Cabot, president of the State Street Investment Company, Governor William Tudor Gardiner, chairman of Incorporated Investors of Boston, and a Calvin Bullock official from New York.

As for the legal profession, its representatives descended on Washington in force at the summons of investment company officials. Yet out of the confusion emerged two names that will be generally remembered in connection with investment company legislation. One is Alfred Jaretzki, Jr., of New York, a Sullivan and Cromwell partner, the recognized authority on the legislation, who negotiated with the SEC the compromise on which the present Act is based and later participated in the drafting of the Act. The other is Warren R. Motley, a member of Gaston, Snow, Motley and Holt, of Boston, who specialized in open-end matters and also helped in the drafting of the Act.

While the Investment Company Act of 1940 was the consummation of efforts to police the investment company industry, by no means was it the only effort.

Back in 1924, the New York Stock Exchange passed a resolution warning its members of disciplinary action if they organized or managed or identified themselves with an investment trust which did not properly protect investors' interests. The National Association of Securities Commissioners in 1927 created a committee to study investment trusts and make appropriate recommendations; two years later the committee suggested strengthening "blue sky" laws.

In 1928 the Attorney General of New York state, after a special study, made a report, discussing certain abuses in the investment trust field and recommended that trusts organized under New York laws be required to incorporate under the banking laws of New York, which would bring them under the supervision of the state banking superintendent. No legislation, however, ensued.

The Investment Bankers Association of America at its fall convention in 1928, heard its investment trust committee recommend that a code of practice be drawn up for investment trusts. Again, in 1929, the New York Stock Exchange made a second study of investment trusts and adopted special requirements for listing their securities.

But it took the federal government to finally do the job. And the job was well done. And it was the first time in history that government representatives and representatives of an industry to be regulated both appeared before congressional committees and urged the enactment into law of such regulation.

7

Milestone

THE INVESTMENT COMPANY ACT OF 1940 became effective on November 1, 1940. Some slight amendments thereto became law on November 10, 1954. Major provisions contained in the Act's sixty-five pages of fine print are broadly summarized in this chapter.

DEFINITION

An "investment company" is defined as a company engaged "primarily in the business of investing, reinvesting, or trading in securities"—or engaged "in the business of issuing face-amount certificates of the installment type"—or engaged in the business of investing, trading in, or owning securities provided more than 40 percent of its assets consist of investment securities—not including United States government securities or securities of a majority owned subsidiary which is not an investment company.

This last definition is an attempt to distinguish an investment company from a holding company, but there are several other criteria for determining whether a company is to be considered an investment company. For example, the common trust fund of a bank is not classified as an investment company, although it has investment company characteristics; nor does a company with less than a hundred stockholders constitute an investment company.

CLASSIFICATION

Investment companies are divided into three principal classes: (1) Face-amount certificate companies, (2) Unit investment trusts, and (3) Management companies.

Management companies are divided into open-end and closed-end companies, defined as follows:

1. "Open-end company" means a management company which is offering for sale or has outstanding any redeemable security of which it is the issuer. (A redeemable security is one which the company must redeem on demand. Thus an open-end company need not be, although generally is, a company which is continually selling its own capital stock.)
2. "Closed-end company" means any management company other than an open-end company.

Management companies are futher divided into diversified companies and non-diversified companies:

1. "Diversified company" means a management company which meets the requirements that at least 75% of the value of its total assets is represented by cash and securities, in which the securities of no issuer except the U. S. Government represent more than 5% of the assets of the investment company or more than 10% of the voting securities of such issuer.
2. "Non-diversified company" means any management company other than a diversified company.

There are exemptions from the Act. For example, an investment company with assets of less than $100,000 need not conform to the provisions of the Act.

REGISTRATION

Jurisdiction over an investment company is obtained upon its registration. No investment company, unless registered, may use the mails or any means or instrumentality of interstate commerce. This likewise applies to foreign investment companies, none of which, until recent years, has been registered. Registration of foreign companies is discretionary with the SEC and is made under rules designed to subject such companies to regulation of the same type as applied to domestic investment companies. To date most registered foreign investment companies have been Canadian open-end companies, and there has been one South African closed-end company.

Every registered investment company must file a comprehensive registration statement with the SEC, including a declaration of its policy as to which classification and subclassifications it proposes to operate under, its policies with respect to borrowing money, issuing senior securities, engaging in underwriting, concentrating investments in a particular industry or group of industries, purchase and sale of real estate and commodities, lending money, and turning over its portfolio—plus any other matters it considers fundamental policy. These policies cannot be changed without the vote of shareholders.

These provisions are designed to prevent certain happenings of the 1920s and their aftermath. Occasionally shareholders would discover that their companies were engaging in entirely different activities and employing quite different policies from those followed at the time shareholders had made their original investment. A company might suddenly change its classification completely. It might borrow money or issue senior securities and become more speculative. It might get involved in a large and unsuccessful underwriting. It might sell a diversified list of securities from its portfolio and concentrate heavily in a single industry. It might lend money where it never did before, perhaps even to its officers. It might buy and sell portfolio securities vigorously to create stock exchange commissions in which its sponsors had an interest.

AFFILIATIONS OF DIRECTORS

No registered investment company may have a board of directors more than 60 percent of whom are investment advisers of such investment company or who are persons affiliated with this investment adviser. Nor may more than 60 percent of the directors be officers or employees of the investment company.

A majority of the board must be persons not affiliated with the company's "regular broker," with the principal underwriter, with any investment bankers, or with any one bank. An exception is that an open-end company, sponsored and managed by an investment counsel, which sells its shares at asset value and meets certain other requirements, need have only one "independent" director on its board.

"Conflict of interest" was a phrase in constant use during the SEC investigation of investment companies. Undoubtedly conflicts did occur, and, in some instances, the investment adviser, employee, broker, underwriter, investment banker, or bank did fare better than the investment company itself. It seemed wise, therefore, to require that a majority of directors have no connection with the above functions, except the investment advisory and management functions. Even in the latter instance a minority of directors would keep a watchful eye on possible "conflicts."

Except as permitted by the SEC, no registered investment company may purchase a security during the existence of any underwriting or selling syndicate with respect to such security if any director, officer, or employee of the investment company is connected directly or indirectly with the underwriting or selling group, unless the investment company is itself the underwriter. This provision was occasioned by occurrences in the 1920s where an investment company was used to help bail out an underwriter or selling group member with respect to a flotation that was not overly successful.

SELLING PRICE AND OFFERS OF EXCHANGE

Generally speaking, sales of stock of open-end investment companies may be made at the public offering price only. Offers of exchange to the shareholders of any other open-end company may be made only on a basis of relative net asset values, except with the approval of the Commission.

This is to prevent insiders from acquiring shares at less than the public offering price as sometimes happened before. But the provision that offers of exchange by one company for another company's shares may be made only on a basis of asset value for asset value cures one of the greatest abuses that the open-end field used to witness. Over many years there was vigorous solicitation of open-end investment company shareholders to trade their shares for another investment company's shares. Consequently the investor would have to pay a second sales charge. The most frequent beneficiary was the salesman who suggested the trade.

ACTIVITIES

Investment companies are prohibited from buying on margin or selling short. They are prohibited from participating in a joint venture with affiliated persons in contravention of rules of the Commission. When investment companies bought stocks on margin or sold stocks short, and when the judgment of such companies' managements proved incorrect, the resultant losses to shareholders were greatly magnified. Often, indeed, shareholders were not informed that their companies were engaged in such speculative practices. Moreover, when affiliated persons entered into joint ventures with investment companies there were instances where the investment companies came out second best.

Open-end companies may not act as a distributor of their own securities, except through an underwriter, without the Commission's approval. This prevents merchandising costs and sometimes losses from sales efforts being charged against an investment company shareholder.

No diversified investment company may enter an underwriting if its commitment in such underwriting, plus existing underwriting commitments it may have, plus its investment in securities (other than an investment company security) of any issuers of which it owns more than 10 percent of the voting securities would exceed 25 percent of its assets. This is to prevent a diversified investment company from unbalancing its portfolio in the case of an unsuccessful underwriting.

Investment companies are prohibited from acquiring stock of other investment companies which would result in a holding of more than 3 percent of the voting stock of such other investment company, except in the case of a company whose policy is to concentrate its investments in a particular group of industries, in which case the percentage may be 5 percent. If an investment company already owned 25 percent or more of the voting stock of another investment company at the time the Act became effective, it is exempted from this prohibition. This prohibition is to prevent situations, often seen in 1929, in which one investment company would control another and that company another—in short, to eliminate the possibility of an individual or small group of men who controlled a top holding or so-called investment company from extending their control all the way down a large pyramid. This used to be one of the most undesirable and, indeed, dangerous practices of other days.

Similar prohibitions, with like exemption, cover purchases of stocks of insurance companies beyond a limit of 10 percent of the voting stock of any insurance company. Nor may an investment company own part of a brokerage, trading, underwriting, or investment advisory organization unless entire ownership thereof is in the hands of one or more investment companies. Because of many conflicts of interest in the 1920s and their aftermath where investment companies had an interest in brokerage, trading, underwriting, or other operations it was deemed wise to prevent this in the future except where one or more investment companies completely owned, for instance, an investment advisory organization, which would probably service them at less cost than was customary.

Investment companies may, however, invest up to 5 percent of their assets in another corporation—originally sold for investment to investment companies only—if its capital does not exceed $100,000,000 and if it proposes to engage in underwriting, furnishing capital to industry, financing promotional enterprises, purchasing securities for which no ready market exists, reorganizing companies or similar activities. This provision is to enable investment companies to participate in venture capital operations on a small scale, which few would otherwise be inclined to do.

SIZE

An investment company must have a minimum net worth of $100,000. There is no maximum size, but the Commission is authorized

> at such times as it deems that any substantial further increase in size of investment companies creates any problem involving the protection of investors or the public interest, to make a study and investigation of the effects of size on the investment policy of investment companies and on security markets, on concentration of control of wealth and industry, and on companies in which investment companies are interested, and from time to time to report the results of its studies and investigations and its recommendations to the Congress.

Too many investment companies started on a shoestring and collapsed for want of capital. Under the provision quoted above, the Commission has recently undertaken an investigation of the size of existing investment companies, delving extensively into all aspects of the companies' operations.

INVESTMENT ADVISORY AND UNDERWRITING CONTRACTS

Stockholders must approve investment advisory contracts. Such contracts may only run two years from the date of their execution, but may be renewed annually by stockholders or by the vote of a majority of directors independent of the investment adviser. Directors or stockholders may terminate the contract upon sixty days notice and there is automatic termination in the case of its "assignment" by the investment adviser, as defined in the Act. "Assignment" includes sale of a controlling block (presumptively more than 25 percent) of the stock of an investment advisory corporation.

Similar, but not identical, provisions hold for underwriting contracts.

This is an important provision. Often investment advisory contracts would run for long periods and would be sold to a new and sometimes less desirable group of men without shareholders having anything to say about the investment company coming under new supervision. Occasionally this also happened with respect to underwriting contracts.

CHANGES IN BOARDS OF DIRECTORS

In the future, no person shall serve as a director of an investment company unless elected by the holders of its outstanding voting securities, except that, in effect, vacancies not exceeding one-third of the board occurring between meetings of stockholders may be filled in any otherwise legal manner. However, with respect to existing strict trusts, where no provision is made for election of trustees, the bill does not require an affirmative election of trustees but provides a procedure for their removal by certificate holders.

If directors are elected in classes, none may be for a shorter term than one year or for a longer term than five years.

Before the passage of the Act there were instances of an entire new board of directors coming into being, none of whom had been elected by shareholders. The method used was to have one director resign and a new director immediately elected by the remaining members of the board. The procedure would be repeated until the entire board was replaced. The new management could, and on several occasions did, misappropriate the funds of the company before stockholders even knew that there had been a change of management.

TRANSACTIONS OF AFFILIATED PERSONS AND UNDERWRITERS

No affiliated person or promoter or underwriter, or any affiliated person of these, may act as principal in selling any security or other property to or in buying such security from an investment company—except in cases specifically approved by the Commission. A flagrant abuse of other days was that of an underwriting house or person affiliated with an investment company unloading undesirable or even unsalable securities into the investment company's portfolio. Moreover, the question of price itself always should be subject to arm's-length bargaining. No one, even though he be acting in good faith, can properly sit on both sides of the table.

Every registered management company must place its securities in the custody of a bank with specified qualifications or of a company which is a member of a national securities exchange; or, it may hold such securities itself under rules prescribed by the Commission. Officers and employees must be bonded if they have access to securities or cash. The purpose here is to assure shareholders maximum physical safety of their property—which, on more than one occasion, was purloined by the unscrupulous.

No legal instrument of any investment company may contain provisions protecting any director or officer against any liability to which he would otherwise be subject by reason of willful misfeasance, bad faith, gross negligence, or reckless disregard of the duties involved in the conduct of his office.

CAPITAL STRUCTURE

These restrictions apply to securities issued after the passage of the Investment Company Act. It is now unlawful for any closed-end company to issue any debt unless such debt has an asset coverage of at least 300 percent. No dividend may be paid on its common stock nor may the company repurchase any of its own stock if such asset coverage falls below 300 percent. Nor may it pay a dividend on any preferred stock it may have outstanding if asset coverage on debt falls below 200 percent.

Provision must be made that if asset coverage on debt is less than 100 percent for a year, the debt holders may elect a majority of the board until coverage equals or exceeds 110 percent; or, in the alternative, if coverage is less than 100 percent for two years, an event of default occurs.

Any preferred stock of an investment company must have an asset coverage of at least 200 percent. No dividend may be paid on the common stock if the coverage is less. Such stock must have certain specified voting rights.

No closed-end investment company may have more than one class of debt or of preferred stock.

No open-end company may issue any senior securities. It may, however, borrow from a bank provided the loan has 300 percent coverage.

No warrant or right may be issued that expires later than 120 days after issuance.

All capital stock now issued by investment companies must have voting rights. Capital structures of investment companies in the earlier days were frequently unsound. Too many classes of securities were issued. The public too often held shares that had no voting rights. The heavily pyramided companies, with top-heavy debt and senior securities, were bound to register great losses to the common stockholder when leverage began working in reverse. Shares with no underlying asset value often controlled the company. These important provisions relating to capital structure are designed to avoid one of the most expensive pitfalls of the past.

DIVIDENDS

No investment company may pay a dividend, except from the company's "accumulated undistributed net income, determined in accordance with good accounting practice and not including profits or losses realized upon the sale of securities or other properties," or from "such company's net income so determined for the current or preceding fiscal year," without adequately disclosing the source of such payment. In the case of certain closed-end companies of the 1920s, "dividends" were paid not only from investment income, but also from profits from sales of securities, including profits made when shares of another affiliated trust were sold which latter shares' appreciation had probably been influenced by operations of a third affiliated trust. Even worse, dividends were also paid from paid-in surplus—or surplus created by the reduction of capital—when no net income was available. Unless adequately informed, a stockholder would not realize that his "dividend" was in essence a return of capital. Then, in the heyday of fixed trusts, in some instances the advertised "yield" was based, not only on investment income but also on similar return of capital.

PROXIES, VOTING TRUSTS, CIRCULAR OWNERSHIP

Solicitations of proxies are subject to the rules of the Commission. These rules are the same for all companies listed on the New York or other national securities exchange.

Voting trusts are prohibited.

No company may buy any voting stock of any other corporation if either company would own more than 3 percent of the voting stock of the other or of a group of companies.

LOANS

An investment company may not lend money or property to anyone if its fundamental policy statement does not permit such action, nor may it lend to a person who controls or is under common control with the investment company. This is to prevent loans to persons or organizations affiliated with investment companies, which not only was improper but resulted in serious losses in the past.

DISTRIBUTION, REDEMPTION, AND REPURCHASE OF REDEEMABLE SECURITIES

A securities association registered under the Securities Exchange Act of 1934 (such as the National Association of Securities Dealers) is given jurisdiction over its members—as is the Commission—in respect of certain matters dealing with pricing and redemption of open-end shares. One of the early problems of the open-end investment companies was dilution of the value of existing shares when new shareholders came into the company in a rising market. Uniform trust funds of some banks sometimes used to evaluate their fund once a month, then accept participations at a firm price until the next month's evaluation. If the market advanced considerably meanwhile, this would be an extreme case of dilution. Open-end investment companies, even those pricing their shares once a day, suffered dilution because the newcomer in a rising market would get his shares, until the stock market closed, at the lower price determined after the close of the market of the previous day. When the Second World War commenced in September, 1939, the stock market had a severe break; then, on one day, September 5, it had a 7 percent rise. Several open-end investment companies voluntarily refused to accept the flood of orders that ensued because they would have unquestionably militated against the interest of existing shareholders. The National Association of Securities Dealers has now required that the price of shares be determined twice a day; as a result, dilutions of previous shareholders' interests are brought to an irreducible practical minimum.

Open-end investment companies may sell shares only through a principal underwriter at the public offering price, except upon offerings to its shareholders, on offers of exchange, and as permitted by the Commission.

No open-end company may restrict the transferability or negotiability of its shares or issue any shares for the services or property other than cash or securities. There was one instance of an open-end company, originally with a self-liquidation feature, which withdrew the feature and, in effect, became a closed-end investment company.

DISTRIBUTION AND REPURCHASE OF SECURITIES OF CLOSED-END COMPANIES

Closed-end companies are prohibited from issuing any securities or from selling any of their stock below its net asset value except (1) "in connection with an offering to the holders of one or more classes of its capital stock," (2) "with the consent of a majority of its common stockholders," (3) "upon conversion of a convertible security in accordance with its terms," (4) "upon the exercise of any warrant outstanding on the date of enactment of this Act," or (5) with the approval of the Commission. There were instances of closed-end companies in mergers issuing new shares below asset value. Obviously this diluted the value of existing shares.

No closed-end company can purchase any of its own securities except (1) "on a securities exchange or such other open market as the Commission may designate. In this event shareholders must have been informed of the investment company's intention within the preceding six months," (2) "pursuant to tenders," or (3) "under such other circumstances as the Commission may permit." These provisions assure all shareholders equal treatment and prevent an interested party (as has been done in the past) from selling back a large block of stock to a closed-end company without others having an equal right.

PLANS OF REORGANIZATION

If the investment company or 25 percent of any class of its security holders request it to do so, the Commission is authorized "to render an advisory report in respect of the fairness of any such plan." The Commission may bring proceedings in a District Court of the United States to enjoin the consummation of any plan of reorganization, and the Court may enjoin its consummation if it shall determine the plan to be grossly unfair or to constitute gross misconduct or gross abuse of trust.

UNIT INVESTMENT TRUSTS

Trust indentures of unit investment trusts must provide for a bank of $500,000 aggregate capital, surplus, and undivided profits or more as trustee or custodian, which cannot resign unless the trust has been liquidated or a successor appointed. Additional conditions are enumerated covering activities of depositor and trustee. In earlier days, trustees of unit trusts were on occasion persuaded to resign. The trust property was then turned over to the depositor corporation. Individuals connected therewith did not always have the highest ethics.

PERIODIC PAYMENT PLANS

No periodic payment plan certificates may be sold with a sales load of more than 9 percent; no more than one-half of the first twelve monthly payments may be deducted for sales load; the sales load deducted from any of such first payments must not exceed proportionately that deducted from other first payments, and deductions from any subsequent payments must be proportionately the same; no first payment may be less than $20, nor any subsequent payment less than $10. The Commission has authority to determine the reasonableness of certain other charges. Previous charges on certain periodic payment plans have been known to be unduly high and other provisions burdensome on shareholders.

FACE-AMOUNT CERTIFICATE COMPANIES

Face-amount certificate companies must have a minimum capital of $250,000 and maintain specified reserves. Qualifications are laid down as to character of such companies' investments, ratios to be maintained, and general operations, as well as procedures in case of bankruptcy. Prior to this the ability of some companies to meet their obligations was questioned.

PERIODIC REPORTS, RECORDS, AUDITS

Every investment company must file annually with the Commission the same information that companies listed on a national securities exchange must file. All reports sent to stockholders must be filed. Such stockholder reports must contain, semiannually, a balance sheet, list of securities owned, income account, surplus account, aggregate remuneration paid by the company to directors, officers, and affiliated persons, as well as purchases and sales of portfolio securities. The Commission may require that such figures be publicly audited annually. Available information on certain investment companies had left much to be desired. A large number were not in the habit of revealing what securities comprised their portfolio.

An investment company must maintain such records as the Commission may prescribe, and these are subject to periodic or special examinations by the Commission, which may issue regulations for a reasonable degree of uniformity in accounting policies and principles.

Public accountants must be appointed annually by a majority of the investment company's independent directors and the appointments ratified by stockholders.

MISCELLANEOUS

An investment company must notify the Commission of the details of the settlement of any civil action against its directors, officers, investment advisers, trustee or depositor. It is

unlawful for any person, in issuing or selling any security of which a registered investment company is the issuer, to represent or imply in any manner whatsoever that such security or company has been guaranteed, sponsored, recommended, or approved by the United States or any agency or officer thereof.

No investment company may adopt a name which the Commission finds deceptive or misleading. This is to prevent any investment company having a name as easily misinterpreted as that of a relatively unimportant New York bank which failed in 1930. It was called Bank of United States, and numerous depositors thought their money was in a government institution. Hence no investment company, for example, investing primarily in automotive shares would be permitted to call itself the "Jones Balanced Fund."

The Commission may bring action in the proper District Court of the United States alleging gross misconduct or gross abuse of trust on the part of any officer, director, member of advisory board, investment adviser, depositor, or principal underwriter of an investment company. If such charges are established, the Court may either permanently or temporarily enjoin any such person from acting in the capacity in which such gross misconduct or gross abuse was committed.

Under this section an investment company was placed in receivership when the trustees of the trust invested the assets in a race track, to their personal profit. On the other hand, the courts have refused to uphold the position of the Commission that sale of a controlling block of stock of an investment advisory company at more than book value constitutes a gross abuse of trust.

Any person who willfully violates any provision of the Act or of any rule, regulation, or order of the Commission thereunder faces the same penalty as one who commits larceny or embezzlement. Upon conviction there is a fine of not more than $10,000, or imprisonment for not more than two years, or both.

Contracts made in violation of the Act or of rules and regulations issued thereunder are void.

The Commission has general powers of enforcement of the Act comparable with powers it possesses in the case of several other acts administered by the Securities and Exchange Commission. In this connection it may make an investigation to determine whether any person has violated or is about to violate the Act and may bring proceedings in the appropriate United States District Court to enjoin such threatened violation and to enforce compliance with the Act or any rule, regulation, or order thereunder.

Information contained in any registration statement or other document filed with the Commission is available to the public unless the Commission "finds that public disclosure is neither necessary nor appropriate in the public interest."

The general concept of the Act is that prohibited acts are specifically enumerated, and that the Commission has broad powers to grant exemptions either by rule, regulation, or order in a particular instance.

8

Public Approval

THE INVESTMENT COMPANY ACT OF 1940 was indeed a milestone in the history of investment companies in the United States. It cleared the atmosphere; it codified the rules of the game. Public confidence began to return.

There was a natural hiatus in the growth of investment companies during the war. For one thing, war financing came first, especially the merchandising of War Bonds to some eighty-five million estimated purchasers. For another thing, a proud number of investment company personnel saw service in the armed forces. Among executives, the most distinguished record belonged to Colonel William Tudor Gardiner, former governor of Maine and chairman of Incorporated Investors, who, with General Maxwell D. Taylor, the recent Army Chief of Staff, as Allied agent went behind German and Italian lines into Rome to ascertain whether an American air drop was feasible.

From 1945 on, however, public acceptance of investment companies has been spectacular. In neighboring Canada where there is no regulation of investment companies as such, there has been a comparable growth. Yet the weight of opinion is that the passage of investment company legislation was a factor in the growth of American mutual funds, even though growth no doubt would have been vigorous anyway because of the economic boom, the attendant upsurge in securities markets, and the increasing number of investors during the postwar years. Since the passage of the Act the SEC, in its policing

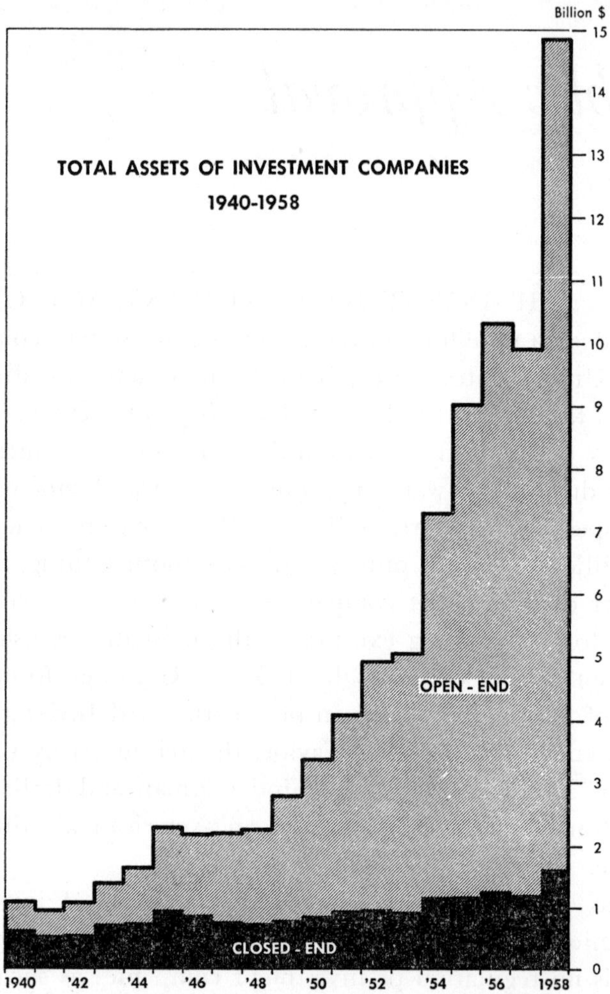

role, up to a year ago was compelled to take action for malpractice against only two unimportant investment companies, these with combined assets of a mere $5 million. Since then there have been three other proceedings, one involving a company with assets of approximately a million dollars, the two others much more substantial. In one of these latter instances, however, the court failed to sustain the SEC. But, notwithstanding the fact that action has been taken against less than half a dozen companies, the SEC has exerted a restraining and salutary influence in many cases. Unofficially, it exercises a policing power in its processing of proxy statements and of registrations under the Securities Act of 1933.

The new army of investors in 1945 had a broad selection of investment companies to choose from—some 70 open-end and some 40 closed-end companies, the first group with assets of slightly over a billion and the second group with assets of slightly less than a billion dollars. In the 1920s closed-end companies had dominated the field. The 1930s saw many open-end companies organized. But, even though no new closed-end company of any consequence had been formed since the Panic, until 1944 total assets of the closed-end group had always exceeded assets of the open-end group. Since 1945 total closed-end assets have remained relatively unchanged, in the neighborhood of a billion to a billion and a half dollars, and the number of closed-end companies has declined—through merger or being changed into open-end companies or ceasing to be classified as investment companies—to not much more than half the number existing in 1945. The number of open-end companies, on the other hand, has more than doubled from the number existing in 1945, and their assets have increased more than tenfold.

What accounts for the tremendous growth of open-end companies and the relatively static condition of the closed-end group?

The primary reason existing closed-end companies have not raised any new capital to speak of is that the common stocks of most of them for a long time have been selling below their asset value, whether they be leverage companies or companies with a simple capital structure. Occasionally rights to subscribe for new shares have been offered, but no appreciable amount of new money has been raised by the closed-end group. While they could, of course, usually raise new money by issuing preferred stock and debentures, the tendency has been to reduce leverage. Originally most closed-end companies were leverage companies; now leverage companies are in the minority. New closed-end companies have not been formed because, naturally, the public is not likely to be attracted by a closed-end common stock at a premium above asset value when so many can be bought at a discount. There are always exceptions to any generality and a notable one is the Lehman Corporation, the capital stock of which, because of widespread information respecting the company's good management, in recent years has usually sold at a premium. Another interesting case is that of State Street Investing Corporation, actually an open-end company, but one which has not issued new shares for some time, where again, because of its prestige, the bid price for its shares has frequently been at a premium above asset value.

It is obvious why open-end or mutual funds have grown. There is no historical background of serious troubles as a result of the Panic. Their self-liquidating feature guarantees that their shares should always bear a direct relationship to their asset value. Whereas financing of closed-end companies as a rule is done by forming a syndicate which takes an outright commitment (and risk) in the new issue to be sold, in the case of open-end or mutual funds an investment dealer customarily receives an order from a client first, before he commits himself to purchase shares of the mutual fund. (A few mutual funds recently have been syndicated as closed-end companies, but with a proviso that they would be open-ended at a specified early date). Finally, mutual funds have been vigorously merchandised. It is doubtful if the securities business has ever witnessed as effective a promotional effort as that identified with mutual funds.

The major growth of mutual funds has of course been in the post-war years. From 1946 through 1958 gross sales of new shares of mutual funds have exceeded $10 billion. The price that the public pays includes a sales charge, averaging about 7½ percent of the offering price, although, on substantial amounts, the sales charge is materially reduced. From 75 to 80 percent of the sales charge is paid to investment dealers who sell shares to their customers. It may be estimated, therefore, that there has been in the years since the war certainly over $100 million, and perhaps not too far below $150 million, available to underwriters of mutual funds—the vast bulk of which has been used for merchandising costs. These include paying commissions to the wholesale representatives of the underwriter, the costs of prospectuses and other forms of literature, costs of qualifying shares for sale in the various states of the union, newspaper and other advertising, and miscellaneous sales and servicing costs.

The commission incentive to investment dealers has undoubtedly been a major factor in the growth of funds and the figures indicate that the sales and merchandising techniques have been effective. However, important as the sales charge may be in mutual fund distribution (and it is considerably less than the comparable costs of selling life insurance, for example), it is unlikely that the volume of sales attained could have been possible were it not for the essential soundness of the mutual fund principle and the widespread public need for diversification and supervision in common stock investing. Moreover, the results obtained for investors over the years— and published in detail every six months—must be considered as a controlling factor in this growth, especially in recent years.

There are a handful of organizations, such as the gigantic

Investors Syndicate, which have sales forces of hundreds of salesmen who approach investors directly. For the most part, however, merchandising by the underwriters of mutual funds is done by their wholesale representatives, who call on thousands of investment dealers throughout America. There may be 500 such representatives making daily calls. The sales literature used by mutual funds is expertly prepared and rigidly policed, newspaper advertising is extensive, and moving pictures and radio, as well as virtually every modern method of communication, are in some instances used. The only industry of a financial nature which employs substantially more aggressive merchandising methods is life insurance.

PUBLIC EDUCATION

Public education as to the merit of investment companies, closed-end as well as open-end, has been furthered by two organizations in particular. One is the National Association of Investment Companies, with its public information committee, a part of whose responsibility it is to maintain and disseminate pertinent facts and figures relative to the investment company industry. The other is the New York Stock Exchange firm of Arthur Wiesenberger & Co. In 1940 Mr. Wiesenberger, convinced of the inherent merit and future growth of the investment company movement, notwithstanding the fact that public apathy permitted common stocks of numerous closed-end companies to sell at illogical discounts below their asset values and even before open-end companies had attained their momentum, published the first of his famous manuals called *Investment Companies.* These have been revised and issued each succeeding year, and their comprehensive and objective picture of each company, as well as the industry as a whole, is invaluable to investor as well as student.

NATIONAL ASSOCIATION OF INVESTMENT COMPANIES

The National Association of Investment Companies is a non-profit organization maintained by the great majority of important registered investment companies. It is an outgrowth of the informal group of individuals who cooperated with the SEC in drafting the Investment Company Act of 1940. Following the passage of the Act these individuals thought it advisable to form a permanent committee to cooperate with the SEC in formulating the rules and regulations necessary to the proper functioning of the Act; the Committee likewise proposed to keep informed as to the trend of any federal and state tax legislation affecting investment companies. A roster of the names of those first serving on this original National Committee of Investment Companies is good historical documentation as to which investment company officials played a major part in cooperating with the SEC in drafting and urging on the Congress the passage of the famous Act. The men were·

Paul Bartholet
F. Wilder Bellamy
Hugh Bullock
Arthur H. Bunker
Paul Cabot
Charles F. Eaton
William Tudor Gardiner
Merrill Griswold
Raymond D. McGrath
David M. Milton
James H. Orr
Cyril J. Quinn
Richard Wagner

Counsel to the Committee were Alfred Jaretzki, Jr., and Warren Motley who have served ever since. The composition of the Committee otherwise changed periodically by selection and election. The Committee itself changed its name to the present one in October, 1941. And, over the years, its responsibilities and activities substantially increased. Originally Paul Bartholet, formerly affiliated with the Tri-Continental Corporation, was executive secretary; in 1945 he was followed by John Sheffey; in 1956 Edward B. Burr succeeded Sheffey with the title of executive director; in May of 1958 Burr was succeeded by Leonard Davis, who was in turn succeeded in January, 1959, by George A. Mooney. The chairman of the executive committee for many years was Dorsey Richardson of the Lehman Corporation; in 1955 he was succeeded by Robert E. Clark of Calvin Bullock; and, in 1957, Joseph E. Welch of Wellington Fund, Inc., followed, with the title of president of the National Association of Investment Companies. His successor in October, 1958, was Herbert R. Anderson of Group Securities.

Besides its functions of public education, liaison with the SEC, keeping an eye on federal and state tax and other legislation affecting investment companies, and other activities, the National Association of Investment Companies has informally exercised a strong influence in maintaining a high standard in the industry.

Such informal influence, however, has not the weight of official action. The investment company industry is governed by the strict standards of the Investment Company Act of 1940. It is subject to the Securities Act of 1933 in raising new capital. It is subject to the Securities Exchange Act of 1934 in so far as listed, closed-end companies are concerned, and for transactions in listed stocks by all investment companies. In raising new capital the industry is also governed by the Blue Sky laws of various states. And underwriters and dealers in investment company securities are subject to the general rules of fair practice and Statement of Policy (covering contents of sales literature, etc.) of the National Association of Securities Dealers, a quasi-governmental regulatory body, with self-policing powers, made up of investment dealers throughout the country. While the old adage "a fool and his money are soon parted" is as valid as it was in the days of our ancestors, nevertheless this generation of investors, particularly in investment companies, has a degree of protection never before known.

ACCUMULATION PLANS

During the years following the Second World War several interesting developments in the investment company industry were initiated or gained momentum. One constructive innovation was that of a voluntary accumulation plan from which an investor might withdraw at any time with no penalty. Dollar cost averaging is as old a principle as the eternal hills and as fundamental as the law of gravity. This means that if an investor places a given amount of money in securities, usually common stocks, and keeps placing an identical amount at regular intervals in such securities, his money will buy more shares of stock, for instance, when prices are down and less shares when prices are high. And it is arithmetically provable that at the completion of a market cycle, namely when prices of a recognized average of common stocks (provided his stock or stocks purchased go up and down more or less in the same fashion as, for example, Dow-Jones Industrial Averages) return in due course to the level existing at the time of the investor's first purchase, he will find to his pleasure that the market value of his holdings exceeds what he paid for such holdings. The Commonwealth Investment Company of San Francisco pioneered in 1946, by offering a "Multiple Purchase Program" based on these principles. A New York sponsor, in 1949, brought out a similar plan under which, however, all functions were performed by an independent banking institution. During subsequent years a hundred other such plans followed.

These plans—confined to mutual funds—permit an investor to deposit a modest amount of money periodically for the purchase of stocks of whichever investment company is concerned. The investor is charged only the usual sales premium, and he may withdraw from the plan at any time and demand the cash and securities that belong to him. Such plans are generally known as Voluntary Accumulation Plans.

A much older plan, dating back to the fixed trust days and employed today by a score of mutual funds, is the Contractual Accumulation Plan. The general principle is the same, except that an investor contracts to put a certain amount of money into the plan over a specified number of years. At the end of the period he takes possession of all his property, but if he defaults on his payments—and thereby withdraws from the plan, particularly in its early stages—he is penalized by having paid most of the charges involved during the first year or two, even though it be a ten- or fifteen-year plan. This is comparable to the method of insurance companies, by which most of the charges involved are deducted in the early stages of life insurance. Indeed, an insurance feature is usually obtainable with such plans. While all the Voluntary Accumulation Plans are offered to the public by the principal underwriter of the mutual fund involved, in the case of Contractual Accumulations Plans an independent organization may base its plan on some mutual fund of its choice. Perhaps the best-known example is First Investors Corporation, which uses Wellington Fund as its base.

The SEC Report states: "The first installment investment plans appeared in 1930, but not until 1932 did their total assets exceed $1,000,000 . . . in 1936, reaching a total of $25,000,000. . . ."[1] These were Contractual Accumulation Plans and, as we have said, were based on fixed trusts, although, as the 1930s progressed, some mutual funds were used as the base. But these plans in turn had an even older first cousin—Face Amount Installment Plans—which the Investment Company Act of 1940

[1] Report of the Securities and Exchange Commission, *Investment Trusts and Investment Companies,* Part Two, chap. II, p. 40.

defines as one of the three types of investment companies. Of these the SEC Report says:

The total assets taken largely at book values of the five companies issuing face amount installment certificates increased each year from $35,000,000 at the end of 1927 to $126,000,000 in 1936, representing 2% of the total assets of the entire investment industry in 1927 and almost 3% in 1936.[2]

Two companies accounted for considerably over 90 percent of these assets—Investors Syndicate and Fidelity Investment Association, organized in 1911. Our story, however, is concerned with Investors Syndicate.

INVESTORS SYNDICATE

This company was formed in 1894 in Minneapolis by a lawyer named John E. Tappan to distribute face-amount installment certificates. A certificate might mature, for instance, in ten years and be worth $1,000 (its face amount) to the investor, who would have paid less than this to the company, the difference representing compound interest. On his part the investor would agree to make small monthly or periodic payments to Investors Syndicate. After deduction of selling charges, the company invested money received primarily in real estate mortgages. By 1929 its assets had reached $29 million.

Over succeeding years its assets greatly expanded, especially after the Investment Company Act had specified amount of reserves and certain other policies such companies could employ. In 1940 the company organized Investors Mutual, Inc., a balanced mutual fund; in 1945 it started Investors Selective Fund, Inc., primarily for investment in bonds and preferred stocks, and, the same year, Investors Stock Fund, Inc. A 1957 venture was Investors Variable Payment Fund, Inc., which invests in common stocks, reinvests dividends, and features provisions for

[2] *Ibid.*, p. 41.

paying out accumulated values in installments which vary in amount depending on the market value of the shares. The company not only merchandised these funds but likewise acted as their investment manager. In 1949 the company changed its name to Investors Diversified Services, Inc., and face-amount certificates are now issued by its subsidiary, Investors Syndicate of America, incorporated in 1940. Another subsidiary, Investors Syndicate of Canada, Ltd., was organized in 1941 to sell face-amount certificates; this in turn organized, in 1950, Investors Mutual of Canada, a Canadian mutual balanced fund, which it managed and sold to the public. Finally, in 1954, the parent company organized Investors Group Canadian Fund, Ltd., a Canadian incorporated company with special tax features, sold only in the United States.

There are two additional subsidiaries—Investors Syndicate Title & Guaranty Company, a $38-million company which conducts a participation certificate business in New York state, the assets of which are invested primarily in mortgages; the other subsidiary is the $5-million Investors Syndicate Life Insurance and Annuity Company, which writes completion insurance for purchases of certificates issued by this New York company and Investors Syndicate of America. It also conducts a regular life insurance business.

The Minneapolis Investors group story is indeed an interesting one. The parent company, Investors Diversified Services, Inc., today is essentially an underwriting and investment management organization. It employs approximately 3,000 salesmen to sell the product of its subsidiaries, direct to the public, whereas, with one or two other important exceptions, almost all investment company securities reach the ultimate investor via the principal underwriter of the investment company and then through the investor's broker or dealer. The face-amount subsidiary, Investors Syndicate of America, had 1958 year-end assets of $500 million; the largest mutual fund, Investors Mutual, Inc., with year-end assets of $1,336 million, is now the largest balanced fund in existence; Investors Stock Fund had assets of $432 million, Investors Selective Fund, Inc., assets of $25 million, Investors Variable Payment Fund, Inc., $56 million, Investors Group Canadian Fund $173 million, and the parent company itself had assets of $180 million.

This 2¾-billion-dollar institution represents the largest aggregation of capital under any one aegis within the investment company industry, even though a fifth of it is in face-amount certificates backed primarily by real estate. Meanwhile, in 1956, control of the Canadian face-amount subsidiary, which likewise merchandised and managed the Canadian mutual fund, was placed directly in the hands of the parent company's shareholders, certain of whom sold their interest so that substantial ownership is now held by Canadians. As for control of the parent American company, Investors Diversified Services, Inc., and its predecessor, Investors Syndicate, after more than one change in ownership the majority of the voting stock today is reported to be divided between the Murchison family in Texas and the Alleghany Corporation. The company's president is Joseph M. Fitzsimmons.

CANADIAN INVASION

Another development of the post-war years was the formation, in Canada or the United States, of mutual funds specializing in Canadian securities for purchase by American investors. From 1932 until the war imposed currency restrictions, the oldest Canadian incorporated mutual fund, Canadian Investment Fund, Ltd., was sold in the United States as well as in Canada. Then, in 1952, the same sponsor, Calvin Bullock, Ltd., organized Canadian Fund, Inc., the first United States incorporated company for investing in Canada.

Two years later an interesting variation occurred. Scudder,

Stevens & Clark organized the Scudder Fund of Canada, Ltd., the first of the so-called nonresident-owned ("NRO") companies to issue its stock to the public. Incorporated in Canada, such a company, to gain certain tax advantages, must be almost entirely owned (95 percent or more) by investors who are not Canadian citizens. The nonresident-owned companies pay no dividends and plow back earnings. If an American investor wants to liquidate his holdings and should realize a profit on his original investment, since there is no capital gains tax in Canada, his principal tax liability would be his United States federal tax on the gains realized. While there are some minor Canadian taxes against the company or the investor (for which a credit against U. S. taxes can usually be claimed), unquestionably the nonresident-owned company is of interest to the wealthy individual or investor uninterested in current income.

Several other nonresident-owned companies followed Scudder's. Names, organization dates, and recent assets are:

Scudder Fund of Canada, Ltd.	1954	$ 62,000,000
Canada General Fund Limited	1954	94,000,000
New York Capital Fund of Canada, Ltd.	1954	28,000,000
United Funds Canada, Ltd.	1954	23,000,000
Keystone Fund of Canada, Ltd.	1954	16,000,000
Investors Group Canadian Fund, Ltd.	1954	173,000,000
Templeton Growth Fund of Canada, Ltd.	1954	3,000,000
Canadian International Growth Fund Limited	1956	6,000,000

LARGEST UNDERWRITING

One of the most interesting events of the 1950s, in addition to the formation of the several Canadian Investment companies, was the largest underwriting ever attempted in investment company history. In 1929 Lehman Brothers had floated one of the hundred-million-dollar companies of the 1920s—the Lehman Corporation being the last large investment company issue before the Panic. Twenty-nine years later, in May of 1958,

Lehman Brothers entered the mutual fund field for the first time by organizing the One William Street Fund, Inc. A nationwide underwriting group provided the company with $183 million to start business, and simultaneously the Fund issued additional shares to purchase the $37 million of assets of Aurora Fund, a private investment company identified with executives of the Ford Motor Co.

The One William Street Fund is an orthodox mutual fund aiming "to achieve reasonable growth of capital through selective participation in the long-term progress of American business and industry, and to provide a fair and reasonable current return on capital invested." It was one of several mutual funds of recent years initially underwritten as a closed-end fund and open-ended at a specified early date. President is Dorsey Richardson, a vice-president of the Lehman Corporation and former chairman of the executive committee of the National Association of Investment Companies. The Fund has retained Lehman Brothers as investment adviser.

Lehman's successful venture was shortly followed by the $117-million Lazard Fund. Three decades ago Lehman and the international banking house of Lazard Frères had formed General American Investors, but, in 1958, Lazard went it alone. Their fund, syndicated as a closed-end company, was then open-ended. But, like State Street Investment Corporation, no day by day raising of capital is contemplated. The Lazard Fund is distinguished by an exceptionally able board of directors, chaired by Dr. Albert J. Hettinger, Jr.

In mid-1958 Dillon Read & Co., who had launched the then largest closed-end trust in 1924, pioneered again by successfully syndicating the $33-million American-South African Investment Company, Limited. This is the first important, orthodox, closed-end investment company to be offered the American public since the 1929 Panic. Incorporated in the Union of South Africa, the company has a simple capital structure of

15,000,000 ordinary shares of £1 par value. It has been organized primarily to provide a medium for investment in the common shares of companies engaged in business in South Africa, particularly gold mining companies. Chairman of the board and a principal factor in the company's management is Charles W. Engelhard, a well-known authority on precious metals and chairman of Rand Mines, Limited, in Johannesburg.

In May of 1959 a second interesting closed-end investment company was underwritten by Glore, Forgan & Co. and others—the predecessor firm of which had been identified with seven such companies more than a quarter of a century before. This is the $19-million Eurofund, Inc., formed primarily to invest in the European common market countries. The company has a simple capitalization of 8,000,000 authorized shares of common stock, and its intention, under favorable conditions, is to invest essentially in common stocks of European corporations, although it has chosen to be classed as a non-diversified investment company. The company has European and American investment advisers—the former owned by E. Gutzwiller & Cie of Basel (in recent years unusually active in the investment company field) and R. deLubersac & Cie of Paris. The European adviser in turn receives advice from four prominent continental banks. The American investment adviser is owned by Glore, Forgan & Co. and receives advice from the Bankers Trust Co. The two investment advisers receive total compensation of 9/16 of 1 percent per annum of the average value of the company's net assets from Eurofund. The company has an unusually prominent directorate, chaired by S. Sloan Colt, formerly head of the Bankers Trust Company.

FIDUCIARIES

The post-war years also saw an accelerated use by trustees of mutual funds. The purchasing power of the pre-war dollar had

Photograph by Fabian Bachrach

MERRILL GRISWOLD

DORSEY RICHARDSON

been cut in half, and, since common stocks appeared to give far greater protection against inflation than bonds, fiduciaries took a much more favorable view than formerly of investment companies whose portfolios generally were characterized by equities. State law of course was the final criterion, but, whereas a minority of the states of the Union at the beginning of the postwar period had adopted the so-called Prudent Man Rule, a decade later this rule had been adopted by the large majority. The rule sets up a standard of conduct of normal prudence—in the place of detailed requirements—for the purchase of securities. Where, however, a trust agreement or a will covers this subject, these, of course, govern.

COMMON TRUST FUNDS

The first common or "uniform" or "composite" trust fund of a bank appeared in 1927, created by the Security National Bank Savings and Trust Company of St. Louis. Two eastern banks shortly became prominent in this field: the City Bank Farmer's Trust Co. (the trust division of the then National City Bank of New York) and the Brooklyn Trust Company. While details of these funds differed, the general principles were the same. Participation by the public was restricted to trust estates of which the trustee was the bank that had created the fund. Banks used these "commingled" funds, after special permission, to take care of some of their smaller trust accounts—under $100,000. A participant would be charged 1 percent of the value of his principal to enter the arrangement, a management fee of ½ of 1 percent per annum and another 1 percent of principal to withdraw from the arrangement. He would own, in effect, his proportionate share of the broad list of securities comprising the fund and obtain exceptionable diversity with, say, $25,000. The idea, however, grew slowly, only about ten funds being created by the end of 1929 with assets of slightly over $30 million. Today something over two hundred such funds exist with assets approximating $2 billion.[3]

PERSONALITIES

In addition to a Boston lawyer named Mayo Shattuck, no one worked more diligently to secure the adoption by various states of the "Prudent Man Rule" than did Merrill Griswold, today honorary chairman of the advisory board of Massachusetts Investors Trust and one of the true deans of the industry. Indeed, for the score or more of years that Mr. Griswold was chairman of the board of trustees of Massachusetts Investors, he either led or was at the forefront of almost every movement to improve the operations, standing, and public acceptance of mutual funds. A partner of the Boston law firm of Gaston, Snow, Saltonstall & Hunt, he became a trustee of Massachusetts Investors Trust as early as 1925 and was chairman from 1932 to 1953. We have already noted that he was a principal leader during the government-industry cooperative effort that resulted in the Investment Company Act. Shrewd, gruff, conservative yet imaginative, with a keen sense of public relations, for many years he has commanded the respect and liking not only of individuals within his industry but also of government regulatory bodies. His monument is the $1½-billion Massachusetts Investors Trust, with record and reputation of which he can be proud.

The choice of what personalities to mention from the field of some two hundred investment companies, most of them mutual funds, the smaller group being the older closed-end companies, is always difficult. For certain large closed-end companies have only recently become classified as investment companies and some mutual funds as well as individuals have attained prominence only in the last decade. The criterion here used is what

[3] Arthur Wiesenberger, *Investment Companies, 1958* (New York, 1959), p. 67.

names would be apt to come first to mind in a backward look over a generation and a half of American investment company history—names identified with constructiveness and progress in the industry.

Some New York names like Calvin Bullock and Floyd B. Odlum have already been mentioned. But Boston figures heavily in investment company lore. And there is no name more identified with Boston's investment world than that of Paul C. Cabot, since 1924 an officer of the State Street Investment Corporation—president since 1934, chairman since April, 1958—treasurer of Harvard University, a director of Morgan Guaranty Trust Company, a Brahmin with a Yankee twang, integrity, and unusual ability.

Two other early Boston investment company executives were officers of Incorporated Investors in 1925. George Putnam, a descendant of Justice Samuel Putnam who promulgated the Prudent Man Rule, was originally president of Incorporated but formed the successful George Putnam Fund of Boston in 1937; he was succeeded as president of Incorporated in 1933 by William A. Parker, chairman since 1954, a keen executive and equally keen skipper, known as "Brother" to his host of business and sailing friends.

Blunt, forthright Charles F. Eaton, Jr., head of one of the earliest Boston investment counsel firms, Eaton & Howard, Inc., formed his two highly successful mutual funds in 1931 and 1932. Over many years he has stood for high ethics in his profession, acknowledgment of which was his election as one of the two strictly investment company presidents who to date have served as a governor of the Investment Bankers Association of America.

The largest aggregation of Boston investment company assets, more than $2 billion, is sponsored by Vance, Sanders & Co., the successor firm to Massachusetts Distributors. Popular Henry T. Vance is president of two of the funds in his group and a director of all but one of the others. Along with Merrill Griswold (succeeded by Dwight P. Robinson, Jr., in 1954 as chairman of Massachusetts Investors) to him belongs credit in the last score of years for making Massachusetts Investors Trust the best known of all investment companies. In many other ways he is one of the outstanding leaders of his profession.

Closed-end investment companies have always primarily centered on New York rather than Boston. The largest closed-end company, Tri-Continental Corporation, and the other open-end companies of the J. & W. Seligman group have been headed for the past eighteen years by trim, military Francis Randolph, a man with a distinguished service record in the First World War, although Minneapolis-born Cyril J. Quinn has been active and even better known through the investment company industry. Until his death in 1940 Earle Bailie headed this group, and it was he who fathered the acquisitions by Tri-Continental of other investment companies with the objective of spreading the cost of operations over a larger amount of assets. Arthur Bunker, forceful principal spokesman for the industry in the 1940 Washington legislative days, transferred from the Lehman Corporation to become an industrialist, and vice-president Dorsey Richardson, with his interesting State Department background, did yeoman's work during the post-war years, not only for his own company but as top man in the National Association of Investment Companies. We have noted that, in 1958, Richardson officially identified himself for the first time with the open-end field by becoming president of Lehman Brothers' important new mutual fund. Finally, George E. Clark, president of the Adams Express group, has been another prominent New York closed-ender.

In the New York open-end field, Hardwick Stires of Scudder, Stevens & Clark, an executive of high integrity, has long been a constructive element in the industry, along with accountant-trained Harry I. Prankard, II, of Affiliated Fund, Inc., Hugh

W. Long, head of one of the largest groups in the country, and Herbert R. Anderson of Group Securities, Inc.

Walter L. Morgan, slow-spoken, distinguished president of the gigantic Wellington Fund of Philadelphia for three decades, has been a potent factor in the industry. Mention should also be made of two Boston executives: S. L. Sholley, long head of the Keystone group, and Edward C. Johnson, II, of Fidelity Fund, as well as Henry J. Simonson, Jr., head of the National Securities Group of New York. The saying "there are always two opinions—your own and the wrong one" is pertinent; other authorities on investment company history would undoubtedly list some different and, certainly, additional names. While additional names unquestionably deserve to be listed, it is believed that those chosen, however imperfect the choice, represent an objective selection of personalities who have left their mark upon one of the most interesting institutions to appear in the financial world. Such men are not infallible. Many, including the author, would be the first to admit to mistakes, honorable mistakes of judgment, at some point in their business careers. But the highly respected positions they occupy today have been earned by integrity and constructive action over many years. This is not to say that, as in every industry, there have not been unsavory characters or individuals whose actions have been harmful to the public. For colorful and juicy tidbits, however, the reader will have to search elsewhere than in this book, because it endeavors, perhaps at the expense of vivid episode and epigram, to tell the story of investment companies with sober accuracy and true perspective.

9

Canadian Experience

CANADA'S EXPERIENCE in the evolution of her investment company industry was similar to that of her neighboring country to the south. There was the formation of closed-end companies in the 1920s, patterned after their British ancestors, some of them indistinguishable from holding companies, particularly in the field of electric light and power. The sequel to the Crash of 1929 was only slightly different from that in the United States. For a year or two fixed trusts struggled to make progress. Then, in 1932, the first mutual fund appeared. Over succeeding years this was followed by numerous others in increasing tempo until today mutual funds dominate the scene, although not quite to the same degree as in the United States.

The story of investment companies in Canada in the 1920s is primarily the story of three groups, centered around the well-known investment banking houses of Wood, Gundy & Co., Ltd., whose home office was in Toronto but whose investment companies were in Montreal; Nesbitt, Thomson & Co., Ltd., in Montreal; and a distinguished Toronto citizen, the Right Honourable Arthur Meighen. By the end of 1929 the assets of these groups represented 75 percent of so-called investment company assets in Canada.

NESBITT, THOMSON & CO. GROUP

The first of these companies appears to have been formed in 1920 under the name of Canadian Pulp & Power Investments, Ltd. This name was changed some three years later to Canadian Power & Paper Investments, Ltd. It was a modest company for several years, but in the late 1920s $2,500,000 in 5 percent debentures and $2,500,000 in 5 percent convertible preferred stock were issued. The 1929 year-end assets at cost were reported as $6,700,000. A. J. Nesbitt and P. A. Thomson of Montreal were respectively president and vice-president, comprising two of the five-man directorate.

In 1925 Nesbitt, Thomson and Co. formed its large investment holding company, Power Corporation of Canada, Ltd. Many would class this company as a utility holding company because of its control and management of several important utility properties, even though the bulk of its assets represented minority investment in a score of other Canadian and American utilities. By December, 1929, its assets had grown to a cost figure of $47 million.

Another Nesbitt company, Foreign Power Securities Corporation, Ltd., formed in 1927 and financed in conjunction with A. Iselin & Co. of New York for investment in securities of French utilities, in 1929 had assets at cost of $14 million, but it did not consider itself an investment trust.

Nesbitt's 1929 company, Great Britain and Canada Investment Corporation, Ltd. (again financed by A. Iselin & Co., New York, as well as by Nesbitt, Thomson & Co., plus Govett Sons & Co. in London), of all these companies was the most typical investment company, patterned and diversified after the British model. There were three Canadian, three American, and four English directors, and $6,000,000 in 4½ percent convertible debentures, $4,000,000 in 5 percent convertible preferred stock, and 350,000 shares of common stock were sold, realizing approximately $11,000,000.

WOOD, GUNDY GROUP

In March of 1927 the first of the Wood, Gundy companies was formed, the Hydro-Electric Bond & Share Corporation, ostensibly an investment trust, but related to a public utility holding company. Sir Herbert S. Holt, a bank president who was also head of Montreal Light, Heat & Power, was president. The company's outstanding capital consisted of $3,430,000 in 5 percent bonds secured by pledge of collateral worth over $8,000,000, $2,000,000 in income debentures, and 200,000 shares of common stock.

In May of 1927 the second Wood, Gundy company was organized, jointly financed by A. Iselin & Co. of New York with their excellent Swiss background and connections. This was Investment Bond and Share Corporation, not a finance company, not a public utility holding company, but a true investment trust. Sir Herbert S. Holt, the prominent and able president of the Royal Bank of Canada again was the company's president. The company issued $4,000,000 in 5 percent debentures, $1,750,000 in 6 percent preferred, and 140,000 shares of common. Market value of assets at the 1929 year-end was $6,401,000.

The third Wood, Gundy company, formed in May of 1928, found Sir Herbert Holt once more as president. This was strictly an investment company, called London Canadian Investment Corporation, with three British directors on its eight-man board. Management fees for the first time were defined as simply ½ of 1 percent of assets up to $5,000,000 and ¼ thereafter, as well as a statement of investment restrictions. The company issued $6,000,000 in 4½ percent debentures, $4,000,-

000 in 5 percent preferred, and 350,000 shares of common. Assets at market value on December 31, 1929, were $11,635,000.

The last Wood, Gundy company of the 1920s, incorporated in February, 1929, was the largest of their group—Consolidated Investment Corporation of Canada. This time J. H. Gundy, who had been on all previous boards, was president. Holt was a director as was George H. Montgomery. The latter, a lawyer, was chairman of the large Hydro-Electric Securities Corporation, vice-president of International Holdings & Investment Co., Ltd., and had been on the other three Wood, Gundy investment company boards. The company issued 4½ percent collateral trust bonds, as well as 5 percent preferred, ahead of its common. Its 1929 year-end assets exceeded $30,000,000.

MEIGHEN GROUP

Of the investment companies operating in Canada in the 1920s, those identified with the Right Honourable Arthur Meighen, in the broad diversification of their portfolios and their lack of any resemblance to holding companies, represented more closely than most the concept of British investment trust companies. Mr. Meighen had served twice as Prime Minister, from 1920 to 1921 and 1925 to 1926. He was an able barrister, Canada's greatest Shakespearian scholar, and Toronto's most distinguished citizen. Affiliated with him in his four business ventures was W. W. Evans, president of Traders Finance Corporation, Ltd.

In late 1926 Canadian General Investment Trust, Ltd., was incorporated, with Meighen as chairman and Evans as president. On their prominent sixteen-man board was Sir Ronald Waterhouse of Price, Waterhouse in London. The company was managed by a management company, Canadian General Securities, Ltd., for one-half of 1 percent of assets plus a fifth of any profits earned over 7 percent. The company operated under strict investment restrictions. Interestingly enough, it published its portfolio, which, by 1930, included over 400 bonds, preferred and common stocks of Canadian, American, and a few European corporations. Its capitalization, differing from a typical British investment trust company, consisted solely of common stock, and its assets by the end of 1929 exceeded $11,000,000.

In October of 1927 Second Canadian General was formed with virtually the same pattern. Assets at market value at December 31, 1929, were $8,954,000. Third Canadian General came in February, 1928, with a London advisory board and 1929 year-end assets of $3,352,000. Fourth Canadian General was organized in late 1928, but had grown to less than $1,000,000 by the time of the Panic.

One of the largest "Canadian" companies of the 1920s, Hydro-Electric Securities Corporation, was incorporated in September, 1926, by Belgian interests to specialize in public utility securities. In 1929, jointly with Central States Electric of New York, it formed Electric Shareholdings Corporation and, in conjunction with the Founders group, helped to form U. S. Electric Power Corporation. While recently its portfolio has been broadly diversified, its character in the earlier period was that of a typical holding company. G. H. Montgomery was its early chairman and Victor M. Drury is its current president—both of Montreal. The company's assets at the 1929 year-end were reported to be over $60,000,000.

Another substantial "Canadian" Company, International Holding & Investment Co., Ltd. (changed a decade later to International Holdings Limited) was formed in 1927; its major interest was in the artificial silk industry of France. It shortly acquired, however, a large interest in Hydro-Electric Securities Corporation. Typically it was a holding company. Once again the names of Montgomery and Belgian interests appear, and recently its management has been the same as Hydro-Electric Securities, their fiscal agent being J. Henry Schroder & Co. of London and New York. Both Hydro-Electric Securities and International Holding, however, while technically Canadian companies, have been prevented from owning Canadian securities and therefore fall outside the mainstream of our Canadian story. Like several other well-known companies they were incorporated in Canada under a tax designation known as "4K," paying only a nominal Canadian tax, but prohibited from deriving income from or having property located in Canada. In January, 1959, they ceased to have any Canadian flavor by merging under a Maryland charter, the new company being called International Holdings Corporation.

There were approximately fifty investment companies existing in Canada by the end of 1929. With the exception of three or four fixed or semi-fixed trusts, all were closed-end companies, most with leverage, of the general management type. Unquestionably four or five of these, like Power Corporation of Canada, Ltd., were holding companies rather than investment trusts. Almost none published their portfolio holdings. In number and size the companies favored Montreal for location over Toronto, with the rare exception located elsewhere. Only twelve had assets of $5,000,000 or more. At the 1929 peak Canadian investment company assets may have reached a figure of over $250 million.

Canadian investment companies, with estimated 1929 year-end assets where available, are listed in the Appendix. The ten largest groups and their assets in 1929 were as follows:

		Assets (in millions of dollars)
Nesbitt, Thomson	Total	79.5
Power Corporation of Canada, Ltd.		47.0
Foreign Power Securities Corp., Ltd.		14.2
Great Britain & Canada Investment Corp.		11.6
Canadian Power & Paper Investments, Ltd.		6.7

		Assets (*in millions of dollars*)
Wood, Gundy	Total	60.4
Consolidated Investment Corp. of Canada		30.3
Hydro-Electric Bond & Share Corp.		12.1
London Canadian Investment Corp.		11.6
Investment Bond & Share Corp.		6.4
Meighen	Total	24.5
Canadian General Investment Trust, Ltd.		11.3
Second Canadian General Investments, Ltd.		9.0
Third Canadian General Investment Trust, Ltd.		3.4
Fourth Canadian General Investment Trust, Ltd.		0.8
Cochrane, Hay	Total	7.2
Dominion-Scottish Investments, Ltd.		4.0
Economic Investment Trust, Ltd.		3.2
Upper Canada Investment Trust, Ltd.	Total	6.2
Basic Investments of Canada, Ltd.	Total	5.1
Foster	Total	4.7
Diversified Standard Securities, Ltd.		1.8
Second Diversified Standard Securities, Ltd.		2.8
Third Diversified Standard Securities, Ltd.		0.1
Canadian International Investment Trust, Ltd.	Total	4.2
Aldred Investment Corp.	Total	3.4
Dominion and Anglo Investment Corp., Ltd.	Total	2.6

After the Panic the word "investment trust" was as unpopular in Canada as in the United States. Fixed trusts made little headway, and only a few American fixed trusts attempted to sell their shares on the other side of the border.

In the closed-end field there were the usual reorganizations and liquidations and disasters among the fringe element, but it is interesting to note that, with some change of name and consolidation here and there, generally the major elements of 1929 exist and operate successfully today. Canadian General has two closed-end companies instead of four. Power Corporation is still a large and successful holding company, the $34-million Hydro-Electric Securities and $35-million International Holdings have considered themselves true investment companies—but were still "Canadian" only in a technical sense and now have merged and incorporated in the United States—and the most important of the Wood, Gundy interests operate under the name of United Corporations, Limited, of which Ney K. Gordon of Montreal is president.

CANADIAN INVESTMENT FUND, LTD.

At the depth of the Depression in 1932 the first mutual fund appeared in Canada. This was Canadian Investment Fund, Ltd., organized by Calvin Bullock and chaired by the man who was Canada's great Prime Minister during the First World War, the Right Honourable Sir Robert Laird Borden. Included among its ten early directors were Sir Edward Beatty, president of Canadian Pacific; Sir Charles Gordon, president of the Bank of Montreal; the Honourable Charles A. Dunning, former Minister of Finance; Senator C. C. Ballantyne, likewise a former Cabinet member; the Right Honourable Arthur B. Purvis, head of Canadian Industries; Norman J. Dawes, head of National Breweries; and the Right Honourable L. A. Taschereau, former Premier of Quebec. For the next quarter century it was the leader in this new and growing field. During the 1930s two other open-end companies or mutual funds were also actively raising capital: Commonwealth International Corp., Ltd., and Corporate Investors Limited.

ARGUS CORPORATION LIMITED

The first half of the 1940s comprised the grim war years, and those of the Canadian investment fraternity who were not in uniform were for the most part busy on War Loan issues. But, in the fall of 1945, an interesting company was organized by E. P. Taylor of Toronto, partially financed by Atlas Corporation interests in the United States. The company, Argus Corporation Limited, was unique in being the only closed-end investment company of any consequence newly organized on the North American continent since the Panic. Technically it is a non-diversified management investment company, but many would call it more simply a holding company because of its half dozen major holdings and its influence in the managerial aspects of such holdings. It is highly pyramided with $15 million in notes and two preferred issues outstanding ahead of its common stock. With November 30, 1958, assets of $103,364,255 it is the largest closed-end investment company in Canada. Power Corporation, with assets of 80 million, is the second largest.

CURRENT SCENE

The 1950s have seen numerous new mutual funds organized. In 1950 Canafund Company, Ltd., was organized by Lombard Odier & Cie and Hentsch & Cie of Geneva, primarily for European investment in Canada. As early as 1947, however, the Montreal investment and brokerage firm of L. G. Beaubien & Cie had formed Beaubran Corporation for the same purpose. In 1952 Canadian Fund, Inc., was formed in the United States to invest in Canada. Its sponsorship and directors were identical with those of Canadian Investment Fund, Ltd. It was followed by another United States company, Canada General Fund, Inc., organized by Vance, Sanders of Boston.

Investors Syndicate of Canada, Ltd., a subsidiary of Investors Syndicate of Minneapolis, had formed, in 1948, a Canadian mutual fund called Investors Mutual of Canada, Ltd. Shares were first publicly offered in Canada in 1950, and the company's rapid growth has carried it to the position of being the largest investment company of any type in Canada. Investors Syndicate of Canada, which specializes in selling face-amount certificates, in 1956 became an independent company whose effective sales force of several hundred individuals specialize in raising capital for Investors Mutual as well as for their face-amount certificate company. The headquarters of both companies are in Winnipeg.

The Minneapolis Investors Syndicate in 1949 changed its name to Investors Diversified Services, Inc., and in 1954 formed Investors Group Canadian Fund, Ltd., a so-called nonresident-owned, non-dividend-paying Canadian company whose shares are sold only in the United States. With 1958 year-end assets of $167,412,984 it is the largest of the nonresident-owned companies.

We have noted that the Scudder Fund of Canada, Ltd., formed in the spring of 1954, was the pioneer of the nonresident-owned companies. Such a company is incorporated in Canada, invests primarily in Canada, reinvests its earnings instead of paying dividends, and 95 percent of its stock must be owned by persons who are not Canadian citizens. If a United States citizen owns shares of one of those companies, he pays no tax until he chooses to sell. Then his major tax liability, if he sells at a profit, is the United States federal tax on his capital gains, there being no tax on capital gains in Canada. Half a dozen other companies in this category besides Scudder's and Investor's Group Canadian Fund were formed within a very short time. But Canadian investment companies, in order to market their shares in the United States, must submit to the jurisdiction of the Securities and Exchange Commission under the Investment Company Act and to special requirements which the Commission has imposed.

Canada General Fund Limited was organized in 1954. Having raised some $32,000,000 through an initial underwriting, the company was merged with Vance, Sanders' two-year-old United States company, Canada General Fund, Inc. The company is supervised by the Boston Management & Research Company. The Right Honourable Arthur Meighen, chairman of closed-end Canadian General Investments, Ltd., of Toronto, is one of Canada General's directors, of whom nine are American and seven Canadian. The company's 1958 year-end assets were $92,000,000.

In October, 1958, Vance, Sanders incorporated their first Canadian mutual fund, the North American Fund of Canada Limited, tailored for Canadian investors. The company's investment adviser has a contract, like Canada General, with Boston Management & Research Company. Directors are prominent Canadians and Americans, and William F. Shelley of Boston is president. Wood, Gundy & Co. raised some $7 million in an initial underwriting.

Other nonresident-owned companies are New York Capital Fund of Canada, Ltd., organized in 1954 by Carl M. Loeb, Rhoades & Co., and the senior officers of the Empire Trust Co. of New York. United Funds Canada, Ltd., was created the same year by Waddell & Reed, Inc., of Kansas City. Three other nonresident-owned companies organized were Canadian International Growth Fund Limited, Keystone Fund of Canada, Ltd., and the Templeton Growth Fund of Canada, Ltd. (now Axe-Templeton).

While investment companies in Canada are generally similar to those in the United States, there are interesting differences in Canadian legislative and tax matters. As in Great Britain, where investment companies operate under the Companies Acts, there is no special federal regulatory Act for investment companies, as such, in Canada. The fact that the major elements of the industry in Canada, especially for the last quarter of a century, have generally acquitted themselves creditably is sometimes advanced as a reason why the Canadian Companies Act and legislative requirements for investment companies of various provinces have proved adequate by way of regulation.

Canadian tax authorities, like those in the United States, accept the philosophy that qualifying Canadian investment companies should not be subjected to additional taxes on dividends received from a Canadian corporation which has already paid the federal corporation tax, and the tax on foreign dividends and interest received from bonds, etc., at a special low tax rate, is not burdensome. As has already been noted, there is no Canadian tax on capital gains (unless classified as a trading operation, in the discretion of the Finance Minister, in which event capital gains are taxed as regular income). Moreover, individual shareholders resident in Canada benefit from the proviso of a 20 percent tax credit which they may take on preferred or common dividends received from Canadian tax paying corporations. In 1957 another constructive piece of legislation was passed respecting the creation of retirement savings plans, which has stimulated interest in those Canadian investment companies and other institutions that have organized such plans.

It will be remembered that at the end of 1929 there were about fifty Canadian investment companies, virtually all closed-end leverage companies, with total estimated assets of about $220 million. Of these only seven companies exceeded $10 million in size. Today the number of companies is about the same, but companies are much larger as witnessed by the fact that 28 companies report assets of $10 million or more. Total assets today approximate $1.3 billion, 25 mutual funds having assets of $878 million and 24 closed-end companies $436 million. An interesting variation in location of investment company assets has occurred since 1929. Montreal still leads with assets of $402 million, followed by Toronto's $244 million and Winnipeg's $185 million. But if U. S. incorporated and non-resident-owned funds are considered, Toronto is management headquarters for investment company assets of $616 million, Montreal of $468 million, and Winnipeg of $185 million.

Companies reporting assets of $1 million or more at the beginning of the year 1959 are listed in the Appendix. The ten major Canadian groups and their assets at market at the start of 1959 were as follows:

		Assets (in millions of Canadian dollars)
Investors Syndicate	Total	185
Investors Mutual of Canada, Ltd.		170
Investors Growth Fund of Canada, Ltd.		15
Investors Diversified Services		
Investors Group Canadian Fund, Ltd.	Total	167
Calvin Bullock	Total	165
Canadian Investment Fund, Ltd.		120
Canadian Fund, Inc.		45
Argus Corporation, Ltd.	Total	103
Vance, Sanders	Total	98
Canada General Fund, Ltd.		91
The North American Fund of Canada, Ltd.		7
Nesbitt, Thomson	Total	92
Power Corporation of Canada, Ltd.		80
Canadian Power and Paper Securities, Ltd.		8
Foreign Power Securities Corp., Ltd.		4
Scudder Fund of Canada, Ltd.	Total	60
Meighen	Total	60
Canadian General Investments, Ltd.		45
Third Canadian General Investment Trust, Ltd.		15
Wood, Gundy	Total	54
United Corporations, Ltd.		30
Investment Bond and Share Corporation		13
London Canadian Investment Corporation		11
Sogemines Limited	Total	29

10

British Trusts Today

THE BARING CRISIS and the First World War were the first two testing periods for British investment trust companies. The aftermath of the 1890 affair separated the early wheat from the chaff; the Great War saw the trusts generally acquit themselves creditably. The third severe testing period was the world financial crisis of 1929 and the prolonged depression that followed.

While more than half of the British investment trust companies were formed prior to the First World War, the rest were launched (as were over 95 percent of their American counterparts) in the later 1920s. Thus, when the crisis came, almost half the British trusts were unseasoned, had little opportunity to build up reserves, and had paid relatively high prices for the securities in their portfolios.

All the British companies were closed-end companies, most with a high degree of leverage. Far more than most American companies, however, their portfolio holdings were comprised of bonds and preference shares rather than equities; moreover, their holdings were world-wide in scope. Yet, for the first time in man's memory, depression gripped the various countries of the world at the same time. And the British theory of selling dear and buying cheap—liquidating portfolio holdings in a country where prices were high to reinvest the proceeds in another area of the world where prices were low—was invalidated.

Obviously, heavy capital losses occurred and dividends were reduced. Yet, few reorganizations were necessary, and no trust was compelled to be liquidated. In 1933, the worst year, only seven pre-war trusts, representing 3 percent of the assets of the pre-war group, passed their dividends. However, over one-third of the post-war organized companies, representing some 40 percent of the assets of the post-war group, omitted dividends. The Securities and Exchange Commission's Report on British trusts states: "The claim of the investment trusts to have administered the national savings in better and more secure fashion than the average investor over a long period does not seem to be fully justified by the facts."[1] But we should remember that the SEC study was conducted in the middle 1930s, after the worst financial holocaust of the twentieth century, and embraced all the British investment trust companies. Many of the older ones had records of which they were and are proud.

The fourth testing period came during the Second World War. With the world convulsed and Britain standing alone for a full year against the most terrible military machine in recorded history, the full six-year period was far more difficult for her men and institutions even than the First World War. But by this time British investment trust companies had built up greater reserves, had enjoyed greater experience, and were in a stronger position than in 1914. George Glasgow is authority for the general statement that they stood up to this test with as much success (even more if one considers the greater difficulty) as they did in the First World War.

[1] Report of the Securities and Exchange Commission, *Investment Trusts and Investment Companies,* "Investment Trusts in Great Britain," p. 9.

FIXED TRUSTS

There was a reaction in Britain after the Panic somewhat comparable to the public reaction in the United States. A flood of fixed or unit trusts began in 1931 in imitation of those on this side of the ocean. By 1936 more than seventy had been organized, and subscriptions from the public may have totaled as high as £80 million. Yet never was the movement in those days more than a fraction of that of the orthodox closed-end investment trust companies and, like their American counterparts, most of the fixed trusts eventually petered out.

Pioneer in the field was the Municipal & General Securities Company which, a decade later, offered its unit shareholders a conversion into a general management company something like our mutual funds. In all, less than a dozen sponsors were involved, the most important being Municipal & General, together with the Bank Insurance and the National groups.

In contrast to anything heretofore known in the United Kingdom, vigorous merchandising methods were employed: branch banks and brokers were urged to recommend shares to their clients: newspaper advertising was extensive. Exigencies of the Second World War stopped the movement, which, however, was on the decline some years before. The post-war years saw little revival until 1958—and nothing comparable to the mutual fund movement in the United States. Today, as for several generations, the closed-end, highly geared, orthodox investment trust company dominates the British scene.

UNIT TRUSTS

For several years Mr. Harold Wincott, editor of the *Investors Chronicle* of London, watching the spectacular growth of mutual funds on the North American continent, has strongly advocated such a movement in the United Kingdom as a practical means of broadening the participation of the average citizen in the ownership of British industry. In recent months, even though the assets of the familiar closed-end British investment trust companies as a group are ten times the size of the so-called unit trust group, it nevertheless appears that the latter may well be on the threshold of substantial expansion.

What is the difference between a unit trust of today and the fixed trusts of a generation ago? Primarily it is that today's trusts have full management discretion and far more prominent sponsorship. How do unit trusts differ from American mutual funds? Essentially they differ in their legal concept. Unit trusts are true trusts, with their assets trusteed and with a terminable date of perhaps twenty or twenty-five years, whereas mutual funds are, for the most part, corporations—though there are American mutual funds, such as Massachusetts Investors Trust, which are common law trusts. Otherwise, the British unit trusts, like our mutual funds, have a self-liquidation feature, issue only one class of stock (which the British call units), register their shareholders, charge an annual management fee of usually one-half of 1 percent of the average value of their assets, and sell their shares to the public at a premium above such asset value. This premium is usually lower than in America, however, being, as a rule, 3¼ percent. The Board of Trade in London, however, which supervises the operations of unit trusts, will permit the premium to be as high as 5 percent provided the management fee is reduced, so that total charges to the public over the life of the trust do not exceed 13¼ percent. Quite different from American mutual funds (in which such action is taken because of tax considerations), neither capital gains nor proceeds from sale of rights is paid out to shareholders.

It is said that the government today is in favor of broader ownership by the British public of shares of industrial corporations; yet, in the post-war years, not until 1957 did a new unit trust group come into being. October, 1957, saw the formation of the Unicorn Trust, today about a $7-million proposition, whose shares for the first time were marketed direct to the public. Other unit trusts like the $18-million "Scotbits," one of the trusts formed by the Bank Insurance interests, the largest group, have been sold through the branches of the Scottish joint stock banks. And most unit trusts are sold through stock brokers or, more recently, occasionally through branches of the "Big Five" banks. Brokers and bank branches receive the customary Stock Exchange commission of something over 1 percent, the remainder going to the sponsors.

November, 1958, marked the first identification of a well-known merchant bank with the unit trust movement. This occurred when Philip Hill, Higginson & Co. Limited made a successful block offering of £2,500,000 of their British Shareholders Trust. The trust's portfolio comprises some sixty leading industrial shares. An investment council of four well-known individuals advises the management, and provisions exist whereby the shares may be purchased by the public in installments. A short time later a famous name in the orthodox investment trust company world entered the unit trust field with the formation of the Robert Fleming Trust Management Ltd. and the offering of one million units at 10 shillings a unit of the Crosby Unit Trust—an existing investment trust company transformed into a new unit trust, approximately a quarter of the portfolio of which is comprised of companies in North America. More leading merchant banks are apparently entering the unit trust field with the announcement that the pioneer Municipal & General Securities are associated with Robert Benson, Lonsdale & Co., and the information that the National group is working with N. M. Rothschild & Co. Following is a recent tabulation of unit trust groups in the United Kingdom, showing their approximate assets at market about January 31, 1959.

	Assets	
	(in millions of pounds)	*(in millions of dollars)*
Bank Insurance (1937)	39.0	109
National (1938)	20.0	56
Municipal & General (1938)	16.5	46
Allied Investors (1942)	8.0	22
Philip Hill, Higginson & Co., Limited (1958; British Shareholders Trust)	5.5	15
A.E.G. (1957)	2.7	8
Unicorn (1957)	2.6	7
N. M. Rothschild & Co. (1959; Shield Unit Fund)	2.5	7
Robert Fleming Trust Management Ltd. (1958; Crosby Unit Trust)	1.9	5

The author is indebted to Mr. Piers Dixon of Philip Hill, Higginson & Co., Limited, for this tabulation and for other useful information.

CHARACTERISTICS

Recently some 38 unit trusts, belonging to nine groups, were quoted in the *Investors Chronicle.* But we must keep our story in perspective and return to our discussion of the dominant type of trust in the United Kingdom. Of 200 British investment trust companies listed in Laing & Cruickshank's manual, all are closed-end companies, all are leverage companies, none has a simple capital structure. The usual ratio of senior capital of the leverage companies to the ordinary shares is about 2 to 1. Most companies have both debenture stock and preference shares ahead of the ordinary shares. Typical ratios, respectively, would be 4 to 2 to 3. It can be seen, therefore, that if a British investment trust company, depending on its reputation and the state of the money market, can borrow money from the public at 2¾ to 4 percent, have somewhere near a 4 percent fixed dividend rate on its preference shares, and then receive a 5 percent return or better from its portfolio investments, the resultant earnings applicable to its ordinary shares, even after deduction of operating expense, can be exceedingly attractive.

While there is high income leverage in the average British investment trust company, there is usually little, if any, capital leverage. This is because the British trusts invest far more in bonds than we do relative to their common stock holdings. They usually buy sufficient bonds and preferreds to offset their pyramided capital structure. Their minds are more on income than is the case in the United States. And, while capital appreciation is obviously an objective, it possibly is not accentuated to the extent it is here. If they realize a capital profit it goes into a reserve—which additional capital investment helps to augment income against a rainy day. Their portfolios, moreover, are much more diversified than ours. They will invest in many countries of the world; in recent years there has again been a trend toward investment in the United States and Canada, especially among the Scottish companies, perhaps 40 percent of the average Scottish trust's portfolio being so invested. A single trust will own several hundred different securities, some over a thousand. In earlier years the accent was on bonds and preferreds, especially those of higher yield, but today equities are strongly favored in most portfolios. Of 200 trusts recently listed by Laing & Cruickshank 197 had over 70 percent of their assets invested in common stocks, and of these 172 had over 80 percent.

COSTS

Costs of raising capital and of management of British investment trust companies have usually been lower than in the United States. Cost of raising capital here has ranged between 5 percent and 10 percent for equity capital and from 3 to 5 percent for senior capital. Comparable British figures would be only half as high. Management personnel of British trusts has been far less extensive than in this country, but management expense would perhaps be little more than half of our ratios.

MARKETABILITY

Debenture stock or preference shares of British investment trust companies are almost always listed but are closely held. They are a preferred trustee investment. Ordinary shares are likewise listed on the London Stock Exchange. Activity is slight, however, and markets narrow.

In the 1920s it was not uncommon for the ordinary shares of most investment trust companies to be quoted at a premium above their break-up value. It is difficult to ascertain whether the ordinary shares of certain companies sell today above or below their actual asset value, because of the conservative practice of carrying portfolio holdings at cost or market—whichever is lower—and even writing down the cost of specific securities, if a portion is sold at a profit, to establish a hidden reserve. A study, however, of the ordinary shares of 182 companies listed by Laing & Cruickshank would indicate that, as of late 1957, 19 were selling above asset value, 2 at asset value, and 161 below asset value—the group on the average selling 11 percent below asset value.

PUBLICITY

Few of the British investment trust companies—other than the fixed or unit trusts—ever publish their portfolios. The London companies are more apt to do so than the Scottish companies. But of 200 British companies listed by Laing & Cruickshank today, only 41 show the investor the names of the actual securities in which his money is invested, and only 2 of these are Scottish. The customary procedure is to give a breakdown of what proportion of investment is in various parts of the world, what percentage is in senior securities as against equities, and what percentage of the investor's dollar is invested in various major industries.

INVESTMENT MANAGERS

Organizers or investment managers of investment companies earlier this century were seldom private or investment bankers or brokers as in this country, but primarily lawyers or accountants. Today the situation is somewhat changed, and more financial houses are identified with such companies. But in Scotland the grouping of investment trusts was usually around firms of solicitors—probably as a result of the latter's investment experience in administering private trust accounts and estates. In England the grouping was more apt to be around accounting firms, although occasionally this is the case in Scotland. It must be remembered that accounting firms in Great Britain have a much broader scope of activity than in the United States and not infrequently act as financial advisers.

To one familiar with the extensive personnel comprising the well-known American investment management organizations, it is something of a contrast to enter a typical office of a prominent British investment trust company. Modest quarters, far fewer personnel, but topped by two or three wise and experienced investment men who have accumulated an enviable reputation over the years. Less original research is done, but full advantage is taken of primary sources of research. Broad contacts with financial men throughout the world are utilized; great attention is paid before investment to the reputation for integrity and ability of an industrial company's management. And all this is accomplished with less cost than is the case on the American scene. Frequently, as a matter of economy, several companies will be grouped in one secretarial office for investment management and administrative responsibilities.

Directors of an investment trust company are relatively few in number, perhaps five or six, and not only take their responsibilities with great seriousness, but devote more time and attention to the affairs of the company than is generally the practice here. They are usually professional investment men, accountants, or solicitors with broad trustee experience.

REGULATION

There is no Investment Company Act in Great Britain, and investment trust companies are registered, as are all other publicly owned corporations, under the Companies Act. Requirements, however, are for periodic reports, full publicity of operations (with the exception of listing portfolio holdings), and ethical business conduct such as is expected by our federal and state laws. Tradition has a strong hold in Britain, and ethics is a characteristic of the British race. Rules are less formal and more apt to be "understood" than written in the supervision of the great financial agencies such as the Bank of England or the Stock Exchange, and every American schoolboy should be familiar with the fact that there is no written British Constitution.

TAXATION

Investment trust companies in Britain pay two kinds of taxes: income tax and profits tax. The income tax rate is 42½ percent on all income from any source, after deducting expense of servicing senior capital as well as management expense. Usually any corporation whose dividends are received by the investment trust company will already have paid this income tax or, if the income is derived from foreign sources, the bank acting as paying agent will have deducted the tax and will have remitted it to the "Inland Revenue." As for income from North American investments and from other countries of the world which have tax conventions with the United Kingdom, credit by the British Investment Trust Company for corporate taxes paid in those countries can be claimed from the Inland Revenue.

The other tax on investment trust companies, the profits tax, in recent years was at a rate of 3 percent on undistributed income and 27 percent on gross dividends—the most recent budget of the Chancellor of the Exchequer, eliminating this differentiation, called for a tax on profits of a flat 10 percent. Dividends received from British companies that have already paid the profits tax themselves are free of this tax so, in effect, only income derived from foreign sources and from bonds is liable to the profits tax. In the case of American investments, for example, this lessens the benefit of double taxation relief and it makes portfolio holdings of debentures less attractive.

FINANCE COMPANIES

Finance companies are taxed on net realized capital profits as if this were income. In short, they pay taxes as any ordinary British corporation does. The new two-tier system consisting of 42½ percent income tax and 10 percent profits tax means, in practical effect, that 52½ percent of corporate profits are paid out in taxes.

To be sure, there is a hazy line between finance companies and investment trust companies. The difference is one of fact and intention. If a company is being run with the provision of income to pay to shareholders the only consideration, capital profits being specifically precluded from distribution as dividends, it will be classified as an investment trust. But if the object is to distribute capital profits by the buying and selling of securities, it will be called a finance company. To repeat—the criterion is whether a company pays out as dividends only investment income or whether it supplements such payments with profits from trading in portfolio securities. An investment trust will virtually never turn over more than one-sixth or one-seventh of its portfolio annually; a finance company is more active in its trading.

On infrequent occasions a company will pass from one category to the other, depending on its activities. Finance companies cover a wider range of activities than pure investment. Sometimes they correspond to our holding companies. Sometimes they are security trading companies. Frequently they perform banking or underwriting functions to a greater extent than the average investment trust company. Sometimes they combine all of these functions. In short, they are veritable department stores of finance.

SIZE

Compared with the fourteen billion dollars invested in American mutual funds and the additional billion and a half invested in American closed-end companies, the total assets of British investment trust companies today exceed £1 billion or approximately $3 billion, with about another $300 million invested in unit trusts.

In the United States there are 30 investment companies with assets of over $100 million. In Great Britain there are seven investment trust companies with assets of over the equivalent of $50 million. The mean size of the typical British company is about £5 million.

In the Appendix will be found an alphabetical list of English and Scottish investment trust companies, taken with the publisher's permission from Laing & Cruickshank's excellent tabulations, giving their date of organization and their approximate asset value as of early 1958.

INVESTMENT TRUST COMPANY GROUPS

In the United Kingdom, even more than in the United States, there are found groupings of investment companies. Occasionally this will occur where they have a common secretariat; often a company is identified as belonging to a particular group because of interlocking directors with other companies. The system of interlocking directors is far more common than in the United States.

The composition of these groups is, to some extent, a matter of opinion, but the following tabulation indicates that which is today most commonly accepted. The figures show gross assets, at market, at various dates in 1957.

		Assets (in millions of pounds)
Baillie Gifford Group, 15 Trusts	Total	124.2
Baillie Gifford-Edinburgh Trusts	Total	43.9
Scottish Mortgage & Trust		13.8
Edinburgh & Dundee		9.1
Scottish Capital Investment		6.4
Scottish Central		5.7
Second Scottish Mortgage & Trust		5.0
Second Edinburgh & Dundee		3.9
Baillie Gifford-London Trusts	Total	15.0
Friars Investment		4.6
Monks Investment		3.9
Abbots Investment		3.8
Winterbottom		2.7
Alliance Trusts, Dundee	Total	42.0
Alliance Trust		30.7
Second Alliance Trust		11.3
Ball Trusts, Edinburgh	Total	23.3
Second Scottish Investment		11.5
Scottish Investment		8.2
U. S. Trust of Scotland		3.6
Fleming Group, 21 Trusts	Total	107.8
Brown Fleming-London Trusts	Total	34.4
British Steamship		11.0
London & Holyrood		6.1
London & Clydesdale		4.3
London & Montrose		3.9
London & Provincial		3.5

		Assets (in millions of pounds)
Second British Steamship		3.0
Capital & National		2.6
Brown Fleming-Glasgow Trusts	Total	31.5
Scottish Western		5.1
Second Scottish Western		4.9
Caledonian		4.4
Clydesdale		4.2
Second Great Northern		3.3
Third Scottish Western		2.8
Second Clydesdale		2.7
Second Caledonian		2.1
Third Caledonian		2.0
Murray Trusts, London	Total	34.2
Investment Trust Corp.		18.4
Metropolitan		6.4
London Maritime Investment		4.8
U. S. & General Trust Corp.		4.6
Berry Trust, London		
Sterling	Total	7.7
Touche Group, London, 8 Trusts	Total	83.8
Touche Trusts	Total	41.2
Atlas Electric & General		17.7
Sphere		8.7
Trust Union		6.2
Continental Union		5.0
Cedar Investment		3.6
Herbert Trusts	Total	42.6
Industrial & General		25.7
Trustees Corporation		13.3
Second Industrial		3.6
Crichton-Govett Group, London, 12 Trusts	Total	73.8
Crichton Trusts	Total	39.4
Foreign American & General		10.2
American Investment & General		10.2
Foreign & Colonial		9.2
London Border & General		6.8
Alliance Investment		3.0
Govett Trusts	Total	23.7
Lake View Investment		9.5
Southern Stockholders		5.6

		Assets (in millions of pounds)
Stockholders Investment		4.8
Scottish Stockholders		3.8
Micklem Trusts	Total	9.2
Bankers' Investment		6.5
Army & Navy Investment		2.7
Francis Peek Trust		
Investment Loan & Agency	Total	1.5
Mercantile-Anglo-American Group, London, 7 Trusts	Total	44.8
Mercantile Trusts	Total	28.5
Mercantile Investment & General		15.5
New Mercantile		5.1
U. S. & Mercantile		4.3
Second Mercantile		3.6
Anglo-American Trusts	Total	16.3
Anglo-American Debenture Corp.		5.8
Share & General		5.4
Debenture & Capital Investment		5.1
Wilshaw Group, London, 2 Trusts	Total	44.6
Cable & Wireless		23.8
Globe Telegraph & Trust		20.8
Blair Group, Edinburgh, 3 Trusts	Total	44.3
A. C. Blair Trusts	Total	27.7
British Assets		20.7
Second British Assets		7.0
A. W. Blair Trust		
Scottish American Investment	Total	16.6
Friarfield-Williamson Group, 8 Trusts	Total	35.0
Friarfield House Trusts, Dundee	Total	22.6
Northern American		7.8
Second Scottish American		4.0
Third Scottish American		3.9
Camperdown		3.6
First Scottish American		3.3
Williamson Trusts, Aberdeen	Total	12.4
Scottish Northern		5.3
Second Scottish Northern		4.4
Third Scottish Northern		2.7

		Assets (in millions of pounds)
Drayton-Adeane Group, London, 13 Trusts	Total	34.7
Drayton Trusts	Total	25.6
Premier Investment		5.3
Omnium Investment		5.2
Government Stocks and other Securities		4.5
Consolidated		4.3
Second Consolidated		3.0
English & International		2.0
International Financial Society		1.3
Adeane Trusts	Total	5.8
Municipal		2.2
New York & General		1.9
London & Overseas		1.1
City & Foreign		.6
P. L. Fleming Trusts	Total	3.3
Union Commercial		2.2
Government & General		1.1
Benson Lonsdale Group, London, 7 Trusts	Total	33.2
Benson Lonsdale Trusts	Total	10.0
English & New York		4.7
Charter Trust & Agency		3.2
English & Chicago		2.1
C. E. Benson Trusts	Total	14.0
Merchants		8.5
British American		5.5
Lonsdale-Brunner Trusts	Total	9.2
Lonsdale Investment		5.7
Brunner Investment		3.5
Grahams, Rintoul-Brock Group, 8 Trusts	Total	29.7
Grahams, Rintoul-Glasgow Trusts	Total	17.3
Scottish National		5.7
Second Scottish National		4.1
Third Scottish National		4.1
Glasgow Stockholders		3.4
Grahams, Rintoul-London Trusts	Total	10.3
London & Lomond		4.6
Anglo-Scottish		3.2
London & Strathclyde		2.5

		Assets (in millions of pounds)
Brock Trust, London		
Staveley Investment	Total	2.1
Robertson Group, Edinburgh, 2 Trusts	Total	26.3
British Investment		18.3
Realisation & Debenture Corporation of Scotland		8.0
McGregor Group, Edinburgh, 3 Trusts	Total	19.9
Edinburgh Investment		8.2
Second Edinburgh Investment		6.8
Third Edinburgh Investment		4.9
Cook Group, London, 3 Trusts	Total	18.9
U. S. Debenture Corporation		11.7
London Scottish American		4.3
Second London Scottish American		2.9
De Stein Group, London, 6 Trusts	Total	18.8
Rio Claro		5.6
British Combined Investors		4.0
Anglo-Celtic		3.8
Romney		2.3
Second Anglo-Celtic		1.8
Compass Investment		1.3

THE BRITISH TRUSTS ASSOCIATION, LTD.

This is not a trade association of British investment trust companies comparable to the National Association of Investment Companies in this country. Rather it is a company the stock of which is owned by over 100 British investment trust and finance companies and which performs several useful functions. The most important is to provide underwritings for its members; indeed the success of numerous underwritings depends on the Association's attitude toward them. It also looks after the interests of its members—especially in controversial matters—in ways comparable to our bondholders protective committees, etc.

THE ALLIANCE TRUST COMPANY LIMITED

The Alliance of Dundee for most of its past history was affiliated with no particular group. It is the largest of all the British investment trust companies. Typical of the older and well-managed companies, its background and latest annual report are pertinent to our story.

The company was incorporated in 1888 and succeeded four amalgamated land mortgage companies (and an Oregon Savings bank) the first of which, the Oregon and Washington Trust Investment Co., Ltd., dated back to 1873. Dundee investment companies of the last century were essentially comprised of the Fleming group which invested primarily in American railroad mortgage bonds and a group of land mortgage companies under the aegis of William MacKenzie. One of the latter, the Western and Hawaiian Investment Company, changed its name in 1923 to the Second Alliance Trust Company, Ltd.

For many years land mortgages in America comprised the investment portfolio of the Alliance; then mortgages were gradually liquidated and holdings of general securities took their place. There was likewise a trend toward less American investment. Yet the history of this trust is illustrative of what a factor Scottish and English investment trust companies were in the development of our country in the days when we were a debtor nation.

The Alliance has been managed astutely and its record over the years, as well as its size, places it in the very first rank. The substance of its latest annual report is to be found in the Appendix.

OTHER COUNTRIES

Investment companies of course have existed in some degree for years and are to be found today in increasing numbers in other countries besides the United Kingdom, the United States, and Canada. But the English-speaking peoples developed them, formed a far larger number than were originated elsewhere, and such companies have been much more important in their financial life than, for instance, on the Continent.

Yet there has been recent great activity on the Continent especially in the form of mutual funds. We remember, of course, that the Société Générale de Belgique of Brussels, in so far as research can tell us, is the forerunner of all investment companies. A few companies analogous to investment companies existed in France during the nineteenth century. As the twentieth century progressed perhaps Switzerland, neutral in both World Wars and an international banking center, has done as much to develop the investment company idea as any continental country. There has been much activity in the Low Countries, little or none in Scandinavia. Italy is just starting, and now the West German Republic is witnessing unusual interest. Overseas, Australia has several mutual funds with combined assets of over $100 million. Latin America, needing foreign capital and short on domestic savings, has been no factor in the field. It is self-evident that Socialist and Communist countries, with industry under state control, have no place for investment companies. Generally speaking they are formed and flourish under private enterprise, not in underdeveloped countries which need capital, but in more mature economies where there is some surplus of savings.

In Switzerland the large banks, like the Crédit Suisse and Union Bank of Switzerland in Zurich, and the Geneva private banking houses such as Lombard Odier & Cie and Hentsch & Cie have long been identified with investment companies. The twenty-year-old America-Canada Trust Fund—AMCA—managed by INTRAG in Zurich, the managing director of which is E. G. Renk of the Union Bank of Switzerland, with assets approximating the equivalent of $150 million is perhaps the best-known Swiss open-end company internationally. A Basel group of trusts under the aegis of the Société Internationale de

Placements (SIP) reports assets of over $200 million. In addition to numerous Swiss trusts a considerable number of foreign mutual funds or unit trusts are merchandised in Switzerland. Purchasers are less apt to be the Swiss than other nationalities who have capital there.

The Netherlands' leading investment company, formed in 1933, is the Rotterdamsch Beleggingoconsortium N. V.—"Robeco" for short—with assets approximating $100 million. Another is "Unitas," of almost equal size. Both are in Rotterdam. Three successful open-end companies are sponsored by the Kredetbank of Antwerp, Belgium. "Eurunion" is the first European unit trust to be marketed simultaneously in the six common market countries. Two Swiss trusts, "Europa-Valor" and "Eurit" likewise look to investment in such countries. "Itac" is a new Swiss mutual fund formed to invest in Italy, but closed-end "Invest" (Societa Invest-Sviluppo & Gestione Investimenti) of Milan is larger and better known.

It is in West Germany, however, that greatest present activity is occurring. "Europa I," a unit trust to invest in common market countries, has recently been sponsored by Hardy & Co. of Frankfurt. German, Dutch, and Swiss banking interests, headed by the Commerzbank, sponsor four companies with assets of over $50 million. The Dresdner Bank has three funds with over $100 million in assets, "Concentra" and "Thesaurus" being the best known. Germany's leading bank, the Deutsche Bank, formed "Investia" with over $50 million—contributing to over $250 million of the unit trust total already raised in that country. "Unifonds" is another company formed in 1956 by Hentsch & Cie of Geneva and German interests. The continental scene is ever changing. Indeed, the story of investment companies in other than the English-speaking countries warrants specialized, on-the-ground research that is beyond the scope of this present volume.

11

Current American Scene

THE SCENE IS an impressive one. Almost four decades of active history have witnessed the evolution of the American investment company from a well-conceived but imperfect vehicle to an investment medium of proven merit.

The principle of diversification has always been sound. Ownership of ten comparable securities carries less risk than ownership of one or two; ownership of a hundred carries less risk than ten. With the exception of so-called non-diversified investment companies, many of which are more in the nature of holding companies, the diversification of risk in today's average investment company is very broad.

Professional supervision is the other major tenet of an investment company. The promoters of the earlier days have been superseded by the professionals of today. Investment management is indeed a profession, and to excel therein requires study and preparation and constant attention as do the professions of law and medicine. And just as law and medicine cross the average man's life, so also does the problem of what to do with one's savings. Today's professional investment company men believe they have one of the soundest answers. Mistakes of judgment will of course be made, just as in other professions. Yet a broadly diversified list of securities, watched over by individuals entitled to the designation of experts, should provide most laymen with a better investment experience than they would have on their own.

The required publicity since the passage of the Investment Company Act of 1940 gives the investor the information to which he has always been entitled. He knows in what securities his capital is invested; he knows what expenses are deducted from the investment company's earnings; of the distributions paid to him, he knows which are derived from investment income and which represent return of capital; he receives audited financial statements at least semiannually; no fact of any material consequence—including what the underwriting expenses were at the time he made his original investment—is left unrevealed.

Regulation of investment companies is strict indeed—by federal and state governments as well as supervision by entities within the securities industry. This cannot prevent falling stock markets or bad investment judgment or even unethical practices. But it is protection which the investor of the 1920s did not have. The investor must remember, however, that the most important factors with respect to any investment company are the integrity and ability of the men who run it. It may reassure him to realize that investment company managers of today are considered more experienced and reputable than ever before.

Capital structures of investment companies present a very different picture from those of other days. Not only does the Investment Company Act require this, but also the tendency of managements of closed-end companies is to operate with conservatism, especially with respect to borrowed money. Looking back to the 1920s, it was the heavily pyramided closed-end companies that got into the most serious trouble, and, since their assets represented twenty times the assets of the few open-end companies, the better experience of open-end stockholders was virtually overlooked. Now the relationship is reversed.

Among members of the National Association of Investment Companies (NAIC) in 1959 assets of open-end companies or mutual funds are over eight times those of closed-end companies. And the mutual fund capital structure is the most conservative of any in the investment company field.

The mutual fund indeed is the typical American company, and this is the country of its birth. Great Britain taught us the principles of diversification and professional investment management. Our early fixed trusts, followed by our open-end companies, were characterized by full publicity as to what securities comprised their portfolios, and they pioneered a redemption feature for any shareholder who wanted to secure asset value for his shares—clumsy in the case of the fixed trusts but perfected by the open-end or mutual funds. This self-liquidation feature gives unusual marketability to mutual fund shares and assures that their market price should never be far removed from their asset value. Over the last quarter century it has been Americans who have exported this refinement of the investment company idea to other countries.

CLOSED-END FUNDS

As a potential investor surveys the current American scene he has a broad field of investment companies from which to choose. First of all he may purchase a security of one of the two broad classifications of investment companies, namely, of a closed-end fund. A large majority of these are listed on the New York Stock Exchange or on other security exchanges. There are debentures combining a reasonable yield with a high factor of safety. There are preferred shares of different grades. There are two types of common stocks: one of an investment company with no funded debt or preferred stock, a company without leverage; the other, the common stock of a leverage company. The latter is speculative in greater or lesser degree, but it has been termed "a margin account that almost never can be called." Most closed-end companies today are without leverage. Finally, there are warrants available entitling the owner to purchase common stocks of certain closed-end companies at specified prices. A list of closed-end securities outstanding as of a recent date, as well as a list of mutual funds, appears in the Appendix.

Closed-end companies have differing investment objectives. The majority of their portfolios contain a broadly diversified list of junior securities of American corporations, with a minor proportion of senior securities or United States government bonds. Some, however, are so-called "non-diversified" companies; some concentrate on special situations; some are virtual finance companies; some specialize in utility, railroad, petroleum, insurance, bank, aviation, tobacco, mining or other enterprises.

We have seen that the common stocks of closed-end companies, often because of leverage, because of not being tied to their asset value, and because their price is entirely subject to the law of supply and demand, have fluctuated more widely than shares of open-end companies or mutual funds. The majority for years have sold below their asset value. Lately, however, the discount has tended to narrow and several sell at premiums. Of 23 common stocks of closed-end companies tabulated by The National Association of Investment Companies early in 1959, four were selling at a premium and the remainder were selling at an average discount of 16 percent below their asset value.

MUTUAL FUNDS

The second broad classification of investment companies is of course the open-end companies—the mutual funds. As we know, these have only one class of stock outstanding and the familiar self-liquidating or redemption feature which assures that their shares should command a market closely related to their asset value. The open-end company is so named because it is virtually always repurchasing its shares, and in consequence it is generally issuing new shares, whereas the closed-end company's capital remains relatively unchanged.

The largest class of mutual funds is made up of those confining their portfolios to a diversified group of common stocks. Some go in for "blue chips," some for growth stocks, some for stocks with high income; some specialize in particular fields such as chemicals, electronics, insurance, aviation, utilities, atomic energy; some confine their investments to Canada or to specific sections of the United States. Other mutual funds buy only bonds or preferred stocks. But of all the common stock funds, the largest group comprises those which invest in a broadly diversified list of orthodox common stocks. And next in size of assets to this large group are the so-called balanced funds—funds which own commons, preferred stocks, and bonds.

There were 24 closed-end companies and 151 mutual funds as of the 1958 year-end which were members of the National Association of Investment Companies. These funds vary as to size, capital structure, composition of portfolio, investment objective, management experience, and competence. Like the British investment trust companies, the majority of the more important American companies belong to certain easily identifiable groups. A common management organization or more or less similar directors, or the same sponsor or underwriter is customarily the criterion for considering a company in a particular group. The most important of these groups in 1959, their component parts, whether open- or closed-end, and total assets at the previous year-end are listed below in order of size—certain independent companies being given the position due them. (O = open-end, C = closed-end.)

		Assets (in millions of dollars)	Type
Investors Group, Minneapolis, Minn.	Total	2,023	
Investors Mutual, Inc.		1,337	O
Investors Stock Fund, Inc.		432	O
Investors Group Canadian Fund, Ltd.		173	O
Investors Variable Payment Fund, Inc.		56	O
Investors Selective Fund, Inc.		25	O
Vance, Sanders Group, Boston, Mass.	Total	2,017	
Massachusetts Investors Trust		1,433	O
Massachusetts Investors Growth Stock Fund, Inc.		231	O
Boston Fund, Inc.		197	O
Canada General Fund, Ltd.		94	O
Century Shares Trust		62	O
Wellington Group, Philadelphia, Pa.	Total	895	
Wellington Fund		858	O
Wellington Equity Fund		37	O
Hugh W. Long Group, Elizabeth, N. J.	Total	644	
Fundamental Investors, Inc.		515	O
Diversified Investment Fund, Inc.		93	O
Diversified Growth Stock Fund, Inc.		36	O
J. & W. Seligman Group, New York, N. Y.	Total	636	
Tri-Continental Corporation		392	C
Broad Street Investing Corp.		140	O
National Investors		94	O
Whitehall Fund		10	O
United Group, Kansas City, Missouri	Total	583	
United Accumulative Fund		241	O
United Income Fund		207	O
United Science Fund		74	O
United Continental Fund		38	O
United Funds Canada, Ltd.		23	O
Lehman Group, New York, N. Y.	Total	553	
One William Street Fund, Inc.		277	O
Lehman Corporation		276	C
Lord, Abbett Group, New York, N. Y.	Total	539	
Affiliated Fund, Inc.		511	O
American Business Shares, Inc.		28	O
Calvin Bullock Group, New York, N. Y.	Total	536	
Dividend Shares, Inc.		267	O
Canadian Investment Fund, Ltd.		125	O
Bullock Fund, Ltd.		47	O
Canadian Fund, Inc.		46	O

		Assets (in millions of dollars)	Type
Nation-Wide Securities Co., Inc.		32	O
Carriers & General Corporation		19	C
Keystone Group, Boston, Mass.	Total	425	
Keystone Custodian Funds, Inc.:			
S-2		83	O
B-4		66	O
K-1		58	O
B-3		46	O
S-3		45	O
K-2		40	O
S-4		30	O
S-1		19	O
B-2		13	O
B-1		9	O
Keystone Fund of Canada		16	O
Fidelity Group, Boston, Mass.	Total	416	
Fidelity Fund, Inc.		357	O
Puritan Fund, Inc.		59	O
National Securities Group, New York, N. Y.	Total	413	
National Securities:			
Stock Series		167	O
Dividend Series		103	O
Income Series		69	O
Growth Stock Series		49	O
Preferred Stock Series		19	O
Balanced Series		3	O
Bond Series		3	O
Incorporated Group, Boston, Mass.	Total	412	
Incorporated Investors		307	O
Incorporated Income Fund		105	O
Insurance Securities Inc. Trust Fund, Oakland, Calif.	Total	357	O
Eaton & Howard Group, Boston, Mass.	Total	335	
Eaton & Howard Balanced Fund		200	O
Eaton & Howard Stock Fund		135	O
Capital Research Group, Los Angeles, Calif.	Total	276	
The Investment Company of America		137	O
American Mutual Fund, Inc.		104	O
International Resources Fund, Inc.		19	O
Washington Mutual Investors Fund, Inc.		16	O
Television-Electronics Fund, Chicago, Ill.	Total	236	O

		Assets (in millions of dollars)	Type
State Street Investment Corporation, Boston, Mass.	Total	199	O
Chemical Fund, Inc., New York, N. Y.	Total	196	O
Putnam Group, Boston, Mass.	Total	188	
George Putnam Fund of Boston		181	O
Putnam Growth Fund		7	O
E. W. Axe Group, Tarrytown, N. Y.	Total	181	
Axe Houghton Fund B.		111	O
Axe Houghton Fund A.		49	O
Axe Science & Electronics Corp.		9	O
Axe Houghton Stock Fund		8	O
Axe-Templeton Growth Fund of Canada, Ltd.		4	O
Adams Express Group, New York, N. Y.	Total	178	
Adams Express Company		98	C
American International Corporation		41	C
Petroleum Corporation of America		39	C
Commonwealth Group, San Francisco, Calif.	Total	174	
Commonwealth Investment Co.		145	O
North American Investment Corp.		10	C
Commonwealth Stock Fund		10	O
Commonwealth Income Fund		9	O
Scudder Group, New York, N. Y.	Total	166	
Scudder, Stevens & Clark Fund, Inc.		78	O
Scudder Fund of Canada, Ltd.		62	O
Scudder, Stevens & Clark Common Stock Fund		26	O
Distributors Group, New York, N. Y.	Total	149	
Group Securities, Inc.:			
Industry Classes		77	O
Common Stock Fund		52	O
Fully Administered Fund		10	O
Capital Growth Fund		7	O
General Bond Fund		2	O
Institutional Bond Fund		1	O
Colonial Group, Boston, Mass.	Total	144	
Gas Industries Fund, Inc.		73	O
The Colonial Fund, Inc.		66	O
The Bond Investment Trust of America		5	O
Madison Fund, New York, N. Y.	Total	136	C
Lazard Fund, New York, N. Y.	Total	135	C

		Assets (in millions of dollars)	Type
Financial Industrial Fund, Denver, Colo.	Total	127	O
United States & Foreign Securities Corporation, New York, N. Y.	Total	123	C
United Corporation, New York, N. Y.	Total	114	C
Value Line Group, New York, N. Y.	Total	107	
The Value Line Income Fund, Inc.		88	O
The Value Line Fund, Inc.		10	O
The Value Line Special Situations Fund		9	O
Atlas Corporation, New York, N. Y.	Total	103	C

NUMBER AND SIZE

As of December 31, 1958, the National Association of Investment Companies reports 151 open-end members and 24 closed-end members with total assets of about $15 billion. As of June 30, 1958, the Securities and Exchange Commission reported 453 companies registered under the Investment Company Act of 1940, divided into 238 open-end companies, 111 closed-end companies, 92 unit investment trusts, and 12 face-amount certificate companies. For these 453 companies the SEC reports estimated assets at market value of $17 billion. How can such widely different sets of figures be reconciled?

The broad explanation is that where there are many series of a single investment company the SEC tabulates them separately and the NAIC counts them as only one. Then there are perhaps 40 open-end companies, not of major importance, that are not members of the NAIC. About three-quarters of the so-called closed-end companies are not members of the NAIC, but, as in the SEC study of investment companies a generation ago, most of these are "investment-holding companies," in plain words, holding companies like Christiana Securities and Coca-Cola International. No unit trusts or face-amount certificate companies can be members of the NAIC.

When it comes to size of assets, perhaps 5 percent of open-end companies are not members of the NAIC and more than half of the assets of the "closed-end" companies are outside the NAIC as are assets of all unit trusts and face-amount certificate companies. The unit trusts existing today, incidentally, are used as the base for several periodic payment companies of the contractual type, little known to the investment company fraternity generally.

For purposes of modern investment company figures used in this book we have chosen usually to quote statistics relating to the membership of the NAIC as being representative and descriptive of the industry whose story we are endeavoring to tell. However, according to our own compilation, New York leads in investment company assets with $5,086 million; Boston is second with $4,534 million, Minneapolis third with $1,860 million, Philadelphia fourth with $975 million, Kansas City fifth with $570 million, and Chicago sixth with $400 million. New York has 89 percent of closed-end company assets. Boston has 33 percent of mutual fund assets, actually topping New York's 27 percent.

The New York Stock Exchange estimates that there are 12½ million shareholders of publicly-owned companies. The NAIC estimates that of these 2 million individuals and institutions are investment company shareholders. A shareholder may own of course one or more investment companies. And the estimate is that the number of shareholders of individual investment companies—called "shareholder accounts"—in June, 1959, was over 4 million, mutual fund shareholders outnumbering closed-end shareholders considerably more than ten fold.

STABILIZING FACTOR

There is no question but that present-day investment companies are a stabilizing influence in the stock market. Back in the catastrophic days of the Panic and the grim days of the Great Depression certain individuals discussed the theory of the federal government's forming a gigantic pool under the aegis of the Treasury or the Federal Reserve System to accumulate stocks begging for a buyer—as a means of stabilizing prices. Dissenters looked on the scheme with a jaundiced eye, feeling, in addition to other objections, that it would be a further socialistic step toward government ownership of industry, notwithstanding the suggested provision that not more than 10 percent of the voting stock of any company should be acquired by the government entity. Today the discussion would seem to be academic in view of the fact that private capital of $15 billion in the form of investment companies exists for the purpose of purchasing securities, for the most part common stocks.

In theory, if investment company managements perform as they should, they would accumulate stocks at sound prices and liquidate such stocks if they sold at unreasonably high prices, meanwhile investing proceeds in more attractively priced stocks or bonds, governmental or corporate. While the reasons are not susceptible of proof, certain it is that fluctuations of security prices have been less severe, especially in the years since the Second World War, than they were two or three decades ago. Logical explanations are the regulatory influence of the SEC in securities markets and the stabilizing influence of huge institutional buyers such as pension funds, insurance companies, and investment companies. But was there not $8 billion of investment company money available for these same purposes at the peak of 1929? No. Almost half of it represented holding companies whose function was entirely different, and, while over $4 billion was in the hands of investment companies, they themselves had such involved capital structures and had borrowed so much money that their difficulties accentuated fluctuations in the security markets rather than alleviating them. Today the investment company industry owes very little money and is run along far more conservative and professional lines.

Moreover, most of its assets are represented by mutual funds which are continually raising capital and can throw this additional buying power into the market in bad periods as well as good.

"A RUN ON THE BANK"

Since the vast bulk of investment company assets are represented by mutual funds, all of which have a provision that a shareholder can liquidate his shares at will, the question is sometimes asked as to what would happen to security markets generally if a large percentage of shareholders decided to liquidate more or less at the same time, thus forcing investment companies to sell heavily on balance. Facts are more impressive than theories and, over the history of the industry, every testing period that has been carefully studied indicates that, in times of anything resembling a sharp market decline, more people purchase shares of mutual funds than sell them back to the investment company and demand its cash. Time after time this matter has been studied, more recently at the instigation of the SEC, and every investigation has shown that the public buys from the company more shares than it sells back to the company in periods of declining prices.

The NAIC has figures from its mutual fund members (representing 74 percent of the assets of its mutual fund members) showing that during the 18 percent stock market decline from May to October in 1946, the public purchased shares from such funds valued at $98 million and asked the funds to redeem $39 million worth of their shares. Meanwhile the funds' purchases of portfolio securities were $117 million and their sales of portfolio securities $72 million. Ninety-six percent of the members of the NAIC (by assets) reported that at the outbreak of the Korean War, when the market declined 7 percent during the week ending June 30, 1950, investors purchased $9 million of shares and redeemed $8 million. Meanwhile the mutual funds themselves purchased $14 million of portfolio securities and sold only $6 million. Then, during the week ending September 30, 1955, when President Eisenhower was first taken seriously ill and the market declined over 4 percent, 82 percent of the NAIC mutual fund members (by assets) reported that investors purchased $22 million and redeemed $10 million, and the funds themselves purchased $16 million portfolio securities and sold $13 million. Similarly in the market break from October 1 to 21 in 1957 a survey of mutual funds, the assets of which represented 79 percent of the NAIC memberships', showed that the ratio of the funds' sales of their shares to repurchases of such shares was $47 million to $16 million or almost 3 to 1, while the companies purchased $81 million of portfolio securities and sold only $32 million.

The severest testing time of all, of course, was the period from late 1929 to 1932, and it is pertinent here to repeat the findings of the Commission when they reviewed the experience of Massachusetts Investors Trust:

At the end of September 1929 Massachusetts Investors Trust had 298,687 shares outstanding. From that date until December 31, 1932, it was called upon to repurchase 235,016 of its outstanding shares. Thus, if no new sales of shares had been effected, the amount of assets of the company would have been reduced by almost 80% by virtue of these redemptions alone. However, at the close of 1932 this company had outstanding 951,752 shares.[1]

The SEC Report concludes:

Fortunately, up to the end of 1939 open-end investment companies had not experienced the tremendous liquidations concentrated within brief periods of time comparable to "runs" on banks.[2]

Nor have they since.

[1] Report of the Securities and Exchange Commission, *Investment Trusts and Investment Companies,* Part Three, chap. III, p. 807.

[2] *Ibid.*

MANAGEMENT STRUCTURE

Every American investment company today is owned and controlled by its stockholders. Stockholders annually elect some or all of the directors of those in corporate form, which comprise most of the industry. Directors then elect the company officers. Common law trusts are managed by trustees, but such trustees can be removed by shareholders, and those acting under trust agreements created since the passage of the Investment Company Act must be elected by investors.

A minority of companies maintain their own paid research staff, but the majority employ a management organization, usually for an annual fee ranging from a half to a quarter of 1 percent of the average value of the company's assets, although in a few instances the fee is a percentage of the company's or trust's income. The management organization can never furnish more than 60 percent of the company's directors, and we have seen that a majority of directors must be independent of the company's underwriter. Investment company directors today are a representative group of men, often individuals renowned in industry, economics, investment banking, science, international affairs, and, always, investment management.

The investment research work done by many investment company managements is distinctly scientific. There is a director of research; there are up to a dozen senior security analysts, specialists in various types of industry, who report to him. They have at their disposal every useful tool concerning facts and figures; individual company reports, industry reports, special services, as well as almost all orthodox investment services in the form of manuals and interim supplements. The industrial specialists take numerous field trips to view industries first hand and to interview corporation officials. The investment company would have an able economist on its staff as well as consultive arrangements with other economists and organizations to supplement its information relative to legislative, scientific, engineering, labor, and monetary trends. Finally the investment company's officials make full use of a broad circle of domestic and international contacts in checking and cross checking their judgment.

TYPICAL FUND

A typical American investment company today would be a mutual fund. This means it would have a simple capital structure of just one class of stock outstanding, fully paid and fully voting, and a proviso that shareholders could require the company to repurchase its shares at asset value upon request. The company would be prohibited from borrowing money, buying securities on margin, or selling short. It would be a business corporation with perhaps seven directors, periodically elected by stockholders; such directors would then elect the company's officers.

The company's investment would be in approximately a hundred common stocks of well-known American corporations (never more than 5 percent in any one corporate security at time of original purchase) plus a nominal amount of cash and a small percentage of United States Government bonds. All cash and securities, perhaps totaling $75 million, would be held by a bank as custodian. The custodian would not permit issuance of new shares by the company until cash had first been deposited with it to cover such shares. Another bank might be dividend paying agent.

Dividend checks would be mailed to shareholders quarterly, representing each shareholder's pro rata interest in the income the company received from the securities it owned, less operating expenses. Shareholders would also receive every three months a list of securities the company owned, and every six months complete audited statements. At the company's fiscal year end, if in buying and selling securities for its portfolio a net capital gain had resulted, the company would notify its shareholders and permit them to take their pro rata share either in additional stock or cash. On their income tax returns shareholders would report this as a long term capital gain from sales of securities as differentiated from the actual income they received in the form of quarterly dividends. (British and Canadian investment companies may retain their capital gains without being taxed thereon, but American companies are forced to pay them out to shareholders to escape paying the regular corporation income tax on such gains.)

The company's operating expenses would be primarily a management fee, dividend-paying and custodian fees, auditors' fees, the mailing of reports to shareholders, expenses of stockholders' annual meetings, legal fees, and franchise and local taxes. All these would total perhaps six- or seven-tenths of 1 percent of the average value of the company's assets per year. Of this the management fee would represent one-half of 1 percent of such average assets.

The fee would be paid to the investment management organization that the company employed. Such organization would furnish the company's office space, its officers, administrative and clerical work, and the complicated investment research work necessary in the professional management of the company's portfolio—all subject of course to the control of the board of directors. Three of the seven directors might well be connected with the investment management organization, the other four being independent of any affiliation with the company's investment manager or underwriter. One of these four might be a well-known economist, two of them industrialists, and the fourth a man prominent in the securities business.

The company's underwriter might well be the same organization that furnished it with investment management. The underwriter would buy from the company at asset value and sell the company's shares to investment dealers who in turn would sell them to their clients. The price would be adjusted twice daily representing the asset value of each share to which would be added a premium of perhaps 7½ percent of the selling price. The bulk of this would be paid to the dealer, the remainder covering the underwriter's expenses for sales literature, advertising, blue sky fees, traveling, other items and profit. Now why is the ultimate investor willing to pay a premium above the quoted market price of a broad list of securities to purchase a mutual fund? Evidently because it usually pays him to do so. Prices of New York Stock Exchange securities are quoted in 100-share lots. The investment company itself customarily purchases stocks in 100-share lots. But for an investor to purchase 100 shares of each of 100 different stocks would require a very substantial sum of money. The average investor with not more than $5,000 or so to invest finds that it actually costs him less to purchase and resell shares of the average mutual fund than it would to obtain the same kind of diversity by purchasing and eventually reselling odd lots (one share or more, up to 100) of a hundred different securities, because of odd-lot differentials and commissions and the higher percentage cost of transfer stamps. As for the large investor, the premium or sales charge on a typical mutual fund for a purchase of $25,000 worth would be reduced to 6 percent, $50,000 worth to 4 percent, and $100,000 worth to 3 percent or less.

Why do investors purchase shares of mutual funds at a premium above their asset value when they may buy shares of many closed-end investment companies at a discount? Many indeed do buy closed-end shares but, when they come to sell them, they are likely to receive a price that still represents a discount. The far greater marketability of open-end or mutual fund shares is also probably a factor with investors.

RECENT DEVELOPMENTS

In both the closed-end and open-end fields there are some specialized funds that have existed for many years and, because of record and size, have gained investors' confidence. Among the mutual funds the various Canadian funds are a case in point, as well as the well-managed Chemical Fund. Sometimes, and more recently, if a glamorous industry attains popularity, a new fund is formed to specialize therein. By and large, looking to the future, it would appear that the more broadly diversified funds would perhaps represent an even larger portion of the assets of the investment company industry than the large percentage they do today.

Bond funds as such have historically been the smallest segment of the investment company industry. But, if enabling legislation is some day passed, it is logical that they would have substantial growth. Before two Congresses have been bills to permit a fund consisting of tax exempt bonds to pay its shareholders dividends which would also be tax exempt. Federal income taxes are at sufficient levels in recent years that not only the man considered wealthy in days gone by but also those of scarcely more than moderate means are in a position to secure tax relief by purchasing so-called municipal bonds. The latter, especially, require special guidance as to credit ratings of various cities and townships and market availability. The large purchaser has a degree of sophistication and can secure desirable diversification that the man in medium tax brackets finds difficult. A municipal bond fund, if obtainable, should offer him distinct advantages. One of the problems of such a fund undoubtedly would be the limited marketability of certain municipal bonds that it might have in its portfolio. Only time will tell how much of a problem this would pose. First of all, legislation authorizing such funds must be enacted. Best opinion is that it will come in due course, possibly applying to all tax exempt income of all mutual funds.

In January of 1954 the New York Stock Exchange first announced its Monthly Investment Plan. Officials of the Exchange had watched for some time the success of, and were interested in the dollar cost averaging principle of, the various periodic purchase plans of many mutual funds. The "M.I.P." of the Exchange makes it possible for the client of a member firm to select a specific security which the broker will buy. The customer agrees to deposit with the broker additional fixed amounts of money periodically which the broker will use to purchase for his client additional shares of the same stock. Dollar cost averaging is thus brought into play. The plan is less expensive than if the client purchased a periodic payment plan of an investment company, but the diversification and professional supervision of the latter is missed. One way that brokers have found to overcome these deficiencies is to suggest that their client choose as the security to buy under the "M.I.P." the common stock of one of the well-known closed-end investment companies listed on the Exchange. As of February, 1959, after five years of operation, the Exchange announced that securities purchased under the Monthly Investment Plan had a value of $112 million.

The American investing public has unquestionably been better protected in recent years, as against a generation ago, by regulation of investment companies. Yet over-regulation can sometimes be detrimental. A supreme example is an existing Federal Reserve Board ruling. The most desirable clubs in the business world are the directorates of important banks. There one finds not only bankers but prominent industrialists and professional men who can be said to have had their ability and reputation and prominence recognized by others at the top. Investment bankers, brokers, and others identified with the distribution of securities are resigned to the fact that the Banking Act of 1933 prohibits by law their serving on bank boards, because of the nature of their profession. But a curious and illogical reverse twist was given this philosophy by a ruling of the Federal Reserve Board which prevents a director of any bank which is a member of the Federal Reserve System from likewise serving on the board of a mutual fund. The reason given is that the primary function of a mutual fund is the issuance of securities. Obviously the primary function of a mutual fund or any investment company is the management of its portfolio of securities. By this unreasonable ruling more than a million shareholders of mutual funds are deprived of the additional information and judgment that could benefit them by having numerous leading industrialists and other business leaders serve on such investment company directorates.

Over the years, by trial and error, many investment company problems have been resolved. Accounting problems have been among them. One still unresolved problem, however, concerns itself with the method of the daily pricing of mutual investment company shares. The Investment Company Act correctly prohibits their being sold to the public below their asset value. Asset value obviously is computed by taking the market value of all securities owned, plus cash, minus accrued expenses, and dividing the quotient by the number of outstanding shares. Some of the portfolio holdings will have been bought by the investment company at higher prices and therefore stand on the books at a potential loss if sold; others will have been bought at lower prices and stand on the books at a profit. In recent years most investment companies, balancing both these factors, have substantial unrealized profits. Along comes a new investor and buys new shares of this investment company at asset value plus whatever the sales charge may be in the case of this particular company. Then, by the year's end, the company in addition to its dividend from investment income also declares a distribution from the net capital gains it has realized during the year by selling from its portfolio more securities at a profit than it has sold at a loss. The investor has to pay a capital gains tax, based on his particular bracket, on this return to him of part of his capital. He is even paying a premium on a portion of capital that will later be returned to him and on which he will be taxed. This problem does not arise in the case of a brand new fund that is offering its shares to the public for the first time—obviously because there are no potential capital gains as yet. But as soon as the fund purchases securities and, if successful, accumulates potential profits, it thereupon inherits the problem. The problem also exists, of course, in the case of a particular closed-end investment company, the stock of which is purchased by an investor approximately at or even above its asset value. If the company—as most do—had substantial amounts of unrealized appreciation in the value of its assets, the investor is "buying a tax liability." Numerous complicated solutions have been suggested, such as proposals that equalization accounts be established, that tax laws and Treasury rulings be changed, but no one as yet has come up with a generally accepted formula. Fortunately, with respect to an investor's total investment the matter is not important. But it is typical of still unsolved problems that the investment company industry has before it.

SIZE

The Investment Company Act requires a minimum size for an investment company. There is no limit on maximum size, even though some government officials were inclined to feel that there should be, prior to the passage of the Act. The Act authorizes the SEC, however, "to make a study and investigation of size on the investment policy of investment companies and on security markets, on concentration of control of wealth and industry, and on companies in which investment companies are interested, and from time to time to report the results of its studies and investigation and its recommendations to the Congress," at any time that the SEC feels that such would concern the protection of investors or be in the public interest. The Commission has recently seen fit to initiate such a study. Voluminous data have been requested from each registered investment company by the Securities Research Unit of the Wharton School of Finance and Commerce of the University of Pennsylvania, employed by the SEC to compile the basic facts. From such facts it is presumed that the SEC will endeavor to determine if large size militates against a company's having a good management record, if liquidity of the company's portfolio is impaired, if buying and selling portfolio securities has an undue influence on their price fluctuations in the general market, if there is evidence of undue control of wealth and industry, and if compensation of the managers of investment companies is based on an equitable formula so far as shareholders are concerned. From evidence so far available to the general public it would seem that the largest companies have generally been among those best managed; that, in actual practice, size has not affected the liquidity of the portfolio to the detriment of shareholders; that investment company operations have, if anything, tended to modify fluctuations in the prices of securities; that there has probably been no undue control of industry; and that management compensation has aided the larger companies in providing impressive research facilities. Moreover, all administrative costs usually decline proportionately as size substantially increases.

VARIABLE ANNUITY

In 1952 the Teachers Insurance and Annuity Association, under a special act of the New York state legislature, organized a mutual fund called the College Retirement Equities Fund. A policyholder in the former is permitted to allocate up to 50 percent of his annual premiums for the purpose of accumulating units in the latter, which is invested in common stocks. TIAA thus is the pioneer of the variable annuity idea. In recent years there has been an effort on the part of certain other life insurance companies—the giant Prudential being the leader—to establish and sell "variable annuity contracts." Such a contract would provide for periodic payments for life to contract holders, not of a fixed number of *dollars,* but of a fixed number of *units.* These units would represent a proportionate interest in a portfolio administered by the insurance company. Since the portfolio would presumably be invested largely in common stocks, the value of which would fluctuate, the value of the units would also vary. The purpose of such a contract would be to offer a greater protection to the contract owner's purchasing power than would be provided by fixed dollar payments in periods of rising living costs.

The life insurance industry is divided on the advisability of issuing such contracts, the opposition being led by the largest company of all, the Metropolitan. The securities industry has been almost solidly in opposition, not so much to the principle involved, as to the degree of regulation and the methods of distribution of such contracts. Another major opponent was the SEC. The latter asserts that such contracts are, in effect, securities (most closely akin to mutual fund shares) and should, therefore, be subject to the federal statutes—specifically the Securities Act of 1933, among others—in the public interest. On these grounds the SEC, aided by the National Association of Securities Dealers, sought to enjoin the sale of variable annuity contracts in the District of Columbia. The District Court and the Court of appeals ruled that such contracts appeared to be subject to statutes applying to insurance companies (under the McCarran Act) and the case was appealed to the Supreme Court.

The variable annuity problem is a current center of controversy in several states, most notably in New Jersey and Massachusetts. Hearings held in these and other states found opposition to variable annuities voiced by the president of the New York Stock Exchange, representatives of the IBA, the NAIC, and others.

Competition from the insurance industry with respect to the sale of a contract based on equity securities would, of course, be formidable to the investment firms of the country. However, if the same federal protective provisions surround the regulation and distribution of these contracts, instead of the regulations of the various states in which the life insurance companies are domiciled, such competition may, in the long run, prove beneficial.

On March 23, 1959, the Supreme Court of the United States found that variable annuities were "securities," subject to regulation by the Securities and Exchange Commission. These interesting contracts will no doubt soon be forcefully brought to the attention of the American public.

THE FUTURE

The investment company industry in the United States may well be in somewhat the same position that the insurance industry was a few years after the Hughes investigation in 1905–6. Practices had crept into insurance that were remedied a half century ago with the result that public confidence and the inherent soundness of the principle of insurance have accounted for the admitted assets of insurance companies increasing from a few billion to substantially over a hundred billion dollars. The Investment Company investigation and the subsequent Act of 1940 could prove to be a comparable milestone in relation to investment company history. Be that as it may, if something over $15 billion is the figure for investment company assets today, by the end of this century, partially because of a decline in the purchasing power of our currency, more because of the growth and prosperity of the American industrial plant and its consequent reflection in security prices, mostly because of the dynamic qualities of the industry itself, a figure for the industry's assets of a hundred billion dollars would seem to be conservative; the figure indeed might well be more nearly double that. By that time, of course, most figures relating to the economy of the greatest nation the world has ever known will be far larger than they are today. Yet, because of the inherent soundness of its principle, the investment company industry should, in any event, be in for a spectacular growth.

For one thing, the securities business is becoming increasingly institutionalized. For another, the American public is more prone to want professional guidance in solving its problems. Every investor desires protection of principal, reliable income, good marketability, and opportunity for appreciation. It would seem that these four desiderata combined are present in greater degree in the shares of a soundly managed mutual fund than in almost any other kind of security available. Those indeed who believe in the principle of private enterprise and the politically stabilizing effect of having as many Americans as possible actual owners of American industry would go far to find as satisfactory a medium for such participation as a well-managed mutual fund.

What changes will we see in investment companies of the future? None in fundamental concept. Lower cost of raising capital, somewhat lower cost of operation, more investment in foreign lands, little else. Many more trust companies will organize uniform trust funds. Additional closed-end companies will be formed—the ideal media for private American investment abroad, an activity which investors have heretofore left primarily to their government and secondarily to large industrial corporations. But the mutual fund is the fund of the future.

PERSPECTIVE

This, then, is the story of investment companies during the almost full century of their existence—most of the second half of which witnessed their development in North America. It is important, however, to keep the detail in proper perspective.

The British pioneered the movement, experienced the early growing pains, could have taught us most of the pitfalls; but human beings, from time immemorial, seem to insist on learning lessons for themselves. The lessons of the Baring Crisis of 1890 we had to learn in the extravagant years of the latter 1920s, culminating in the Crash of 1929. What were the lessons?

That economic cycles are just as certain as death and taxes. And, even though no two periods are alike, one who succumbs to talk of "new eras" and "permanently high plateaus" better have an anchor to windward—just in case. That security prices can go down as well as up—and down much faster than up. That highly complicated capital structures can trip up managements and stockholders alike. And that too much debt is dangerous—debt piled on debt piled on debt.

The American movement did not really start until the earliest 1920s, and not until the years 1927 through 1929 did it gain tremendous momentum. Like any highly popular vehicle, "trusts" were overdone. A certain magic attached itself to the name. But there were many misnomers, companies that should never have been called trusts, just as there were numerous trusts that were operated on unsound principles. The 1929 Panic and its aftermath were disastrous, and the pendulum swung too far to the other extreme in the fixed trusts. Of the

$8 billion that was supposed to represent investment company assets in 1929, only about half this amount, or about 4½ billion, represented true investment companies.

Why were investor losses so severe from 1929 to 1932? Because there was an unbelievable decline in security prices—Dow-Jones Industrial Averages declined, for example, almost 90 percent. And securities, primarily common stocks, were the commodity that investment companies owned. This was the most important reason. Indeed there are just as vivid examples of people losing money in industrial and utility and other stocks, especially of holding companies, as in shares of investment trusts. A second important reason, however, was that the very large majority of investment companies in 1929 were heavily pyramided closed-end companies with involved capital structures. Their own common stocks, ahead of which were preferred shares and, often, debentures, suffered precipitous declines when leverage began working in reverse. To be sure, many managements were inexperienced; there were plenty of instances of bad judgment and some cases of outright crookedness. But these reasons contributed far less to investor losses than the two important reasons first mentioned.

All this was a generation ago; let us hope that the expensive lessons of those days have been well learned. While investors must never fail to be on their guard, the scene today is vastly different and the road ahead would seem to be less hazardous.

Economics has advanced as a science. Governmental action to endeavor to cushion depressions is more intelligently and promptly taken than in earlier years; moreover, there exist today impressively effective built-in economic stabilizers such as broad unemployment insurance and old-age benefits. We may be in the process of learning how to modify the most violent fluctuations in our economy. The most potent factor of all, unfortunately, no man can foretell, namely public psychology.

And, until human nature changes, any current period will still be characterized by a given psychology—running from confidence to over-confidence to wildly emotional optimism or, on the other hand, from doubt to pessimism to unreasoning fear. So, prosperity and boom, recession and unemployment, we will see until the end of time; the only hope is that these will be less extreme.

If this be so, and since earning power is the major influence in prices of securities, especially of common stocks, a high school student must know that the stock market will advance and retrogress. The reasoned hope is that the inevitable declines of future years will be less severe than the experience and aftermath of 1929. The Crash was accelerated by billions of previously borrowed money and shoestring margins—factors which do not exist today and, it is to be presumed, will not be permitted to exist in future periods of relatively high levels of stock prices. Moreover, with the securities business becoming more and more institutionalized, institutions buy for cash and their professional managers are less influenced by emotion and necessity for liquidation than private and institutional investors of a generation ago.

The investment company is no cure-all. But the stockholder of an investment company todays owns a very different kind of security from the investment trust that his father may have owned thirty years ago. If he owns shares in a closed-end company, it usually has no debt or, at best, a moderate debt. Far more often, however, he will own shares in a mutual fund with one class of share outstanding, highly marketable, because of its self-liquidating feature. It will have a broadly diversified portfolio, carefully supervised by men who are endeavoring to do the best possible management job for their shareholders. Being human they will make some mistakes of judgment, but they are professionals today—men of integrity and experience gained over many years. The shareholder is informed quarterly of their actions. And his company is under strict governmental regulation.

By trial and error, by baptism of fire, by the application of many minds to the problem over a long period of time, there appears to have been evolved an investment vehicle which is as satisfactory for the average investor as any he is ever likely to find.

Glossary

advisory board	a board other than the directors of an investment company, having advisory functions only.
affiliated person	(1) any person directly or indirectly controlling 5 percent or more of the outstanding voting securities of another person; or (2) any person 5 percent or more of whose outstanding voting securities are directly or indirectly controlled by another person; or (3) any person directly or indirectly controlling, controlled by, or under common control with another person; or (4) any officer, director, partner, co-partner or employee of another person; or (5) any investment adviser of or member of an advisory board of an investment company; or (6) the depositor corporation of a unit trust.
asset value	a company's total resources at market value minus all liabilities, divided by the number of shares outstanding of the security under consideration.
balanced fund	an investment company with substantial stated proportion of senior securities in its portfolio in addition to common stocks.
bankers shares	shares of beneficial interest issued against a block of securities pledged with a trustee.
bearer certificates	nonregistered negotiable certificates carrying dividend or interest coupons.
bearer form	bearer certificates.
blind pool	a securities company speculative in nature, usually not revealing its transactions to its participants.

bond	a debt instrument of a corporation, promising to pay a specified amount of money on a certain date.
bond fund	an investment company which invests essentially in bonds.
bonus stock	stock received free.
break up value	liquidating value.
buying on margin	purchasing a security with borrowed money.
call	an option that gives the holder the right to buy stock from another person at a specified price.
capital gain	a profit realized from the sale of a security.
capital structure	a company's outstanding capitalization; viz., the amount and character of securities it has issued.
closed-end investment company	an investment company with no requirement that it repurchase its shares at approximately asset value. These customarily are companies with relatively fixed capitalizations.
closed-end trust	closed-end investment company.
common law trust	a true trust in the legal sense of the word.
common stock	the security which represents the ownership of the assets of the corporation after deducting the claim of senior securities.
common stock fund	an investment company which invests essentially in common stocks.
common trust fund	separate trusts commingled by a trust company under statutory authority in a single fund of which participants own their respective shares.
contractual plan	an arrangement whereby an investor contracts to purchase a given amount of a security by a certain date and agrees to make partial payments at specified intervals.
custodian	a financial institution that holds an investment company's securities and cash in safe keeping.
dealer	a firm or individual specializing in the buying and selling of securities from or to other firms or the public.
debenture	a bond with no specific security except the general credit of a corporation.

debenture stock	the British term for debentures.
depositor corporation	the corporation which deposits shares of stock with a trustee of a unit trust against which are issued certificates of beneficial interest.
discount	the extent to which the market price of a security is less than its asset value.
distributions	payments to an investment company's shareholders from income or profits realized from sale of securities.
diversified investment company	a management investment company 75 percent of the assets of which are invested so that initially not more than 5 percent represent the securities of any one issuer and which does not own more than 10 percent of such issuer's voting securities.
dollar cost averaging	investment in a given security at regular intervals of the same amount of money.
face amount certificate	a contract which represents an obligation on the part of its issuer to pay a stated sum at a fixed date more than twenty-four months after the date of issuance, in consideration of the payment of periodic installments of a stated amount by the holder.
fiduciary	an individual or institution occupying a position of trust.
finance company	a corporation designed to finance temporarily other corporations rather than to make permanent investment therein. In Great Britain the term has a somewhat different connotation and may mean an investment trust company which shows more than normal activity in buying and selling portfolio securities or one that allocates to its income account profits from sales of such securities.
fixed income security	a debt security or preferred stock which has a stipulated interest payment or dividend rate (occasionally debt security and preferred stocks are not fixed income securities).
fixed trust	a unit trust the investments of which can virtually never be changed.
floating debt	unfunded debt such as bank loans.
funded debt	bonds or longer term notes.

gearing	the British term for leverage.
general management investment company	an investment company in which management has broad discretion.
holding company	a corporation whose primary object is to control or influence the management of companies in which it invests.
independent director	a director who is not an officer or employee of an investment company nor a director, officer or employee of its underwriter or investment adviser.
installment certificate	face-amount certificate.
intermediate banking	lending money to a company on a relatively short term basis similar to a commercial bank's operations.
investment adviser	investment counsel to an investment company; also a manager of an investment company.
investment company	a corporation or trust the primary objective of which is to buy securities for investment.
investment counsel	a firm or individual which furnishes investment advice for a fee.
investment trust	investment company.
investment trust company	the British term for a closed-end investment company.
junior securities	securities subordinate to other securities such as bonds or a higher ranking preferred stock.
leverage	the effect of a senior security in accelerating fluctuations in asset values and per share earnings in respect of junior securities; as a result of the leverage of the senior securities, the fluctuations of the junior securities are greater than the fluctuations of the assets as a whole.
liquidating value	asset value.
management fee	the sum paid to the investment company's adviser or manager for supervising its portfolio and/or operations.
management investment company	an investment company in which management has discretion in choosing its investments.
management investment holding company	holding company.

multiple capital structure	a capitalization that has bonds and/or preferred stock in addition to common stock.
mutual fund	an investment company required to redeem its shares, usually at asset value; these customarily are companies which continuously issue new shares.
negative asset value	a colorful characterization of shares with negative asset value is the remark made by an SEC examiner during the investigation of investment companies in 1939: "The assets had to go up 50% before they were worth nothing."
New York joint stock association	a New York organization whose stockholders have unlimited liability for its debts (comparable in this respect to a partnership).
non-diversified investment company	a company the portfolio of which is not as fully diversified as is required by the Investment Company Act to qualify as a diversified investment company.
odd lot	less than 100 shares.
open-end investment company	mutual fund.
ordinary shares	the British term for common stock.
par value	the amount designated as that portion of the stated capital of the corporation represented by a given security; this seldom has any relationship to actual value.
periodic payment plan	an arrangement whereby investors voluntarily purchase a given security at regular intervals.
portfolio	the securities which an investment company owns.
preference shares	preference stock.
preference stock	a preferred stock.
preferred stock	a stock senior to the common stock of a corporation, with preferred claim on assets in case of liquidation and a specified annual dividend.
premium	the extent to which market price exceeds the asset value of an investment company security.
prospectus	the official circular describing a security.
put	an option that gives the holder the right to sell stock to another person at a specified price.

pyramided capital structure	a capitalization consisting of one or more issues of bonds and/or preferred stocks in addition to one or more issues of common stock.
registered investment company	an investment company registered with the Securities and Exchange Commission.
sales charge	the difference between asset value and the public offering price of a mutual fund or unit trust (see sales load).
sales load	selling charges (see sales charge).
sales premium	selling charges.
self-liquidating feature	the provision in a mutual fund whereby a shareholder can demand that the fund redeem his shares at asset value; this feature in a unit trust permits the owner of a unit of securities to demand that the trustee deliver such securities (or occasionally their cash value) to him upon presentation of his shares.
selling short	selling a security which one does not own.
senior securities	bonds or preferred stock.
shareholders equity	the amount of a corporation's assets belonging to its shareholders (both common and preferred) after satisfaction of any prior claims.
shares of beneficial interest	pro rata interests in a trust fund.
simple capital structure	a corporation or trust with only one class of stock outstanding.
sinking fund	a fund set aside usually from income or profits to purchase and retire outstanding securities.
stock options	rights to purchase a corporation's stock at a specified price.
trading company	a corporation which purchases and sells securities with much more than average frequency.
trust	investment company.
trustee	an individual or institution holding property in trust.
underwriter	an investment firm that purchases a security direct from its issuer for resale to other investment firms or the public or sells for such issuer to the public.
uniform trust fund	common trust fund.

unit trust	a common law trust where a depositor corporation deposits a series of identical units of stocks with a trustee against which are issued certificates of beneficial interest; the term in the United Kingdom today is used to describe what would be designated in the United States as a mutual fund in the form of a trust rather than of a corporation.
voluntary plan	an arrangement whereby an investor indicates his intention to make periodic payments to purchase a given security.
yield	the annual rate of return on his investment which an investor receives from net income; this does not include distributions from capital gains.

Bibliography

GOVERNMENT PUBLICATIONS

UNITED KINGDOM

Great Britain. Parliament. Sessional Papers, 1935–36, Vol. 10, Cmd. 5259. Fixed Trusts: Report of the Departmental Committee Appointed by the Board of Trade, 1936. London, H. M. Stationery Office, 1936.

——— Statutes. The Public General Acts . . . November 8, 1938, to December 31, 1939, . . . chap. 16, pp. 58–90. London, H. M. Stationery Office, 1939. "An act to provide for regulating the business of dealing in securities; to restrict the registration of societies under the Industrial and Provident Societies Act, 1893 . . . ."

UNITED STATES

House of Representatives. Banking and Currency Committee, 66th Cong., 1st Sess., H.R. 473, Ser. 7593. Amendment to Federal Reserve Act, Conference Report to Accompany S. 2472 . . . . Washington, D.C., Government Printing Office, 1919.

——— Banking and Currency Committee, 66th Cong., 1st Sess. Amendment to Federal Reserve Act. Hearing . . . on S. 2472 . . . Parts 1–3. Washington, D.C., Government Printing Office, 1919.

——— Banking and Currency Committee, 66th Cong., 1st Sess., H.R. 408, Ser. 7593. Amending Federal Reserve Act, a Report to Accompany S. 2472 . . . . Washington, D.C., Government Printing Office, 1919.

——— Interstate and Foreign Commerce Committee, 76th Cong., 3d Sess., H.R. 2639, Ser. 10443. Investment Company Act of 1940 and Investment Advisers Act of 1940, Report to Accompany H.R. 10065 . . . . Washington, D.C., Government Printing Office, 1940.

——— Interstate and Foreign Commerce Committee, 76th Cong., 3d Sess. Investment Trusts and Investment Companies. Hearings . . . on H.R. 10065 . . . . Washington, D.C., Government Printing Office, 1940.

Securities and Exchange Commission. Investment Trusts and Investment Companies . . . . Washington, D.C., Government Printing Office, 1939–

42. Part 1: The Origin, Scope and Conduct of the Study, Nature and Classification of Investment Trusts and Investment Companies, and the Origin of the Investment Trust and Investment Company Movement in the United States. Part 2: The Statistical Survey of Investment Trusts and Investment Companies. Part 3: Abuses and Deficiencies in the Organization and Operation of Investment Trusts and Investment Companies. Parts 4–5: Control and Influence over Industry and Economic Significance of Investment Companies.

——— Investment Trusts and Investment Companies. . . . a Report on Commingled or Common Trust Funds Administered by Banks and Trust Companies. Washington, D.C., Government Printing Office, 1939.

——— Investment Trusts and Investment Companies. . . . a Report on Companies Issuing Face Amount Installment Certificates . . . . Washington, D.C., Government Printing Office, 1939.

——— Investment Trusts and Investment Companies. . . . a Report on Companies Sponsoring Installment Investment Plans . . . . Washington, D.C., Government Printing Office, 1940.

——— Investment Trusts and Investment Companies. . . . a Report on Fixed and Semifixed Investment Trusts . . . . Washington, D.C., Government Printing Office, 1940.

——— Investment Trusts and Investment Companies. . . . a Report on Investment Trusts in Great Britain . . . . Washington, D.C., Government Printing Office, 1939.

——— Investment Trusts and Investment Companies. Report of Securities and Exchange Commission . . . Index Digest. Compiled and edited by Adelaide R. Hasse. Washington, D.C., Government Printing Office, 1946.

——— Investment Trusts and Investment Companies. Report . . . Pursuant to Section 30 of the Public Utility Holding Company Act of 1935. Investment Counsel, Investment Management, Investment Supervisory, and Investment Advisory Services. Washington, D.C., Government Printing Office, 1939.

Senate. Banking and Currency Committee, 66th Cong., 1st Sess. Incorporating Institutions to Engage in International or Foreign Banking. Hearings . . . on S. 2472 . . . . Washington, D.C., Government Printing Office, 1919.

——— Banking and Currency Committee, 66th Cong., 1st Sess., Sen. Rep. 108, Ser. 17590. Incorporating Institutions to Engage in International or Foreign Banking, Report to Accompany S. 2472 . . . . Washington, D.C., Government Printing Office, 1919.

——— Banking and Currency Committee, 76th Cong., 3d Sess., Sen. Rep. 1775, Ser. 10430. Investment Company Act of 1940 and Investment Advisers Act of 1940, Report to Accompany S. 4108 . . . . Washington, D.C., Government Printing Office, 1940.

——— Banking and Currency Committee, 76th Cong., 3d Sess. Investment Trusts and Investment Companies. Hearings before a Subcommittee . . . , on S. 3580, a Bill to Provide for the Registration and

Regulation of Investment Companies and Investment Advisers, and for other Purposes . . . . Washington, D.C., Government Printing Office, 1940.

——— Banking and Currency Committee, 84th Cong., 1st Sess., Sen. Rep. 1280. Factors Affecting the Stock Market. Staff Report . . . . Washington, D.C., Government Printing Office, 1955.

——— Banking and Currency Committee, 84th Cong., 1st Sess. Institutional Investors and the Stock Market 1953–55. Staff Report . . . . Washington, D.C., Government Printing Office, 1956.

——— Banking and Currency Committee, 84th Cong., 1st Sess. Stock Market Study. Hearings . . . on Factors Affecting the Buying and Selling of Equity Securities . . . . Washington, D.C., Government Printing Office, 1955.

——— Banking and Currency Committee, 84th Cong., 1st Sess., Sen. Rep. 376. Stock Market Study. Report together with Individual Views and Minority Views . . . . Washington, D.C., Government Printing Office, 1955.

Statutes. The Statutes at Large of the United States of America from May 1919 to March 1921 . . . . Vol. 41, Part 1 . . . , chap. 18, pp. 378–84. Washington, D.C., Government Printing Office, 1921. "An act to amend the act approved December 23, 1913, known as the Federal Reserve Act."

——— United States Statutes at Large: Public Laws . . . Passed by the Seventy-fourth Congress 1935–1936 . . . . Vol. 49, Part 1 . . . , chap. 687, sec. 30, p. 837. Washington, D.C., Government Printing Office, 1936. "An act to provide for control and regulation of public-utility holding companies, and for other purposes . . . ."

——— United States Statutes at Large . . . Second and Third Sessions of the Seventy-sixth Congress . . . 1939–1941 . . . . Vol. 54, Part 1 . . . , chap. 686, pp. 789–858. Washington, D.C., Government Printing Office, 1941. "An act to provide for the registration and regulation of investment companies and investment advisers . . . ."

OTHER PUBLICATIONS

Allen, Edward D., "A Study of a Group of American Management-Investment Companies, 1930–36," *Journal of Business of the University of Chicago,* July, 1938, p. 232.

American Institute for Economic Research. Investment Trusts and Funds from the Investor's Point of View. Great Barrington, Massachusetts, 1937–58.

Barnes, Leo. Your Buying Guide to Mutual Funds and Investment Companies. Larchmont, New York, American Research Council, 1958.

Bialkin, Kenneth J., "The Renascence of the Investment Company in Foreign Investments," *International Investment Quarterly,* 1956.

Bichsel, Fritz. Investment-Trusts; Wesen und Volkswirtschaftliche Bedeutung. Vienna, 1934.

Blumstein, Philipp. Trusts de Placement en Angleterre. Riga, 1930.

Bosland, Chelcie C., "The Investment Company Act of 1940 and Its Background," *Journal of Political Economy,* XLIX (1941), 477, 687.

Bruppacher, C. Investment Trusts. Zurich, 1933.

Bullock, Hugh. The Investment Company in 1945. Address before the twenty-eighth annual convention of the National Association of Securities Commissioners. New York, National Association of Investment Companies, 1945.

——— Remarks before the Federal Bar Association's Briefing Conference on Securities Laws and Regulations. New York, National Association of Investment Companies, 1957.

Burton, Charles Seth, and V. Dushayne. The Investment Trust; a Résumé, Its Adoption in the United States. New York, 1928.

California, State of. Corporation Department. Rules and Regulations Governing Investment Trusts. California Investment Department, Corporation Division. Seventh Biennial Report. Sacramento, Calif., State Printing Office, 1928.

Cam, Gilbert A. A Survey of the Literature on Investment Companies, 1864–1957. New York Public Library, 1958.

Campbell, Edward M., "Some Management Problems of Investment Trusts," *Harvard Business Review,* II (1923–24), 296.

Carter, William D., "Mutual Investment Funds," *Harvard Business Review,* XXVII (November, 1949), 715.

Close, James A., "Investment Companies: Closed-End versus Open-End," *Harvard Business Review,* XXIX (May, 1951), 79.

Durst, Walter N. Analysis and Handbook of Investment Trusts. New York, Rand McNally & Co., 1932.

Du Cann, Edward, M.P. Investing Simplified. London, Newman Neame, Ltd., 1959.

Du Val, Pierre A., and Fred Fredericks. The Money Making Magic of Investment Companies. New York, Long Island City, 1951.

Flynn, John T. Investment Trusts Gone Wrong! New York, New Republic, Inc., 1931.

Foster & Braithwaite, *firm.* Investment Trust Stocks. London, 1957.

Fowler, John F. American Investment Trusts. New York, Harper and Brothers, 1928.

Frederick, Leopold, "Investment Trusts," *Bankers Magazine,* XCVIII (June, 1919), 733.

Gilbert, John C. A History of Investment Trusts in Dundee, 1873–1938. London, P. S. King and Son, Ltd., 1939.

Glasgow, George. Glasgow's Guide to Investment Trust Companies. London, Eyre and Spottiswoode, Ltd., 1935.

——— The English Investment Trust Companies. London, Eyre and Spottiswoode, Ltd., 1930.

——— The Scottish Investment Trust Companies. London, Eyre and Spottiswoode, Ltd., 1932.

Glines, E. Stanley, "Individual and Estate Investing through Investment Trusts," *Journal of Business of the University of Chicago,* January, 1930, p. 22.

Goldschmidt, Rudolf F. Investment Trusts in Deutschland. Mannheim, 1932.

Grayson, Theodore J. Investment Trusts, Their Origin, Development, and Operation. New York, John Wiley & Sons, Inc., 1928.

Guaranty Trust Company of New York. Foreign Financing under the Edge Act, Approved December 24, 1919. New York, 1919.

Haney, Lewis H. The Investment Trust, What It Is, and What It Does. New York, 1928.

Haskins & Sells, *firm*. Investment Trusts: A Study in Relation to Public Accounting. New York, 1930.

Hügi, Bruno. Der Amerikanische Investment Trust. Berne, 1936.

Investment Bankers Association of America. Proceedings. Chicago, 1927–40.

Investors Chronicle, London, April 24, 1954.

Investment Trusts. Geneva, Hentsch & Cie, 1959.

Jaretzki, Alfred, Jr., "The Investment Company Act of 1940," *Washington University Law Quarterly,* 1941.

Joubert, Marc. Les Sociétés de Placement à Long Terme en Valeurs Mobilières, ou "Investment-Trust." Paris, 1932.

Keane, C. P. *Keane's Investment Trust Monthly.* Boston, Financial Publishing Co., 1929–32.

——— Keane's Manual of Investment Trusts. Boston, New York, Financial Publishing Co., 1928–32.

Ketchum, Marshall D., The Fixed Investment Trust. Chicago, 1937. Vol. VII, No. 3, "Studies in Business Administration," supplements to *Journal of Business.*

Kilborne, Russell D., "American Investment Trusts," *Harvard Business Review,* III (1924–25), 160.

Kilgus, Egon. Kapitalsanlagegesellschaften: Investment Trusts. Berlin, 1929.

Kwast, E. H. Th., Investment Trusts. Amsterdam, 1931.

Laing & Cruickshank, *firm.* Investment Trust Companies. London, 1957.

Lander, Jacques de. Les Investment Trusts. Paris, 1929.

Langmuir, Dean. The Fixed Trust: A Statement of Underlying Principles. New York, 1931.

Lazard, Christian. Un Puissant Moyen de Financement Anglo-Saxon: L'investment Trust. Paris, 1929.

Lee, Frederic E. Participating Shares in British Investment Trusts. U. S. Foreign and Domestic Commerce Bureau Trade Information Bulletin No. 530. Washington, D.C., Government Printing Office, 1928.

Leibson, Israel Baruch. Investment Trusts—How and Why. New York, Financial Publishing Co., 1930.

Linhardt, Hanns. Die Anlagepolitik der Britischen Investment Trusts. Munich, 1938.

——— Die Britischen Investment Trusts. Berlin, Industrieverlag Spaeth & Linde, 1935.

——— Die Neuere Entwicklung der Englishchen Investment Trusts. Berlin, 1936.

Livermore, Shaw., "Investment Trusts in 1930," *Journal of Business of the University of Chicago,* October, 1930, p. 432.

Loftus, John A. Investment Management, An Analysis of the Experiences of American Management Investment Trusts. Baltimore, Johns Hopkins Press, 1941.

McFadden, Louis T., "Investment Trusts: Their Benefits and Dangers as Shown by British Experience . . . With Exhibits from Financial Books and Journals," *The Congressional Record,* Vol. 69. Washington, D.C., 1929.

McMartin, John S., "Reporting Investment-Trust Income," *Harvard Business Review,* IX (1931), 491.

Mirimonde, A. P. de. Le Développement de Investment Trusts et ses Causes. Brussels, 1930.

Moffitt, George Wilber, Jr., "Management Achievement of Open-end Investment Companies," *Journal of Business,* April, 1952, p. 71.

Mollet, Walter. Schweizerische Investment-Trusts. Solothurn, Switzerland, 1942.

Moody's Bank & Finance Manual. New York, Moody's Investors Service, 1959.

Motley, Warren, "Federal Regulation of Investment Companies Since 1940," *Harvard Law Review,* 1950.

Moulton, Harold G. The Financial Organization of Society. Chicago, University of Chicago Press, 1921.

National Association of Investment Companies. Annual Report to Members . . . . New York, 1956, 1957, 1958.

——— Investment Companies: A Statistical Summary, 1940–1958. New York, 1955.

——— The Mutual Fund Shareholder—A Comprehensive Study. New York, 1958.

——— A Survey of Stockholders of Closed-end Investment Companies. New York, 1957.

National Association of Securities Commissioners. Proceedings. St. Paul, Minnesota, 1929–44.

Norris Oakley Brothers, *firm.* Investment Trusts. London, 1957.

New York, State of. Report of the Joint Legislative Committee on Banking and Investment Trusts. Albany, J. B. Lyons, 1930.

——— Department of Law. Summary of Results of the Investigation of 100 General Management Trusts in the State of New York Made Under the Direction of the Attorney General. Albany, 1932.

——— Department of Law, Securities Bureau. Investment Trusts, A Survey of Activities and Forms of Investment Trusts with Recommendations for Statutory Regulation. Albany, 1927.

Pabst, Fritz. Industriesgesellschaften: Ein Beitrag zur Frage des Deutschen Wiederaufbaues.

Petersen, Erling. Investment Truster. Oslo, 1931.

Plum, Lester V., and Joseph H. Humphrey, Jr. Investment Analysis and Management. Chicago, Richard D. Irwin, Inc., 1951. Chap. 19, "Investment Trusts."

Powell, Ellis T., "The Evolution of the Money Market (1385–1915) . . . ," *Financial News,* London, 1915.
Prankard, Harry I. Federal Taxation of Investment Companies and Their Shareholders. New York, 1956.
——— Understanding Capital Gain Distributions—A Discussion of the Nature and Effect of Capital Gain Distributions by Investment Companies. New York, 1952.
Richardson, Dorsey. The Investment Companies in 1955: Their Relationship to the Nation's Securities Markets. New York, National Association of Investment Companies, 1955.
Rider, James G. The ABC of Investment Trusts. Philadelphia, 1931.
Robinson, Leland Rex. British Investment Trusts. Washington, D.C., Government Printing Office, 1923.
——— Investment Trust Organization and Management. New York, Ronald Press Co., 1926. Rev. ed., 1929.
——— "Investment Trusts," *Journal of Business of the University of Chicago,* July, 1930, p. 279.
Rosi, Giulio. Investment Trusts. Rome, 1930.
Schwob, Philippe. Les Investment Trusts aux Etats-Unis et la Crise de 1929–30. Paris, 1931.
——— Protection ou Exploitation de L'épargne: une Experience Americaine, L'investment Trust. Paris, 1934.
Scratchley, Arthur. A Practical Treatise on Building Societies and Average Investment "Trusts," or Companies and Societies Investing in Public Securities. London, 1891.
——— On Average Investment Trusts. London, Shaw and Sons, 1875.
Seischab, Hans. Investment Trusts: Versuch einer Theorie und Systematik der Kapitalwertsicherungsbetriebe. Stuttgart, 1931.
Shattuck, Mayo A., "The Legal Propriety of Investment by American Fiduciaries in the Shares of Boston-Type Open-End Investment Trusts," *Boston University Law Review,* 1945.
Speaker, Lawrence M. The Investment Trust. Chicago, A. W. Shaw, 1924.
Steiner, William Howard. Investment Trusts: American Experience. New York, Adelphi Co., 1929.
Stevenson, Alec Brock. Shares in Mutual Investment Funds: Their Use by Trustee and Individual Investors. Nashville, Vanderbilt University Press, 1946.
——— Investment Company Shares: Their Place in Investment Management and Their Use by Trustees. New York, Fiduciary Publishers, Inc., 1947.
Straley, John A. What About Mutual Funds. New York, Harper & Bros., 1954.
Thiesing, T. H. The Investment Trust as a Channel for Investment Abroad. Washington, D.C., U. S. Federal Reserve Board Bulletin, 1921–22.
Thomas, J. Woodrow, "The Investment Company Act of 1940," *George Washington Law Review,* 1949.

Thomas, Joseph A., "Ten Investment Trusts in America—A Three-Year Record," *Harvard Business Review,* IX (1930), 78.

Walker, Charles H., "Unincorporated Investment Trusts in the Nineteenth Century," in *Economic History,* London, Macmillan and Co., Ltd., 1940.

Weissman, Rudolph L. The Investment Company and the Investor. New York, Harper & Brothers, 1951.

Wiesenberger, Arthur. Investment Companies. New York, Arthur Wiesenberger & Co., 1942–59.

Williams, Marshall H. Investment Trusts in America. New York, The Macmillan Co., 1928.

Appendix

American Investment Companies

NOTE. Assets are for December 31, 1929, or the nearest date. Where "1928" appears, it refers to December 31, 1928, or the nearest date.

Assets appear at market prices unless otherwise indicated.

* indicates that portfolio is published.

A dash indicates that information is not available.

† indicates cost price.

†† indicates cost or market, whichever is lower.

	Assets (in millions of dollars)	*Date Founded*
* Adams Express Company	72.2	1929
Adirondack Investors, Incorporated	—	1929
Aeronautical Industries, Incorporated	1.5	1929
* Affiliated Investors Incorporated	1.5	1927
* Air Investors, Inc.	3.2	1928
Aircraft Securities Corp.	—	1929
Airstocks, Inc.	4.2	1928
* Aldred Investment Trust	12.9	1927
Alexander Fund, The	3.9	1907
Alexander Hamilton Investment Corp.	—	1928
* All America General Corp.	4.7	1929
All America Utility Securities Corp.	—	1929
All American Shares Corporation	—	1929
Alliance Investment Corporation	6.6 †	1925
Allied American Industries, Inc.	1.9 †	1928
* Allied International Investing Corp.	3.1	1927
Allied Investors, Inc.	—	1927

	Assets (in millions of dollars)	Date Founded
Allied Investors Securities Corp.	—	1929
American and Foreign Share Corp.	.8	1927
American & General Securities Corp.	17.1	1928
American & Overseas Investing Corp.	1.8	1927
American and Scottish Investment Co.	7.2	1928
American Associated Investors Corp.	—	1928
American Bankers Investment Co.	.8	1928
American Bond & Share Corp.	.5 †	1924
American Bondholders & Share Corp.	1.2 †	1927
* American, British & Continental Corp.	17.6	1926
American Capital Corporation	16.5	1928
American Cash Credit Corporation	1.5 †	1929
* American-Colonial Corporation	.5	1928
American and Continental Corp.	20.8	1924
American Diversified Realty Corp., Ltd.	—	1929
American Electric Securities Corp.	.4	1928
* American European Securities Co.	26.2	1925
American Financial Corp. of N. Y.	—	1928
American Founders Corp.	171.6	1922
* American Industries Participation Shares	—	1928
American Insuranstocks Corporation	—	1928
American International Corp.	60.6	1915
American Investment Company	1.0 †	1914
American Investment Corporation	—	1927
American Investment Trust (Massachusetts)	—	1929
American Investment Trust (of Kentucky)	—	1929
American Investors, Inc.	12.3	1928
American, London & Empire Corp.	—	1928
* American Railway Trust Shares	—	1929
American Securities Shares	—	1927
American Shareholders Finance Corp.	—	1925
American Shares, Inc.	—	1929
American Utilities & General Corp.	6.8	1929
Amoskeag Co.	—	1927
F. L. Andrews Investment Trust	1.3	1926
Anglo-American Holding Corp.	—	1927
Appalachian Corp.	2.6 †	1929
Associated Security Investors, Inc.	2.4 †	1927
* Associated Standard Oilstocks Shares, Series A	—	1929
* Association for Mutual Investment	.2 †	1926
Astor Financial Corp.	1.4 †	1927
* Atlantic Investments, Inc.	.2	1925
Atlantic Midland Corp.	3.8	1929
* Atlantic and Pacific International Corp.	6.8 †	1928

	Assets (in millions of dollars)	*Date Founded*
Atlantic Securities Co.	2.4 †	1928
* Atlantic Securities Corp.	6.9	1927
Atlas Corp.	13.8	1929
* Automotive Participation Shares	—	1928
Aviation Corp. of California	2.0	1928
Aviation Securities Corp. (Delaware)	2.1 ††	1928
Aviation Securities Corp. of New England	2.8 †	1929
Bainryan Corporation	—	1929
Bakers Share Corp.	.3 †	1927
Bancscrip Investment Corp.	.9 †	1929
Bankers Advisory Trust	—	1929
Bankers Holding Trust, Inc.	—	1924
Bankers Investment Trust of America	1.5	1926
Bankers National Investing Corp.	1.3 †	1929
Bankstocks Corp. of Maryland	3.1	1925
Basic Commodities Corp.	—	1929
* Basic Industry Shares	—	1928
Beacon Participations, Inc.	2.2 †	1928
Blue Ridge Corp.	133.5	1929
Boardwalk Securities Corp.	1.2 †	1925
* Bond Investment Trust, The	2.5 †	1923
* Bond Investment Trust of America, The	.2 †	1926
Bond & Share Co., Ltd.	4.1	1928
Bondshare Corp.	—	1928
Boston Personal Property Trust	5.1 †	1893
* Boston Securities Corp.	.5	1928
* British Type Investors, Inc.	10.7 †	1928
* Broad Street Investing Co., Inc.	2.7	1929
Brooklyn Capital, Inc.	—	1929
Brooklyn-Lafayette Corp.	1.3 †	1926
Brooklyn National Corp., The	—	1929
Burco, Inc.	—	1929
Burnham Trading Corp.	—	1929
California Investment Fund, Inc.	.5 †	1925
* Cambridge Investment Corporation	.3	1929
* Capital Administration Co. Ltd.	11.8	1928
Capital Management Corporation	2.3 ††	1928
Central Illinois Securities Corp.	14.9	1929
Central Investors Corporation	—	1927
Central States Investment Trust, Inc.	—	1929
* Century Shares Trust	5.7	1928
* Chain Distributors Trust	.2	1928

	Assets (in millions of dollars)	Date Founded
* Chain & General Equities, Inc.	5.6	1929
* Chain Store Investment Corp.	.8	1927
* Chain Store Stocks, Inc.	5.8	1928
Chainstores Trading Corporation	—	1929
Charter Oak Investors Corporation	—	1929
* Chartered Investors Inc.	10.2	1928
Chatham Phenix Allied Corporation	50.4	1929
Chemical National Associates, Inc.	—	1929
* Chicago Bank Participation Shares	—	1929
* Chicago Bankshares Certificates	—	1929
Chicago Corporation	51.3	1929
* Chicago Investors Corporation	11.3	1927
Chippewa Share Corporation	—	1929
* Cincinnati Combined Securities, Trustee Shares	—	—
City Security Corporation	3.7 †	1929
City Shareholders, Inc.	.8 †	1929
* Claggett Shares Corporation	.3 †	1929
Claremont Investing Corporation	2.0	1927
Coast Foundation, Inc.	.1 †	1929
Colonial Bond and Share Corp.	1.4 †	1929
Colonial Investors Shares, Series A	—	1927
Columbia Investing Corporation	3.4 ††	1927
* Combined Trust Shares (of Standard Oil Group)	—	1929
Commerce Investments Inc. of Cincinnati	—	1929
Commercial Finance Corporation	.9 †	1917
Commonwealth Securities, Inc.	27.6	1923
Community State Corporation	.6	1928
* Compound Interest Company, Ltd.	.1 †	1927
* Connecticut Investment Trust	—	1927
Consolidated Bond & Share Corp.	—	1925
Consolidated Commerce Corporation	—	1928
Consolidated Stock & Debenture Co., Inc.	—	1927
Continental American Bankshares Corporation	.5 †	1927
Continental Chicago Corporation	59.2	1929
Continental Equities, Inc.	—	1929
Continental Investment Co.	2.3	1927
Continental Metropolitan Corp.	1.3 †	1929
Continental Securities Corp.	10.3	1924
Co-operating Investors, Inc.	.1	1925
Corporate Capital Corporation	—	1928
* Corporate Trust Shares	7.9	1929
Corporation Investment Shares Inc.	.3 †	1927
Corporation Securities Co. of Chicago	72.7	1929
* Counselors Securities Trust	1.7	1929
Credit Foncier International, Inc.	1.2 †	1928

	Assets (in millions of dollars)	*Date Founded*
* Deposited Bank Shares, Series B-1 (Bank & Insurance Shares, Inc.)	—	1928
* Deposited Bank Shares, Series CDSP (Diversified Bancshares, Inc.)	—	1929
* Deposited Bank Shares, Series N. Y. (Bank & Insurance Shares, Inc.)	—	1929
* Detroit Bank Participation Shares	—	1928
* Devonshire Investing Corp.	1.6	1928
Diversified Aviation Shares	—	1928
Diversified Investment Trusts, Inc.	2.5 †	1928
* Diversified Trustee Shares	—	1925
* Diversified Trustee Shares, Series B	20.1	1927
* Diversified Trustee Shares, Series C	6.4	1929
Dollar Share Corporation	—	1929
Domestic & Foreign Investors Corp.	4.7 †	1927
Domestic and Overseas Investing Co., Ltd.	—	1928
Dominion Holding Corporation	—	1928
Eastern Bankers Corporation	—	1922
Elbert A. Harvey, Agent Cooperative Account	—	1928
Electric Investors, Incorporated	—	1924
Empire American Securities Corp.	1.5 †	1929
Empire Equities Corporation	—	1929
Empire Western Corporation	—	1929
Engineers Investment Corporation (Del.)	—	1929
* Engineers Investment Corp. (Mass.)	33.4	1929
Equitable Investing Corporation	.6	1928
Equitable Trust Co. Investment Trust (Detroit)	—	1929
Equity Investors Corporation	2.6	1929
Equity Ownership Shares, Inc.	—	1929
Erie Share Corp.	—	—
Federal American Bond & Share Corp.	.1 †	1926
Federal Bond & Share Company	—	1923
Federal National Investment Trust	—	1928
Federated Capital Corporation (1928)	6.8	1927
Federated Industries Inc.	—	1929
Federated Investors, Incorporated	.2	1927
Fidelity Investment Associates	—	1928
* Financial Investing Co. of New York, Ltd.	—	1924
First American Bancorporation, Incorporated	—	1929
First Cincinnati Corporation	—	1929
First Federal Foreign Investment Trust	—	1926
First Guaranteed Trust of America	—	1929
First Holding & Trading Corp.	—	1928

	Assets (in millions of dollars)	*Date Founded*
First Investment Company (1928)	1.2 †	1916
First Investment Counsel Corp.	3.2	1928
First Investors Company of Illinois	.9 †	1927
First Maine Investment Company	—	1927
First National Investors' Corporation of America	—	1928
First Ohio Investment Company	.1 †	1927
First Trust Bank-Stock Corp.	—	1926
Fiscal Bond and Share Corp.	—	1919
* Fixed Trust Shares	5.0	1927
* Fletcher Savings & Trust Company's Half Million Dollar Investment Fund, Trust Fund A	—	1929
Folds Buck Financial Corporation	—	1929
* Foreign Government Bond Trust Certificates	—	1925
Foundation Investment Company, The	.5	1928
Founders Securities Trust	1.5 †	1927
* Fourth National Investors Corp.	23.5	1929
Franklin Bancshares Corporation	—	1928
* General American Investors Co., Inc.	34.2	1927
General American Securities, Inc.	—	1929
General Bancshares Corporation	—	1929
* General Capital Corporation (of Delaware)	10.7	1929
General Empire Corporation	2.9 ††	1929
General Equity Corporation	—	1927
* General Public Service Corporation	36.0	1925
General Stockyards Corporation	4.4 †	1928
General Trustees Corporation	.9 †	1927
General Utilities & Investment Company, Inc.	.3 †	1928
German Credit & Investment Corp.	4.9 †	1926
Gibralter Founders, Inc.	—	1929
Globe Financial Corporation	—	1929
Goddard Securities Corporation	—	1929
Goldman Sachs Trading Corp., The	251.9 ††	1928
Granger Trading Corporation	1.0	1929
* Graymur Corporation	7.8	1929
Great Lakes Share Corp.	—	—
Great Northern Investing Co., Inc.	1.4	1927
* Greenway Corporation	.6 ††	1926
Griggs Investment Trust, Inc.	—	1928
Grover O'Neill Fund, Inc.	—	1929
Guaranty Founders Trust	—	1927
Guaranty Investment Assurance Trust	—	1929
Guardian Bank Shares Investment Trust	—	1929
Guardian Investing Agency	—	1928
Guardian Investment Trust	6.6 †	1927

	Assets (in millions of dollars)	*Date Founded*
* Guardian Investors Corp.	11.4 †	1925
Guardian Public Utilities Investment Trust	—	1929
Guardian Rail Shares Investment Trust	—	1929
Gude Winmill Trading Corporation	—	1929
* Hambleton Corporation, The	7.1 †	1929
Hartley Rogers Trading Corp.	—	1929
Hayes-Jackson Corporation	.2 †	1928
Hub Financial Corporation	—	1927
Hydro-Electric Securities Corp.	61.6	1926
* Hytag Financial Corporation of America	.2	1929
Illuminating & Power Securities Corporation	18.4	1912
Income Producing Corporation (1928)	2.0 †	1925
Incorporated Equities	7.3	1928
* Incorporated Investors	41.2	1925
Industrial & Power Securities Co.	—	1928
* Inland Investors Incorporated	5.4	1927
Insull Utility Investments, Inc.	157.6	1928
Insurance and Bank Stock Trust	—	1927
Insuranshares and General Management Co.	1.1 †	1927
* Insuranshares Certificates, Incorporated	13.4	1929
Insuranshares Corporation (New York)	5.1 †	1927
* Insuranshares Corporation of Delaware	11.9	1929
Interbanc Investors Inc.	1.2 †	1929
Intercontinental Investment Corp.	3.4 †	1927
International American Investment Corporation	—	1928
International and General Corp.	—	1929
International Bankstocks Corp. (Md.)	—	1928
International Bond and Share Corp.	—	1927
* International Carriers, Ltd.	15.6	1929
International Equities Corporation	2.7 †	1927
International Investing Corp.	2.2 †	1928
International Joint Security Corp.	—	1929
International Securities Corp. of America	63.8	1921
* International Security Management Company	2.0	1929
International Share Corporation	15.3	1928
* International Superpower Corp.	11.0	1928
Interstate Equities Corporation	25.2 †	1929
Investment Administration Corp.	—	1928
Investment Co. of America	15.2	1926
Investment Corporation of North America	—	1927
Investment Corporation of Philadelphia, The	1.8	1928
Investment Counsel Fund of Rochester, The	—	1929
Investment Counsel Trust	1.1	1927

	Assets (in millions of dollars)	Date Founded
Investment Fund of New Jersey	.1 †	1929
Investment Stock & Bond Corporation	.2 †	1928
Investment Trust Associates	16.9	1924
* Investment Trust Fund "A"	19.5	1925
* Investment Trust Fund "B"	5.3	1927
* Investment Trust of North America, Inc.	—	1928
* Investment Trust Shares (Investment Corporation of North America)	—	1927
Investment Trust Shares (Investment Shares Corporation, California)	—	1926
* Investment Trust Shares, Series A (Prudential Company)	—	1927
* Investment Trust Shares, Series B (Prudential Company)	—	1927
Investors Alliance Corporation	.2	1925
Investors & Traders, Inc.	.5	1929
* Investors Association, The	3.4 †	1928
Investors Bond & Share Corporation	—	1928
Investors Corporation	4.5 †	1925
Investors Counsel, Inc.	.048 †	1929
* Investors Equity Company, Inc.	28.4	1927
Investors Savings Trust	.3 †	1928
* Investors Securities Company of Massachusetts	4.5	1925
Investors of Washington, Inc.	.8 †	1928
Iroquois Share Corporation	2.6	1929
Jackson & Curtis Investment Assoc.	1.9 †	1928
* Jackson & Curtis Securities Corp.	2.2 †	1924
Joint Investors, Inc.	1.4	1926
Joint Security Corporation	.5 †	1927
Junior Shares, Incorporated	.2 †	1929
* Keystone Investing Corp. (1928)	1.5	1928
* Kidder Participations, Inc.	5.8 †	1926
* Kidder Participations, Inc. No. 2	4.9 †	1927
* Kidder Participations, Inc. No. 3	4.8 †	1928
Knickerbocker National Corporation	—	1929
Leach Corporation, The	—	1929
* Leaders of Industry Shares	—	1929
Lebanon Financial Corporation of America	—	1927
* Lehman Corporation, The	92.4	1929
Liberty Share Corporation	12.0	1929
Lincoln Mutual Investment Trust	.6	1928

	Assets (in millions of dollars)	*Date Founded*
M. & T. Securities Corp.	22.8	1929
McMurray Hill Investment Corp.	.5 †	1929
Manhattan Dearborn Corporation	17.8	1929
Manhattan Financial Corporation	1.7	1927
* Massachusetts Investors Trust	13.5 †	1924
* Massasoit Corporation, The	.2	1929
Mayflower Associates, Inc.	18.8	1928
Metal & Mining Shares, Inc.	7.4	1928
Metropolitan Bankshares Corporation	.3	1929
Minnesota Investors Corp.	.3 †	1929
Mitchum, Tully Participations, Inc.	1.2 †	1927
Mitchum, Tully Participations, Inc. No. 2	1.1 †	1929
Mohawk Investment Corporation	4.8	1928
Mohawk Share Corporation	—	1929
Morristown Securities Corp.	3.6	1925
Municipal Investment Trust	—	1929
Mutual Finance Corporation	1.3 †	1918
* Mutual Investment Co.	.2	1926
* Mutual Investment Trust	.7	1926
Mutual Investors Company	.9	1925
Nassau Management Corporation	—	1929
National Assets Corporation	—	1929
National Aviation Corporation	3.0	1928
* National Bond & Share Corporation	10.3	1929
National Investment Shares, Inc.	.4	1929
National Investors Corporation	5.9 †	1927
National Re-Investing Corporation	—	1929
National Republic Investment Trust	6.6	1929
National Securities Corporation of California	.8	1928
National Securities Investment Company	32.8	1926
* National Units of America Shares	—	1928
* Nation-Wide Securities Company	1.8	1924
Nevis Share Company	.1 †	1928
* New Bedford Investors Trust	.4 †	1927
* New Jersey Bond & Shareholding Corp.	.4 †	1927
New York & Foreign Investing Corp.	9.1	1928
New York & London Management Co., Ltd.	—	1928
Newton Securities Corporation	—	1929
* North American Aviation, Inc.	19.4	1928
North American Investment Corp.	10.3	1925
* North American Trust Shares	33.0	1928
North and South American Corp.	9.3 ††	1929
Northern Securities Corporation	.9	1927

	Assets (in millions of dollars)	Date Founded
Ohio Shares, Inc.	1.0 †	1927
* Oil Shares, Incorporated	9.8	1928
Oilstocks, Limited	8.4 †	1928
* Old Colony Investment Trust	12.1	1927
* Old Line Insurance Shares	—	1929
* Overseas Securities Co., Inc.	6.8	1923
Pacific Associates, Inc.	3.2 †	1924
Pacific Investing Corporation	14.3	1922
Pacific Investment Trust	—	—
Pan-American Share Corporation	—	—
Pan-Continental Investing Corp.	—	1929
Paramount Investment Corporation	—	1929
Parker Trading Corporation	—	1929
Participating Investors Shares Corp.	—	—
Passwall Corporation	4.8	1928
* Pennsylvania Bank Shares & Securities Corporation	6.4	1928
Pennsylvania First National Corp.	—	1929
* Pennsylvania Industries, Inc.	12.0	1927
Pennsylvania Investing Company	2.4 †	1928
Pennsylvania Securities Investment Corp.	.6 †	1928
Pennsylvania Share Company	.3	1928
Petroleum Industries Incorporated	2.3	1928
Petroleum Royalties Co.	2.4 †	1925
Petroleum and Trading Corporation	3.4	1929
Piedmont Associates, Inc.	—	—
* Pittsburgh Bond & Share Corp.	.4	1929
* Pittsburgh Investment Securities Corporation	1.3 †	1926
Power, Gas and Water Securities Corp.	9.5	1928
* Power and Light Securities Trust	4.8	1926
Prince & Whitely Trading Corporation	38.0	1929
Professional Investment Trust, Inc.	—	1929
Provident Trustee Shares	—	1928
Prudential Company, The	—	1927
Prudential Investment Corporation	—	1927
Prudential Investors, Inc.	16.1	1929
Public Investing Company	1.4 †	1929
Public Utilities Corp.	13.4	1910
Public Utility Holding Corp.	66.0	1929
Public Utility Investing Corp.	12.4 †	1917
* Radio Securities Corporation	.4	1929
Railroad and General Securities Corporation	.6 †	1929
* Railroad Investment Shares	—	1929

		Assets (in millions of dollars)	*Date Founded*
	Railroad Shares Corporation	10.6 †	1929
	Railway Equities Corporation	.7	1925
*	Railway & Light Securities Company	18.6	1904
	Railway and Utilities Investing Corp.	4.7	1927
	Reinvestment Associates, Series A	—	1927
	Reinvestment Associates, Series B	—	1929
	Reinvestment Associates, Series C	—	1929
	Reinvestment Associates, Series D	—	1929
	Reinvestment Associates, Series E	—	1929
*	Reliance International Corp.	16.7	1929
*	Reliance Management Corporation	8.5	1929
	Republic Investing Corporation	.2 †	1927
	Research Investment Corporation	1.2	1928
	Reybarn Co.	12.8	—
	Reynolds Brothers, Incorporated	10.1	1929
	Reynolds Investing Company, Inc.	11.4	1928
	Rochester Capital Corporation	—	1928
	St. Louis Aviation Corporation	1.3	1929
*	Seaboard Utilities Shares Corp.	18.3	1929
	Second American Investment Corp.	—	—
	Second Founders Share Corporation	—	1929
*	Second Incorporated Equities	2.0	1929
	Second International Securities Corporation	22.6	1926
*	Second Investment Counsel Corp.	1.1	1928
	Second Investors Corporation	2.5 †	1929
*	Second National Investors Corp.	10.5	1928
	Second Southern Bankers Securities Corp.	.5 †	1929
	Securities Company of New Hampshire, The (1928)	.2 †	1922
	Securities Corporation General	13.4	1912
	Security Investment Trust (Ill.)	—	1929
*	Security Investment Trust, Inc. (Del.)	1.0	1927
	Security Co.	—	1922
	Security National Bond Trust Fund	—	1927
	Security Shares, Incorporated	—	1927
	Selected American Shares	—	1929
	Selected Industries, Inc.	81.0	1928
	Selected Stocks, Inc. (Delaware)	—	1929
*	Selected Stocks, Inc. (New York)	.7	1929
*	Selected Trust Shares	—	1929
	Shareholders Corporation	—	1929
	Shareholders Investment Corp.	1.6 †	1929
	Shares Corporation of Wall Street	.3	1928

	Assets (in millions of dollars)	Date Founded
Shares in Maine, Inc.	.1 †	1928
Shares in the South, Inc.	2.5	1928
Shawmut Association	9.7	1928
Shawmut Bank Investment Trust	8.7	1927
Shaw-Loomis-Sayles Mutual Fund, Inc.	—	1929
Shenandoah Corporation	104.4	1929
Sisto Financial Corporation	6.2 ††	1929
Southeastern Investment Trust, Inc.	.8 †	1929
Southern Bankers Securities Corp.	2.8 †	1927
Southern Bond and Share Corporation	3.0	1928
Southern National Corporation	3.3 †	1929
Southern New York Investment Corp.	—	1929
Southland Realty Investment Trust	—	1929
* Specialized Shares Corporation	.3	1927
* Spencer Trask Fund, Inc.	14.8	1929
* Standard Collateral Trusteed Common Stock Shares	—	1928
Standard Corporations, Inc.	—	1929
Standard Holding Corporation	3.8	1927
Standard International Securities Corporation	—	1927
* Standard Investing Corp.	14.4	1927
* Standard Oil Trust Shares	—	1929
* Standard Shares, Inc.	—	1929
State Street Investment Corporation	18.9	1924
* Sterling Securities Corporation	31.8	1928
S. W. Straus Investing Corporation	15.1 †	1929
Stuyvesant Bond & Share Corporation	.3 †	1925
Sun Investing Company, Inc.	6.7	1929
Syndicate Shares	—	1929
* Third Investment Counsel Corp.	.8	1929
* Third National Investors Corp.	9.1	1929
Tobacco and Allied Stocks, Inc.	2.7	1929
Tonawanda Share Corporation	.2 †	1927
Traders Corporation	.8	1927
* Tri-Continental Corporation	76.5	1929
Tri-National Trading Corporation	1.6 †	1929
* Trustee Standard Oilshares, Series A	—	1928
Underwritings and Participations, Inc.	—	1928
Ungerleider Financial Corporation	14.1	1929
Union American Investing Corp.	6.3 †	1928
Union Financial Corporation of America	3.0 †	1928
Union Investment Trust Units	—	—
United Bond & Share Corporation (Seattle)	—	1925

	Assets (in millions of dollars)	*Date Founded*
United Capital Corporation	.6 †	1928
United Continental Corporation	—	—
United Diversified Securities Corp.	—	1927
United Equities, Inc.	3.8 †	1928
United First National Corporation	—	1929
* United Founders Corporation	208.2	1929
United Hellenic Bank Shares, Inc.	—	1929
United Investment Assurance Trust	1.1 †	1927
United Investors Securities Corp.	1.5 †	1927
United Pacific Corporation	—	1928
United Securities Corporation	.2	1929
* United Securities Trust Associates	11.6	1929
United States & British International Co., Ltd.	17.0	1928
* United States & Foreign Securities Corporation	61.9	1924
* United States & International Securities Corporation	42.3	1928
United States & Overseas Corp.	22.1 †	1929
United States Bond & Share Company	2.9 †	1926
* United States Electric Light & Power Shares, Inc.	36.8	1927
United States Securities Corporation, Ltd.	—	1929
United States Securities Investment Co.	—	1928
* United States Shares Corporation	—	1927
* United States Shares Financial Corp.	3.2	1929
* Utilities Associates, Inc.	.5 †	1929
* Utilities Hydro & Rails Shares Corp.	1.3 †	1929
Utility Equities Corporation	21.2	1928
Vernon Associates, Inc.	.5	1928
* Vick Financial Corporation	12.7	1929
Virginia Investors, Inc.	.3	1929
Wall-Lombard Corporation	—	1926
Wall Street Trading Corporation	—	1929
Wedgwood Investing Corporation	4.7	1928
West Coast Bancorporation, Portland, Ore.	5.2	1928
Westchester First National Corp.	1.8 †	1928
Western New York Securities Corp.	—	1929
* Western Reserve Investing Corp.	6.3	1928
Williamsville Share Corp.	—	1929
Winslow Lanier International Corp.	11.4	1929
Wisconsin Investment Company	2.8	1924
Wisconsin Shares Corp.	—	1929
Yosemite Holding Corporation	2.5	1929

American Investment Company Groups

DECEMBER 31, 1929

		Assets (in millions of dollars)
Founders Group, Jersey City	Total	626.1
United Founders Corporation		208.2
American Founders Corporation		171.6
Public Utility Holding Corporation of America		66.0
International Securities Corporation of America		63.8
Second International Securities Corporation		22.6
United States & Overseas Corporation		22.1
American and Continental Corporation		20.8
American & General Securities Corporation		17.1
United States & British International Company, Ltd.		17.0
Investment Trust Associates		16.9
Goldman Sachs Group, New York	Total	489.8
Goldman Sachs Trading Corporation		251.9
Blue Ridge Corporation		133.5
Shenandoah Corporation		104.4
Insull Group, Chicago	Total	230.3
Insull Utility Investments, Inc.		157.6
Corporation Securities Co. of Chicago		72.7
Field Glore Group, Chicago	Total	110.5
Continental Chicago Corporation		59.2
Chicago Corporation		51.3
Dillon Read Group, New York	Total	104.2
United States & Foreign Securities Corporation		61.9
United States & International Securities Corporation		42.3

		Assets (in millions of dollars)
Reynolds Group, New York	Total	102.5
Selected Industries, Inc.		81.0
Reynolds Investing Co., Inc.		11.4
Reynolds Bros., Inc.		10.1
Lehman Corporation, New York		92.4
Stone & Webster Group, Boston	Total	81.8
General Public Service Corporation		36.0
Utility Equities Corporation		21.2
Railway and Light Securities Co.		18.6
General Stockyards Corporation		4.4
Devonshire Investing Corporation		1.6
Tri-Continental Corporation, New York		76.5
Adams Express Co., New York		72.2
Calvin Bullock Group, New York	Total	65.2
United States Electric Light & Power Shares, Inc., Trust Certificates, Series A		36.8
International Carriers, Ltd.		15.6
International Superpower Corporation		11.0
Nation-Wide Securities Company		1.8
Insuranshares Group, Jersey City	Total	63.3
Sterling Securities Corporation		31.8
Insuranshares Certificates, Inc.		13.4
Insuranshares Corporation of Delaware		11.9
Insuranshares Corporation (New York)		5.1
Insuranshares and General Management Company		1.1
American International Corporation, New York		60.6
Putnam Group, Boston	Total	54.3
Incorporated Investors		41.2
Incorporated Equities		7.3
United Equities, Inc.		3.8
Second Incorporated Equities		2.0
Chatham Phenix Allied Corporation, New York		50.4
National Investors Group, New York	Total	49.0
Fourth National Investors Corporation		23.5
Second National Investors Corporation		10.5
Third National Investors Corporation		9.1
National Investors Corporation		5.9
Total of 16 groups (49 companies)		2,329.1

Closed-End Management Investment Companies

TOTAL ASSETS $10 MILLION OR MORE,

BASE DATE DECEMBER 31, 1929

Source: Report of the Securities and Exchange Commission, *Investment Trusts and Investment Companies,* Part Two, p. 53.

	Assets (in millions of dollars)
Goldman, Sachs Trading Corporation, The (later Pacific Eastern Corporation)	251.9
United Founders Corporation	208.2
American Founders Corporation	171.6
Blue Ridge Corporation	133.5
Shenandoah Corporation	104.4
Lehman Corporation, The	92.4
Selected Industries, Inc.	81.0
Tri-Continental Corporation	76.5
Adams Express Co., The	72.2
Public Utility Holding Corporation (later General Investment Corporation)	66.0
International Securities Corporation of America	63.8
United States & Foreign Securities Corporation	61.9
American International Corporation	60.6
Continental Chicago Corporation (later The Chicago Corporation)	59.2
Chicago Corporation, The	51.3

	Assets (in millions of dollars)
Chatham Phenix Allied Corporation (later Securities Allied Corporation)	50.4
United States & International Securities Corporation	42.3
General Public Service Corporation	36.0
General American Investors Co., Inc.	34.2
National Securities Investment Co.	32.8
Sterling Securities Corporation	31.8
Investors Equity Co., Inc.	28.4
Commonwealth Securities, Inc.	27.6
American European Securities Co.	26.2
Interstate Equities Corporation	25.2
Fourth National Investors Corporation	23.5
M. & T. Securities Corporation	22.8
Second International Securities Corporation	22.6
Utility Equities Corporation	21.2
American and Continental Corporation	20.8
Mayflower Associates, Inc.	18.8
Railway and Light Securities Co.	18.6
Illuminating and Power Securities Corporation	18.4
American, British & Continental Corporation	17.6
American & General Securities Corporation	17.1
United States & British International Co., Ltd.	17.0
Investment Trust Associates	16.9
Reliance International Corporation	16.7
American Capital Corporation	16.5
Prudential Investors, Inc.	16.1
International Carriers, Ltd. (later Carriers & General Corporation)	15.6
Investment Co. of America, The	15.2
Central Illinois Securities Corporation	14.9
Standard Investing Corporation	14.4
Pacific Investing Corporation	14.3
Ungerleider Financial Corporation (later The Financial Corporation)	14.1
Atlas Corporation	13.8
Securities Corporation General	13.4
Public Utilities Corporation	13.4
Insuranshares Certificates, Inc.	13.4
Aldred Investment Trust	12.9
Reybarn Co., Inc.	12.8
Vick Financial Corporation	12.7
American Investors, Inc.	12.3
Old Colony Investment Trust	12.1

	Assets (in millions of dollars)
Liberty Share Corporation	12.0
Capital Administration Co., Ltd.	11.8
United Securities Trust Associates	11.6
Reynolds Investing Co., Inc.	11.4
Chicago Investors Corporation	11.3
International Superpower Corporation	11.0
General Capital Corporation	10.7
Second National Investors Corporation	10.5
Continental Securities Corporation (old)	10.3
National Bond and Share Corporation	10.3
North American Investment Corporation	10.3
Reynolds Bros., Inc.	10.1

Management Investment-Holding Companies

TOTAL ASSETS $20 MILLION OR MORE,

BASE DATE DECEMBER 31, 1929

Source: Report of the Securities and Exchange Commission, *Investment Trusts and Investment Companies,* Part Two, p. 92.

	Assets (in millions of dollars)
Christiana Securities Co.	361.5
United Corporation, The	332.5
Alleghany Corporation	263.7
American Superpower Corporation	225.5
Chesapeake Corporation, The	169.9
Solvay American Investment Corporation	165.1
Central States Electric Corporation	161.0
Continental Shares, Inc.	140.2
Petroleum Corporation of America	93.5
Eastern Utilities Investing Corporation	78.9
Niagara Share Corporation of Maryland	74.4
American I. G. Chemical Corporation	72.3
Electric Shareholdings Corporation	51.0
American Cities Power and Light Corporation	50.5
Empire Power Corporation	49.1
International Utilities Corporation	47.0
International Power Securities Corporation	43.7
Italian Superpower Corporation	38.9
Utility and Industrial Corporation	35.8
Hutchins Securities Co., The	35.4
American Equities Co.	34.5
Bankers Securities Corporation	30.4
Marine Union Investors, Inc.	30.3
International Holding & Investment Co., Ltd.	28.5
Electric Power Associates, Inc.	26.9
Warren Brothers Co.	23.0
Eastern States Corporation	20.8
Old Colony Trust Associates	20.5

Unclassified Management Investment Companies

TOTAL ASSETS $10 MILLION OR MORE,
BASE DATE DECEMBER 31, 1929

Source: Report of the Securities and Exchange Commission, *Investment Trusts and Investment Companies,* Part Two, p. 95.

	Assets (in millions of dollars)
Insull Utility Investments, Inc.	157.6
G. E. Employees Securities Corporation	96.4
Corporation Securities Co. of Chicago	72.7
Inter-Continental Corporation	68.9
Hydro-Electric Securities Corporation	61.6
Electrical Securities Corporation	56.1
Newmont Mining Corporation	55.5
Chemates, Inc.	40.0
Intercoast Trading Co.	32.7
Public Utilities Securities Corporation	20.0
Seaboard Utilities Shares Corporation (Mass.)	18.3
International Share Corporation	15.3
Setay Co., Inc.	12.7
Pennsylvania Industries, Inc.	12.0
Insuranshares Corporation of Delaware	11.9
Winslow Lanier International Corporation, The	11.4
Case, Pomeroy and Co., Inc.	10.4

12 Open-End Management Investment Companies

ASSETS $10 MILLION OR MORE AT ANY YEAR-END, 1927–36

Source: Report of the Securities and Exchange Commission, *Investment Trusts and Investment Companies*, Part Two, p. 56.

	Assets (in millions of dollars)									
	1927	*1928*	*1929*	*1930*	*1931*	*1932*	*1933*	*1934*	*1935*	*1936*
Massachusetts Investors Trust	6.5	10.9	14.5	15.1	14.1	13.6	21.0	30.8	81.4	130.3
Incorporated Investors	5.4	45.7	41.2	28.1	15.4	15.3	32.0	37.3	57.0	77.5
State Street Investment Corporation	4.3	12.8	18.9	11.9	8.0	7.5	21.5	28.6	44.9	52.3
Quarterly Income Shares, Inc.	—	—	—	—	—	0.1	15.7	27.0	38.6	46.5
Dividend Shares, Inc.	—	—	—	—	—	9.9	25.2	16.9	24.8	38.5
Investment Trust Fund A	15.4	17.8	19.5	14.2	7.8	4.8	5.9	4.8	5.6	5.9
Spencer Trask Fund, Inc.	—	—	14.8	7.5	3.4	3.2	6.9	5.1	6.8	7.8
Century Shares Trust	—	3.6	5.7	3.9	2.0	1.8	1.7	2.7	8.1	13.5
First Investment Counsel Corporation	—	2.0	3.2	4.3	3.1	3.3	5.3	7.0	10.2	12.7
Selected American Shares	—	—	—	—	—	—	3.9	5.4	8.2	11.8
Maryland Fund Inc., The	—	—	—	—	—	—	—	0.2	5.2	11.7
Supervised Shares, Inc.	—	—	—	—	—	0.2	7.6	7.7	9.2	11.0

Fixed and Semi-Fixed Investment Trusts

ASSETS $10 MILLION OR MORE AT ANY YEAR-END, 1927–35

Source: Report of the Securities and Exchange Commission, *Investment Trusts and Investment Companies,* Part Two, p. 98.

	Assets (in millions of dollars)								
	1927	*1928*	*1929*	*1930*	*1931*	*1932*	*1933*	*1934*	*1935*
North American Trust Shares, 1953	—	—	33.0	96.3	32.3	5.2	5.0	3.7	4.2
Corporate Trust Shares (original series)	—	—	7.9	74.7	25.3	3.3	2.9	2.2	2.4
United States Electric Light & Power Shares, Inc., Trust Certificates, Series A	7.5	35.8	36.8	27.3	15.3	10.5	7.0	5.4	7.5
North American Trust Shares, 1956	—	—	—	—	12.4	21.2	25.1	20.0	23.2
North American Trust Shares, 1955	—	—	—	—	10.9	19.7	24.1	19.5	22.2
Diversified Trustee Shares, Series B	—	6.1	20.1	7.8	3.8	1.4	1.4	1.0	1.1
Diversified Trustee Shares, Series C	—	—	6.4	18.7	12.0	9.2	9.7	8.1	9.7
United States Electric Light & Power Shares, Inc., Trust Certificates, Series B	—	—	—	13.0	17.6	13.6	7.1	3.4	5.3
Super-Corporations of America Trust Shares, Series A	—	—	—	10.8	15.9	1.6	1.1	0.6	0.7
Corporate Trust Shares, Accum. Series and Accum. Series (Modified)	—	—	—	—	10.3	14.7	12.1	7.9	8.6
Corporate Trust Shares, Series AA and Series AA (Modified)	—	—	—	—	9.2	12.3	9.1	5.6	5.9
Diversified Trustee Shares, Series D	—	—	—	—	3.5	5.9	9.3	7.1	10.3
Deposited Insurance Shares, Series A	—	—	—	0.1	0.4	1.5	2.4	5.4	10.2
Fixed Trust Shares (original series)	2.6	10.1	5.0	2.9	1.3	0.9	1.2	0.9	1.1

Canadian Investment Companies, 1929

A dash indicates that no figures are available. † indicates cost price. †† indicates market price. * indicates estimated size. ** indicates cost or market, whichever is lower.

	Date Founded	*Size (in millions of dollars)*	*Main Office*
Aldred Investment Corp. (Canada)	1928	3.4 †	Montreal
Alliance Investments, Ltd.	1929	1.2 *	Toronto
Basic Investments of Canada, Ltd.	1929	5.1 *	Toronto
Canadamerica Investment Corp., Ltd.	1929	0.3 *	Montreal
Canadian Bank Stock Trust Shares, Series D (United States Shares Corp.)	1927	—	New York
Canadian Bankstocks, Inc.	1927	0.02 *	New York
Canadian & Foreign Corp., Ltd.	1926	0.1 *	Toronto
Canadian General Investment Trust, Ltd.	1926	11.3 ††	Toronto
Canadian International Investment Trust, Ltd.	1929	4.2 ††	Montreal
Canadian Investors Corp., Ltd.	1929	2.4 ††	Toronto
Canadian Mining Securities Corp., Ltd.	1929	1.8 *	Montreal
Canadian Power & Paper Investments, Ltd.	1920	6.7 †	Montreal
Consolidated Investment Corp. of Canada	1929	30.3 ††	Montreal Toronto
Diversified Investment Trust, Ltd.	1927	0.2 †	

	Date Founded	Size (in millions of dollars)	Main Office
Diversified Investments, Ltd.	1929	0.3 *	St. John's, Newfoundland
Diversified Mining Securities, Ltd.	1929	—	Calgary
Diversified Standard Securities, Ltd.	1927	1.8 †	Montreal
Dominion & Anglo Investment Corp., Ltd.	1928	2.6 †	Toronto
Dominion-Scottish Investments, Ltd.	1929	4.0 ††	Toronto
Economic Investment Trust, Ltd.	1927	3.2 †	Toronto
Foreign Power Securities Corp., Ltd.	1927	14.2 †	Montreal
Founders Investment Trust, Ltd.	1927	0.4 †	Ottawa
Fourth Canadian General Investment Trust, Ltd.	1929	0.8 *	Toronto
Great Britain and Canada Investment Corp.	1929	11.6 ††	Montreal
Hydro-Electric Bond & Share Corp.	1927	12.1 ††	Montreal
Hydro-Electric Securities Corp.	1926	61.6 ††	Montreal
International Holding & Investment Co., Ltd.	1927	28.5 ††	Montreal
Investment Bond & Share Corp.	1927	6.4 ††	Montreal
Investment Foundation, Ltd.	1929	2.3 ††	Montreal
Investors Equity Corp., Ltd.	1929	0.6 *	Toronto
Lombard Bond & Share Corp., Ltd.	1928	0.5 *	Winnipeg
London Canadian Investment Corp.	1928	11.6 ††	Montreal
Mohawk Investment Trust	1929	—	Winnipeg
Montreal London & General Investors	1929/1930	3.6 *	Montreal
Montroy Investment Corp., Ltd.	1928	0.7 *	Montreal
Power and Industrial Securities, Ltd.	1929	1.1 *	Toronto
Power Corporation of Canada, Ltd.	1925	47.0 †	Montreal
Public Utility Investment Co.	1927	0.3 ††	Montreal
Quebec Diversified Securities, Ltd.	1929	—	Montreal
Research Investment Trust, Ltd.	1929/1930	—	Toronto
Royalties and Standardshares, Ltd.	1929	0.2 *	Toronto
Second Canadian General Investments, Ltd.	1927	9.0 ††	Toronto
Second Diversified Standard Securities, Ltd.	1928	2.8 †	Montreal
Second Public Utility Investment Co.	1927	1.1 *	Montreal
Securities Holding Corp., Ltd.	1928	2.2 *	Toronto
Third Canadian General Investment Trust, Ltd.	1928	3.4 ††	Toronto
Third Diversified Standard Securities, Ltd.	1929	0.053 *	Montreal
United Bond & Share Corp. (Quebec)	1927	0.8 **	Montreal
Upper Canada Investment Trust, Ltd.	1928	6.2 *	Toronto

Canadian Investment Companies, 1958

BASE DATE DECEMBER 31

* indicates figures that are approximations.

	Total Net Assets at Market (in millions of Canadian dollars)
Mutual Funds Owned Primarily in Canada	
All-Canadian Dividend Fund & Compound Fund	19
American Growth Fund, Ltd.	3
Canadian Investment Fund, Ltd.	120
Commonwealth International Corp. Ltd.	20
Corporate Investors Limited	9
Grouped Income Shares Limited	7
Investors Growth Fund of Canada, Ltd.	15
Investors Mutual of Canada Ltd.	170
Leverage Fund of Canada Ltd.	2
Mutual Accumulating Fund & Mutual Income Fund	18
North American Fund of Canada Ltd.	7
Savings & Investment Corp. Mutual Fund of Canada Ltd.	1
Timed Investment Fund Limited	2
Fixed Trusts	
Diversified Income Securities	2*
Trans-Canada Shares	12*
Mutual Funds Owned Primarily Abroad	
Beaubran Corporation	15
Canafund Company Ltd.	23
Dominion Equity Investments Ltd.	9

	Total Net Assets at Market (in millions of Canadian dollars)
United States Incorporated Mutual Fund for Investment in Canada, Owned Primarily in the United States	
Canadian Fund, Inc.	45
Nonresident-Owned Companies Owned Primarily in the United States	
Axe-Templeton Growth Fund of Canada, Ltd.	4
Canada General Fund Limited	91
Canadian International Growth Fund Ltd.	6
Investors Group Canadian Fund Ltd.	167
Keystone Fund of Canada Ltd.	15
New York Capital Fund of Canada Ltd.	27
Scudder Fund of Canada Ltd.	60
United Funds Canada Ltd.	23
Closed-End Investment Companies	
Canadian & Foreign Securities Co. Limited	7
Canadian General Investments Limited	45
Canadian International Investment Trust Ltd.	7
Central Canada Investments, Ltd.	13
Consolidated Diversified Standard Securities, Ltd.	1
Debenture & Securities Corp. of Canada	4
Dominion & Anglo Investment Corp. Ltd.	9
Dominion-Scottish Investments Ltd.	8
Economic Investment Trust Limited	11
Foreign Power Securities Corp. Ltd.	4
Great Britain & Canada Investment Corp.	13
Investment Bond & Share Corp.	13
Investment Foundation, Ltd.	5
London Canadian Investment Corporation	11
Montreal London & General Investors, Ltd.	4
Pacific Atlantic Canadian Investment Co. Ltd.	2
Toronto & London Investment Company Ltd.	11
Third Canadian General Investment Trust Ltd.	15
United Corporations Limited	30
Westburne Oil Company Limited	6
Investment-Holding Companies	
Argus Corporation Limited	103
Canadian Power & Paper Securities, Ltd.	8
Magnum Fund, Ltd.	4
Power Corporation of Canada Limited	80
Sogemines, Ltd.	29

200 British Investment Trusts

OCTOBER, 1957

Source: Laing & Cruickshank, *Investment Trust Companies* (London, 1957).

	Assets at Market Value (in millions of pounds) Various Dates, 1956–57
Alliance Trust	30.7
Industrial & General	25.7
Cable & Wireless	23.8
Globe Telegraph	20.8
British Assets	20.7
Investment Trust Corp.	18.4
British Investment	18.3
Atlas Electric and General	17.7
Scottish American Investment	16.6
Mercantile Investment	15.5
Scottish Mortgage & Trust	13.8
Trustees Corp.	13.3
Philip Hill Investment	12.6
U. S. Debenture Corp.	11.7
Second Scottish Investment	11.5
Second Alliance Trust	11.3
British Steamship	11.0
Foreign American & General	10.2
American Investment & General	10.2
Witan	10.0

	Assets at Market Value (in millions of pounds) Various Dates, 1956–57
Lake View Investment	9.5
Investors' Mortgage Security	9.4
Foreign & Colonial	9.2
Edinburgh & Dundee	9.1
Sphere Investment	8.7
Merchants	8.5
London Trust	8.2
Debenture Corp.	8.2
Edinburgh Investment	8.2
Scottish Investment	8.2
Continental & Industrial	8.1
Realisation & Debenture Corp. of Scotland	8.0
Northern American	7.8
Great Northern Investment	7.8
Sterling	7.7
Rhodesia Railways Trust	7.5
River Plate Trust, Loan & Agency	7.5
Second Investors' Mortgage Security	7.5
Second British Assets	7.0
London Border & General	6.8
Second Edinburgh Investment	6.8
Scottish American Mortgage	6.6
Bankers' Investment	6.5
Metropolitan	6.4
Scottish Capital Investment	6.4
Trust Union	6.2
Scottish United Investors	6.2
London & Holyrood	6.1
Scottish Eastern Investment	6.0
Aberdeen & Canadian	5.8
Anglo-American Debenture Corp.	5.8
Scottish Central Investment	5.7
Scottish National	5.7
Lonsdale Investment	5.7
Southern Stockholders Investment	5.6
Rio Claro Investment	5.6
British American & General	5.5
Share & General Investment	5.4
Premier Investment	5.3
Scottish Northern Investment	5.3
Omnium Investment	5.2
Scottish Western	5.1

	Assets at Market Value (in millions of pounds) Various Dates, 1956–57
New Mercantile	5.1
Debenture & Capital Investment	5.1
Standard	5.1
Clyde & Mersey	5.0
Continental Union	5.0
Second Guardian	5.0
Second Scottish Mortgage & Trust	5.0
General Investors & Trustees	4.9
International Investment	4.9
Second Scottish Western	4.9
Third Edinburgh Investment	4.9
American Trust Co.	4.8
Guardian Investment	4.8
London Maritime	4.8
Stockholders Investment	4.8
Trust Co. of London & Scotland	4.7
English & New York	4.7
Friars Investment	4.6
London & Lomond	4.6
U. S. & General Trust	4.6
Second Scottish Eastern	4.6
Government Stocks and Other Securities	4.5
Second Scottish Northern	4.4
Caledonian	4.4
London & Clydesdale	4.3
Consolidated	4.3
London Scottish American	4.3
U. S. & Mercantile Investment	4.3
Home & Foreign	4.3
Clydesdale	4.2
Second Scottish National	4.1
Third Scottish National	4.1
Second Scottish American	4.0
Third Guardian	4.0
British Combined Investors	4.0
London & Montrose	3.9
Monks Investment	3.9
Trans-Oceanic	3.9
Melville	3.9
Second Edinburgh & Dundee	3.9
Third Scottish American	3.9
Second American	3.8

	Assets at Market Value (in millions of pounds) Various Dates, 1956–57
Scottish Stockholders Investment	3.8
Anglo-Celtic	3.8
Abbots Investment	3.8
General Consolidated Investment	3.7
Mid-European Corp.	3.7
Securities Trust of Scotland	3.7
U. S. Trust Company of Scotland	3.6
Camperdown	3.6
Second Mercantile	3.6
Second Industrial	3.6
Cedar Investment	3.6
Broadstone Investment	3.5
Brunner Investment	3.5
City & International	3.5
London & Provincial	3.5
Glasgow Stockholders	3.4
First Scottish American	3.3
Nineteen Twenty-Eight Investment	3.3
East of Scotland	3.3
Second Great Northern	3.3
Charter Trust & Agency	3.2
Anglo-Scottish	3.2
London Electrical & General	3.1
Second Consolidated	3.1
Second Scottish United Investors	3.0
St. Andrew	3.0
General Scottish	3.0
Second Consolidated	3.0
Second British Steamship	3.0
English & Caledonian	3.0
Alliance Investment	3.0
Greenfriar Investment	2.9
Nineteen Twenty-Nine Investment	2.9
Second London Scottish American	2.9
Dominion & General	2.8
Third Scottish Western	2.8
Second Securities Trust of Scotland	2.8
Second Clydesdale	2.7
London Scottish	2.7
Army & Navy Investment	2.7
Winterbottom	2.7
Third Scottish Northern	2.7

	Assets at Market Value (in millions of pounds) Various Dates, 1956–57
Pentland Investment	2.7
Indian & General	2.6
Capital & National	2.6
London & New York	2.5
London & Strathclyde	2.5
London General Investment	2.5
Oregon Mortgage	2.5
English & Scottish Investors	2.4
C. L. R. P. Investment	2.3
Law Debenture Corp.	2.3
River Plate & General	2.3
Romney	2.3
Union Commercial	2.2
Municipal	2.2
Canadian & Foreign	2.2
English & Chicago	2.1
Grange	2.1
Stavely Investment	2.1
Scottish & Dominion	2.1
Second Caledonian	2.1
Third Caledonian	2.0
Perham Investment	2.0
English & International	2.0
Investors Trust Association	1.9
London & Westminster	1.9
Nelson Financial Trust	1.9
New York & General	1.9
Plate Investment	1.9
Aberdeen, Edinburgh & London	1.9
U. S. Investment	1.9
Second Anglo-Celtic	1.8
Charterhouse Investment	1.8
British Isles & General	1.8
Cardinal Investment	1.8
General & Commercial	1.7
Ailsa Investment	1.7
Scottish Allied Investors	1.6
Dundee & London	1.6
Investment Loan & Agency	1.5
Phoenix Investment	1.5
Coldstream Investment	1.5
Scottish International	1.3

	Assets at Market Value (in millions of pounds) Various Dates, 1956–57
International Financial Society	1.3
Compass Investment	1.3
Independent Investment	1.3
London & Overseas	1.1
Debenture Securities	1.1
Government & General	1.1
London & Colonial	1.1
New Investment	1.0
General Funds Investment	1.0
Brewery & Commercial	.9
Imperial Colonial Investment	.7
City & Foreign	.6

Members of the National Association of Investment Companies

APRIL 1, 1959

NOTE. Of 180 companies, 152 are open-end, 24 are closed-end, and 4 associate members. C = Closed-end. O = Open-end. ON = Open-end not offering shares. A = Associate member (Canadian corporation).

		Net Assets at Market Value December 31, 1958 (in millions of dollars)
O	Aberdeen Fund, New York	13.1
C	Adams Express Company, The, New York, N. Y.	97.6
O	Advisers Fund, Inc., Philadelphia, Pa.	1.2
O	Affiliated Fund, Inc., New York, N. Y.	511.0
O	American Business Shares, Inc., New York, N. Y.	27.6
C	American Electric Securities Corporation, New York, N. Y.	1.7
C	American European Securities Company, Jersey City, N. J.	18.6
C	American International Corporation, New York, N. Y.	40.7
O	American Investment & Income Fund, Inc., Washington, D. C.	—

		Net Assets at Market Value December 31, 1958 (in millions of dollars)
O	American Mutual Fund, Inc., Los Angeles, Calif.	103.5
C	American Research and Development Corp., Boston, Mass.	14.8
O	Associated Fund Trust, St. Louis, Mo.	32.7
O	Atomic Development Mutual Fund, Inc., Washington, D. C.	60.9
O	Automation Shares, Inc., Washington, D. C.	0.2
O	Axe-Houghton Fund A, Inc., Tarrytown, N. Y.	48.5
O	Axe-Houghton Fund B, Inc., Tarrytown, N. Y.	110.6
O	Axe-Houghton Stock Fund, Inc., Tarrytown, N. Y.	7.8
O	Axe Science & Electronics Corp., Tarrytown, N. Y.	9.4
O	Blue Ridge Mutual Fund, Inc., New York, N. Y.	32.2
O	Bond Investment Trust of America, The, Boston, Mass.	4.5
O	Boston Fund, Inc., Boston, Mass.	197.1
C	Boston Personal Property Trust, Boston, Mass.	17.7
O	Broad Street Investing Corporation, New York, N. Y.	139.6
O	Bullock Fund, Ltd., New York, N. Y.	46.9
O	California Fund, Inc., Los Angeles, Calif.	3.1
A	Canada General Fund Ltd., Toronto, Ontario	93.6
O	Canadian Fund, Inc., New York, N. Y.	46.2
C	Carriers & General Corporation, New York, N. Y.	19.0
C	Central Securities Corp., New York, N. Y.	26.7
O	Century Shares Trust, Boston, Mass.	61.7
O	Chase Fund of Boston, The, Boston, Mass.	7.3
O	Chemical Fund, Inc., New York, N. Y.	196.4
O	Colonial Fund, Inc., The, Boston, Mass.	66.4
O	Commonwealth Income Fund, San Francisco, Calif.	9.1
O	Commonwealth Investment Company, San Francisco, Calif.	144.8
O	Commonwealth Stock Fund, Inc., San Francisco, Calif.	9.7
O	Composite Bond and Stock Fund, Inc., Spokane, Wash.	6.3
O	Composite Fund, Inc., Spokane, Wash.	9.3
O	Concord Fund, Inc., Boston, Mass.	13.7
C	Consolidated Investment Trust, Boston, Mass.	67.8
O	Continental American Fund, New York, N. Y.	3.8
O	Crown Western Investments, Inc., Dallas, Texas	5.7

		Net Assets at Market Value December 31, 1958 (in millions of dollars)
O	Delaware Fund, Inc., Philadelphia, Pa.	72.1
O	Delaware Income Fund, Inc., Philadelphia, Pa.	3.8
O	De Vegh Investing Company, Inc., New York, N. Y.	6.0
ON	De Vegh Mutual Fund, Inc., New York, N. Y.	18.9
O	Diversified Growth Stock Fund, Inc., Elizabeth, N. J.	36.4
O	Diversified Investment Fund, Inc., Elizabeth, N. J.	92.7
O	Dividend Shares, Inc., New York, N. Y.	267.4
O	Dodge & Cox Fund, San Francisco, Calif.	6.6
C	Dominick Fund, Inc., The, New York, N. Y.	35.8
O	Dow Theory Investment Fund, Inc., Hammond, Ind.	0.9
O	Dreyfus Fund, Inc., New York, N. Y.	36.6
O	Eaton & Howard Balanced Fund, Boston, Mass.	200.0
O	Eaton & Howard Stock Fund, Boston, Mass.	134.6
O	Energy Fund Incorporated, New York, N. Y.	5.8
O	Equity Fund, Inc., Seattle, Wash.	15.0
O	Fidelity Capital Fund, Inc., Boston, Mass.	0.3
O	Fidelity Fund, Inc., Boston, Mass.	357.1
O	Fidelity Trend Fund, Inc., Boston, Mass.	—
O	Fiduciary Mutual Investing Company, Inc., New York, N. Y.	7.5
O	Financial Industrial Fund, Inc., Denver, Colo.	127.1
O	Florida Growth Fund, Inc., Palm Beach, Fla.	1.6
O	Florida Mutual Fund, Inc., The, St. Petersburg, Fla.	3.8
O	Franklin Custodian Funds, Inc., New York, N. Y.	3.6
O	Fundamental Investors, Inc., Elizabeth, N. J.	515.0
O	Gas Industries Fund, Inc., Boston, Mass.	72.6
C	General American Investors Company, Inc., New York, N. Y.	68.4
O	General Capital Corporation, Boston, Mass.	18.3
O	General Investors Trust, Boston, Mass.	6.2
C	General Public Service Corporation, New York, N. Y.	44.8
O	General Securities, Inc., Minneapolis, Minn.	1.3
O	Group Securities, Inc., Jersey City, N. J.	149.0
O	Growth Industry Shares, Inc., Chicago, Ill.	16.2
O	Guardian Mutual Fund, Inc., New York, N. Y.	6.8
O	Hamilton Funds, Inc., Denver, Colo.	102.9

		Net Assets at Market Value December 31, 1958 (in millions of dollars)
O	Income Foundation Fund, Inc., Boston, Mass.	8.5
O	Incorporated Income Fund, Boston, Mass.	105.0
O	Incorporated Investors, Boston, Mass.	307.0
O	Institutional Income Fund, Inc., New York, N. Y.	27.0
O	Institutional Shares, Ltd., New York, N. Y.	83.1
O	Insurance Securities Trust Fund, Oakland, Calif.	356.9
C	Insuranshares Certificates, Inc., Wilmington, Del.	6.9
O	International Investors Incorporated, New York, N. Y.	0.5
O	International Resources Fund, Inc., Los Angeles, Calif.	19.1
O	Investment Company of America, The, Los Angeles, Calif.	136.7
O	Investment Trust of Boston, Boston, Mass.	54.7
O	Investors Mutual, Inc., Minneapolis, Minn.	1,337.0
O	Investors Selective Fund, Inc., Minneapolis, Minn.	25.2
O	Investors Stock Fund, Inc., Minneapolis, Minn.	432.1
O	Investors Variable Payment Fund, Inc., Minneapolis, Minn.	56.3
O	Istel Fund, Inc., New York, N. Y.	16.0
O	Johnston Mutual Fund, Inc., The, New York, N. Y.	7.9
O	Keystone Custodian Funds (10 funds), Boston, Mass.	408.0
A	Keystone Fund of Canada, Ltd., Montreal, Quebec	15.6
O	Knickerbocker Fund, New York, N. Y.	14.3
O	Knickerbocker Growth Fund, Inc., New York, N. Y.	0.9
O	Lazard Fund, Inc., The, New York, N. Y.	135.2
C	Lehman Corporation, The, New York, N. Y.	275.8
O	Lexington Trust Fund, New York, N. Y.	6.5
O	Lexington Venture Fund, Inc., New York, N. Y.	2.7
O	Liberty Income Fund, Inc., Houston, Texas	1.1
ON	Life Insurance Investors, Inc., Chicago, Ill.	15.8
O	Life Insurance Stock Fund, Inc., Dallas, Texas	1.2
O	Loan Star Fund, Dallas, Texas	1.9
O	Loomis-Sayles Mutual Fund, Inc., Boston, Mass.	71.7
C	Madison Fund, Inc., New York, N. Y.	135.8
O	Managed Funds, Inc., St. Louis, Mo.	72.3
O	Massachusetts Investors Growth Stock Fund, Inc., Boston, Mass.	231.3
O	Massachusetts Investors Trust, Boston, Mass.	1,432.8

		Net Assets at Market Value December 31, 1958 (in millions of dollars)
O	Massachusetts Life Fund, Boston, Mass.	49.0
O	Minnesota Fund, Inc., Minneapolis, Minn.	8.1
O	Mutual Income Foundation, Columbus, Ohio	9.9
O	Mutual Investment Company of America, New York, N. Y.	0.4
O	Mutual Investment Fund, Inc., New York, N. Y.	24.3
O	Mutual Securities Fund of Boston, Boston, Mass.	0.3
O	Mutual Shares Corp., White Plains, N. Y.	1.6
O	Mutual Trust, Kansas City, Mo.	10.2
C	National Aviation Corporation, New York, N. Y.	25.4
O	National Investors Corporation, New York, N. Y.	94.0
O	National Securities Series, New York, N. Y.	414.3
O	Nation-Wide Securities Company, New York, N. Y.	31.8
O	Nelson Fund, Inc., New York,, N. Y.	1.2
O	New England Fund, Boston, Mass.	15.6
A	New York Capital Fund of Canada, Ltd., Toronto, Ontario	28.1
C	Niagara Share Corporation, Buffalo, N. Y.	57.2
C	North American Investment Corporation, San Francisco, Calif.	10.0
O	One William Street Fund, Inc., The, New York, N. Y.	276.7
C	Overseas Securities Co., Inc., New York, N. Y.	2.5
C	Penn Investment Company, Philadelphia, Pa.	0.2
C	Petroleum Corporation of America, New York, N. Y.	38.6
O	Philadelphia Fund, Inc., Camden, N. J.	8.6
O	Pine Street Fund, Inc., New York, N. Y.	17.4
O	Pioneer Fund, Inc., Boston, Mass.	30.4
O	Plymouth Fund, Inc., Miami, Fla.	0.2
O	T. Rowe Price Growth Stock Fund, Inc., Baltimore, Md.	16.8
O	Prudential Fund of Boston, Inc., The, Boston, Mass.	1.1
O	Puritan Fund, Inc., Boston, Mass.	59.0
O	George Putnam Fund of Boston, The, Boston, Mass.	180.5
O	Putnam Growth Fund, The, Boston, Mass.	6.8
A	Scudder Fund of Canada, Ltd., Toronto, Ontario	61.8
O	Scudder Special Fund, Inc., New York, N. Y.	—

		Net Assets at Market Value December 31, 1958 (in millions of dollars)
O	Scudder, Stevens & Clark Common Stock Fund, Inc., Boston, Mass.	25.7
O	Scudder, Stevens & Clark Fund, Inc., Boston, Mass.	78.4
O	Securities Fund Incorporated, Englewood, N. J.	2.3
O	Selected American Shares, Inc., Chicago, Ill.	91.1
O	Shareholders' Trust of Boston, Boston, Mass.	27.7
O	Southern Industries Fund, Inc., Savannah, Ga.	1.3
O	Sovereign Investors, Inc., Philadelphia, Pa.	2.9
ON	State Street Investment Corp., Boston, Mass.	199.0
O	Stein Roe & Farnham Balanced Fund, Inc., Chicago, Ill.	34.1
O	Stein Roe & Farnham Stock Fund, Inc., Chicago, Ill.	6.1
O	Sterling Investment Fund, Inc., Charlotte, N. C.	4.0
O	Supervised Shares, Inc., Des Moines, Iowa	3.5
O	Television-Electronics Fund, Inc., Chicago, Ill.	236.4
O	Texas Fund, Inc., Houston, Texas	37.9
O	Townsend U. S. & International Growth Fund, Inc., Short Hills, N. J.	2.6
C	Tri-Continental Corporation, New York, N. Y.	392.1
O	Twentieth Century Investors, Inc., Kansas City, Mo.	0.4
C	United Corporation, The, New Rochelle, N. Y.	113.8
O	United Funds, Inc., Kansas City, Mo.	559.7
C	United States & Foreign Securities Corp., Morristown, N. J.	123.2
O	Value Line Fund, Inc., The, New York, N. Y.	9.6
O	Value Line Income Fund, Inc., The, New York, N. Y.	88.0
O	Value Line Special Situations Fund, Inc., The, New York, N. Y.	8.8
O	Wall Street Investing Corporation, New York, N. Y.	8.7
O	Washington Mutual Investors Fund, Inc., Washington, D. C.	15.6
O	Wellington Equity Fund, Inc., Philadelphia, Pa.	36.7
O	Wellington Fund, Inc., Philadelphia, Pa.	858.0
O	Whitehall Fund, Inc., New York, N. Y.	10.4
O	Winfield Growth Industries Fund, Inc., San Francisco, Calif.	1.0

Companies Registered under The Investment Company Act of 1940

DECEMBER 31, 1958

NOTE. * indicates that the company has filed an application, pursuant to Section 8(f) of the Act, requesting an order declaring that it has ceased to be an investment company. M-C-D = Management–closed-end–diversified. M-C-N = Management–closed-end–non-diversified. M-O-D = Management–open-end–diversified. M-O-N = Management–open-end–non-diversified. U = Unit. FA = Face-Amount.

	Classifications
Abacus Fund	M-C-N
Aberdeen Fund	M-O-D
Aberdeen Investor Programs	U
Accumulated Shares, Ltd., Inc.	M-O-D
Adams Express Co.	M-C-D
Advisers Fund, Inc.	M-O-D
Affiliated Fund, Inc.	M-O-D
Alaska Fund, Inc.	M-O-D
All States Management Co., Plan to Accumulate Shares of Lone Star Fund, Inc., Industrial Growth Fund Series	U
Alleghany Corp.	M-C-N
Leon B. Allen Fund, Inc.	M-O-D
Allied Resources Fund, Inc.	M-O-N

	Classifications
American Automation Development Fund, Inc.	M-O-D
American Business Shares, Inc.	M-O-D
American Electric Securities Corp.	M-C-N
American Enterprise Fund Inc.	M-O-N
American European Securities Co.	M-C-D
American Financial Fund, Inc.	M-O-D
American Growth Fund Inc.	M-C-D
American Income Fund, Inc.	M-O-N
American International Corp.	M-C-D
American Investment and Income Fund, Inc.	M-O-D
American Investment and Income Fund Investment Plans	U
American Investment Trust	U
American Investors Fund, Inc.	M-O-D
American Mutual Fund, Inc.	M-O-D
American Research & Development Corp.	M-C-N
American-South African Investment Co., Ltd.	M-C-D
Amoskeag Co.	M-C-N
Arcady Corporation	M-C-N
Arisaig Corp.	M-C-D
Arkansas Fund	U
Armfield Plan	U
Associated Fund Trust	M-O-D
* Associated General Utilities Co.	M-C-N
Associated Motion Pictures Industries, Inc.	M-C-N
Atlas Corp.	M-C-N
Atomic Development Mutual Fund, Inc.	M-O-N
Automation Fund, Inc.	M-O-D
Automation Investments Co.	M-C-N
Automation Shares, Inc.	M-O-D
Axe Houghton Fund A, Inc.	M-O-D
Axe Houghton Fund B, Inc.	M-O-D
Axe Houghton Stock Fund, Inc.	M-O-D
Axe Science & Electronics Corp.	M-O-D
Axe-Templeton Growth Fund of Canada, Ltd.	M-O-N
Baldwin Securities Corp. (Pa.)	M-C-N
Baldwin Securities Corp. (Del.)	M-C-D
Bank Fiduciary Fund	M-O-D
Bankers Southern Inc.	M-C-N
Bareco Oil Co.	M-C-N
Betco Corp.	FA
Blue Ridge Mutual Fund, Inc.	M-O-D
Bond Fund of Boston, Inc.	M-O-D
Bond Investment Trust of America	M-O-D
Bonds, Inc.	M-O-N
Bondstock Corp.	M-O-D

	Classifications
Boston Fund, Inc.	M-O-D
Boston Personal Property Trust	M-C-D
Broad Street Investing Corp.	M-O-D
Brown Fund of Hawaii, Ltd.	M-O-D
Bullock Fund, Ltd.	M-O-D
California Fund, Inc.	M-O-D
California Pacific Trading Corp.	M-C-N
Canada General Fund Limited	M-O-D
Canadian Fund, Inc.	M-O-D
Canadian International Growth Fund, Ltd.	M-O-D
Canadian National Commodities Corp.	M-C-D
Capital Securities Fund, Inc.	M-O-D
Cardinal Investors Fund	M-C-D
Carriers & General Corp.	M-C-D
Central Illinois Securities Corp.	M-C-N
Central States Electric Corp.	M-C-N
Century Investors, Inc.	M-C-N
Century Shares Trust	M-O-D
Champion Industries, Inc.	M-C-N
Chase Fund of Boston	M-O-D
Chemical Fund, Inc.	M-O-D
China Industries, Inc.	M-C-N
Christiana Securities Co.	M-C-N
Civil and Military Investors Mutual Fund, Inc.	M-O-D
Coca Cola International Corp.	M-O-N
Colonial Equities	M-O-D
Colonial Fund, Inc.	M-O-D
Columbia Financial Development Co., Inc.	U
Combined Metals, Inc.	M-C-N
Commonwealth Fund, Plans A & B	M-O-D
Commonwealth Fund, Plans C & D	M-O-D
Commonwealth Income Fund, Inc.	M-O-D
Commonwealth Investment Co.	M-O-D
Commonwealth Stock Fund, Inc.	M-O-D
Composite Bond and Stock Fund, Inc.	M-O-D
Composite Fund, Inc.	M-O-D
Concord Fund, Inc.	M-O-D
Connecticut Fiduciaries Fund Inc.	M-O-D
Consolidated Investment Trust	M-C-D
Consumers Investment Fund, Inc.	M-O-D
Continental American Fund, Inc.	M-O-D
Corporate Leaders Trust Fund, Series A & B	U
Corporate Trust Shares	U
Corporate Trust Shares Accumulative Series	U
Corporate Trust Shares Accumulative Series Modified	U

	Classifications
Corporate Trust Shares, Series AA	U
Corporate Trust Shares, Series AA Modified	U
Cosmopolitan Hotel Co. of Dallas, Inc.	M-C-N
Counselors Investment Fund, Inc.	M-O-D
Crown Western Investments, Inc.	M-O-D
D & Z Employees' Trust Fund	M-O-N
Delaware Fund, Inc.	M-O-D
Delaware Income Fund, Inc.	M-O-D
Delaware Realty and Investment Co.	M-C-N
Detroit and Cleveland Navigation Co.	M-C-N
De Vegh Income Fund, Inc.	M-O-D
De Vegh Mutual Fund, Inc.	M-O-N
Development Securities Corporation	M-C-D
Diversified Growth Stock Fund, Inc.	M-O-D
Diversified Investment Fund, Inc.	M-O-D
Diversified Trustee Shares, Series C	U
Diversified Trustee Shares, Series E	U
Dividend Shares, Inc.	M-O-D
Dodge & Cox Fund	M-O-D
Dominion Plan	U
Dominion Plan, Series TS	U
Dow Theory Investment Fund, Inc.	M-O-D
Dreyfus Fund, Inc.	M-O-D
Dreyfus Investment Program	U
Eastern States Corp.	M-C-N
Eaton & Howard Balanced Fund	M-O-D
Eaton & Howard Stock Fund	M-O-D
Electronics Investment Corp.	M-O-D
Electronics Investment Program	U
Elfun Trusts	M-O-D
Energy Fund, Inc.	M-O-N
Equity Corp.	M-C-N
Equity Fund, Inc.	M-O-D
Equity Trust Shares in America	U
Equity Underwriters, Inc.	FA
Executive Investment Trusts	M-O-D
F.I.F. Plan Corp., Series XD Periodic Payment and Fully Paid Plans	U
Federal United Corp.	M-C-D
Federated Fund	M-O-D
Fidelity Capital Fund, Inc.	M-O-D
Fidelity Fund, Inc.	M-O-D
Fidelity Trend Fund, Inc.	M-O-D

	Classifications
Fiduciary Mutual Investing Co., Inc.	M-O-D
Filbert Corp.	M-C-N
Financial Fund, Inc.	M-O-D
Financial Independence Founders, Series D, Periodic Payment and Fully Paid Plans	U
Financial Industrial Fund	U
Financial Industrial Fund, Inc.	M-O-D
First Guardian Securities Corp.	M-C-N
First Investors Corp., Plans for the Accumulation of Shares of Wellington Fund Inc.	U
First Investors Corp., Plans for the Accumulation of Shares of Mutual Investment Fund Inc.	U
First Investors Corp., Plans for the Accumulation of Shares of Fundamental Investors, Inc.	U
First National Mutual Fund, Inc.	M-O-D
First Securities Corp. of Syracuse	M-C-N
First Southern Investment Trust for the Accumulation of Shares of Nucleonics, Chemistry & Electronics Shares Inc.	U
First Springfield Corporation	M-C-N
Fixed Trust Oil Shares	U
Florida Growth Fund, Inc.	M-O-D
Florida Mutual Fund, Inc.	M-O-D
Foundation Investment Co.	M-C-D
* Foundation Plan Trust Agreement dated Jan. 1, 1933	U
* Foundation Plan Trust Agreement, N. Y., dated May 1, 1935	U
* Foundation Trust Shares, Series A	U
Founders Mutual Fund	U
Benjamin Franklin Foundation Certificates	U
Franklin Custodian Funds, Inc.	M-O-D
Fundamental Investors, Inc.	M-O-D
Fundamental Trust Shares, Series A	U
Fundamental Trust Shares, Series B	U
Fundamerican Trusteed Certificates, Series 2, Plans A, B, and C	U
Future Planning Corp.	U
Future Planning Corp., Plans for the Accumulation of Shares of Knickerbocker Fund	U
G. M. Shares, Inc.	M-O-N
Gas Industries Fund, Inc.	M-O-D
Gauley Mountain Co.	M-C-N
General American Investors Co., Inc.	M-C-D
General Capital Corp.	M-O-D
General Industrial Enterprises Inc.	M-C-N
General Investors Trust	M-O-D
General Public Service Corp.	M-C-D

	Classifications
General Securities, Inc.	M-O-D
Gibco, Inc.	M-C-N
* Graham Newman Corp.	M-O-N
Graham-Paige Corp.	M-C-N
* Great American Life Underwriters, Inc.	FA
Griesedieck Company	M-C-D
Group Securities, Inc.	M-O-D
Growth Industry Shares, Inc. (Md.)	M-O-D
Guardian Mutual Fund, Inc.	M-O-D
HBNS Corporation	M-C-N
Hamilton Fund	U
Hamilton Funds, Inc.	M-O-D
Hamilton Trust Shares	U
Haydock Fund, Inc.	M-O-D
Heritage Fund, Inc.	M-O-N
* Home & Foreign Securities Corp.	M-C-N
* Howe Plan Fund, Inc.	M-O-D
Imperial Growth Fund Inc.	M-O-D
Imperial Income Fund Inc.	M-O-D
Income Foundation Fund Agreements & Certificates of Trust Plans A, B, C, D, E	U
Income Foundation Fund, Inc.	M-O-D
Income Foundation Fund Investment Plans	U
Income Fund of America, Inc.	M-O-D
Income Fund of America Unit Plans	U
Income Fund of Boston, Inc.	M-O-D
Incorporated Income Fund	M-O-D
Incorporated Investors	M-O-D
Individual Assured Estates 1933	U
Inland Investors, Inc.	M-C-D
Institutional Income Fund, Inc.	M-O-D
Institutional Investors Mutual Fund, Inc.	M-O-D
Institutional Shares, Ltd.	M-O-D
Instoria, Inc.	M-C-N
Insurance Investors Fund, Inc.	M-O-D
Insurance Securities, Inc. Trust Fund	M-O-D
Insuranshares Certificates, Inc.	M-C-N
Insurors Mutual Fund, Inc.	M-O-D
Inter-Canadian Corp.	M-C-N
* Intercontinental Holdings, Ltd.	M-C-N
International Holdings Corp.	M-C-D
International Investors, Inc.	M-O-D
International Power Securities Corp.	M-C-N
International Resources Fund, Inc.	M-O-D

	Classifications
Investment Company of America	M-O-D
Investment Trust of Boston	M-O-D
Investors Diversified Services, Inc.	FA
Investors Group Canadian Fund Ltd.	M-O-D
Investors Mutual, Inc.	M-O-D
Investors Planning Corp., Plans for the Accumulation of Shares of Axe-Houghton Fund B, Inc.	U
Investors Planning Corp. of America	U
Investors Selective Fund, Inc.	M-O-D
Investors Stock Fund, Inc.	M-O-D
Investors Syndicate of America, Inc.	FA
Investors Trust Co.	M-C-N
Investors Variable Payment Fund, Inc.	M-O-D
Israel Development Corp.	M-C-N
Israel Enterprises Inc.	M-C-N
Israel Investors Corp.	M-C-N
Israel Investors Inc.	M-C-N
Istel Fund, Inc.	M-O-D
Jefferson Custodian Fund, Inc.	M-O-D
Johnston Mutual Fund, Inc.	M-O-D
Kerr Income Fund, Inc.	M-O-D
Keystone Custodian Fund, Series B1	M-O-D
Keystone Custodian Fund, Series B2	M-O-D
Keystone Custodian Fund, Series B3	M-O-D
Keystone Custodian Fund, Series B4	M-O-D
Keystone Custodian Fund, Series K1	M-O-D
Keystone Custodian Fund, Series K2	M-O-D
Keystone Custodian Fund, Series S1	M-O-D
Keystone Custodian Fund, Series S2	M-O-D
Keystone Custodian Fund, Series S3	M-O-D
Keystone Custodian Fund, Series S4	M-O-D
Keystone Fund of Canada, Ltd.	M-O-D
Kirk Industries, Inc.	M-C-N
Knickerbocker Fund	M-O-D
Knickerbocker Growth Fund Inc.	M-O-D
Lazard Fund Inc.	M-O-D
Lehman Corp.	M-C-D
Lennon Company Aetna Life Stock Investment Programs	U
Lennon Company Connecticut General Stock Investment Programs	U
Lennon Company Travelers Stock Investment Programs	U
Lexington Accumulation Plans	U
Lexington Foundation Trust Certificates	U

	Classifications
Lexington Funds, Inc.	M-O-D
Lexington Trust Fund	M-O-D
Lexington Trust Fund Plans	U
Liberty Income Fund, Inc.	M-O-D
Liberty Income Fund, Inc., Monthly Purchase Plan	U
Life Insurance Fund, Inc.	M-O-D
Life Insurance Investors, Inc.	M-O-D
Life Insurance Stock Fund, Inc.	M-O-D
Lone Star Fund, Inc.	M-O-D
Lone Star Fund Unit Plan	U
* Long Island Securities Corp.	M-C-N
Loomis Sayles Mutual Fund, Inc.	M-O-D
Loomis Sayles Second Fund, Inc.	M-O-D
Louisville Investment Co.	M-C-N
Mairs and Power Fund Inc.	M-O-D
Managed Funds, Inc.	M-O-D
Managed Funds Personal Investment Plan	U
Managed Funds Personal Investment Plan (Electric Shares)	U
Managed Funds Personal Investment Plan (Metal Shares)	U
Managed Funds Personal Investment Plan (Paper Shares)	U
Managed Funds Personal Investment Plan (Petroleum Shares)	U
Managed Funds Personal Investment Plan (Special Investment Shares)	U
Managed Funds Personal Investment Plan (Transport Shares)	U
Manhattan Bond Fund, Inc.	M-O-D
Horace Mann Fund, Inc.	M-O-D
Massachusetts Investors Growth Stock Fund, Inc.	M-O-D
Massachusetts Investors Trust	M-O-D
Massachusetts Life Fund	M-O-D
* Master Fund, Inc.	M-C-D
McPhail Candy Corp.	M-C-N
Midwest Technical Development Corp.	M-C-N
Minnesota Fund, Inc.	M-O-D
Missiles-Jets & Automation Fund, Inc.	M-O-D
Missouri Kansas Pipeline Co.	M-C-N
Motion Picture Investors Inc.	M-C-N
Moss Fund Inc., Preston	M-O-N
Multnomah Canadian Fund, Ltd.	M-O-N
Municipal Investment Trust Fund, Series A	U
Municipal Tax Free Income Fund Inc.	M-O-D
Mutual Income Foundation	M-O-D
Mutual Income Foundation, Monthly Purchase Plan	U
Mutual Investment Company of America	M-O-D

	Classifications
Mutual Investment Fund, Inc.	M-O-D
Mutual Investment Fund of Connecticut, Inc.	M-O-D
Mutual Investment Trust for Profit Sharing, Retirement Plans, Inc.	M-O-D
Mutual Investors Company	M-C-D
Mutual Securities Fund of Boston	M-O-D
Mutual Shares Corp.	M-O-D
Mutual Trust	M-O-D
Nassau Fund	M-O-D
Nation-Wide Securities Co., Inc.	M-O-D
National Aviation Corp.	M-C-N
National Investors Corp. of Maryland	M-O-D
National Plan, Inc.	U
National Reserve Association, Inc.	FA
National Securities Series	M-O-D
National Shares Corp.	M-C-D
National Union Investment Co. of Baltimore	M-C-N
Nelson Fund Inc.	M-O-N
New England Fund	M-O-D
New Jersey Investing Fund Inc.	M-O-D
New York Bank Trust Shares	U
New York Capital Fund of Canada, Ltd.	M-O-N
New York Dock Company	M-C-N
Niagara Share Corp.	M-C-N
Nineteen Corporation	M-C-N
North American Bond Trust	U
North American Investment Corp.	M-C-D
North American Planning Corp., Plans for the Accumulation of Shares of Boston Fund, Inc.	U
North American Trust Shares 1955	U
North American Trust Shares 1956	U
North American Trust Shares 1958	U
North River Securities Co., Inc.	M-C-N
Northeast Investors Trust	M-O-D
Nucleonics Chemistry & Electronics Shares, Inc.	M-O-D
* Oils & Industries, Inc.	M-C-N
Old Dominion Growth Stock Fund Inc.	M-O-D
Old Dominion Investors' Trust, Inc.	M-O-D
One William Street Fund Inc.	M-O-D
Oppenheimer Fund Inc.	M-O-N
Over-the-Counter Securities Fund, Inc.	M-O-D
Overland Corp.	M-C-N
Overseas Securities Co., Inc.	M-C-D

	Classifications
Pacific Investment Fund, Ltd.	M-O-D
Pallas Corp.	M-C-N
Palmer Co.	M-C-N
Paramount Mutual Fund Inc.	M-O-D
Peckham Plan Fund Inc.	M-O-D
Penn Investment Co.	M-C-D
Penn Square Mutual Fund	M-O-D
Pennroad Corp.	M-C-N
Peoples Investment Program	U
Peoples Securities Corp.	M-O-D
Periodic Purchase Plans for Accumulation of Shares of Beneficial Interest of Mutual Trust	U
Petroleum Corp. of America	M-C-N
Philadelphia Fund, Inc.	M-O-D
Pine Street Fund, Inc.	M-O-D
Pioneer Fund, Inc.	M-O-D
Pioneer National Corp.	FA
Plans for the Accumulation of Shares of Franklin Custodian Funds Inc.	U
Plans for the Accumulation of Shares of Nucleonics Chemistry & Electronics Shares, Inc.	U
Plymouth Fund, Inc.	M-O-D
Portsmouth Steel Corp.	M-C-N
Potomac Plan	U
Potosi Investment Co.	M-C-N
T. Rowe Price Growth Stock Fund, Inc.	M-O-D
Professional Research Fund Inc.	M-O-D
Protected Investors of America Trust 1934	U
Protected Investors of America Trust 1937	U
Providentia, Ltd.	M-C-N
Prudential Fund of Boston, Inc.	M-O-D
Prudential Investment Corp. of South Carolina	M-C-D
Puritan Fund, Inc. (Mass.)	M-O-D
George Putnam Fund of Boston	M-O-D
Putnam Growth Fund	M-O-D
Quaker City Mutual Fund, Inc.	M-O-D
Quarterly Distribution Shares, Inc.	M-O-D
Quinby Plan for Accumulation of Common Stock of American Telephone and Telegraph Co.	U
Quinby Plan for Accumulation of Common Stock of E. I. duPont de Nemours & Co.	U
Quinby Plan for Accumulation of Common Stock of Eastman Kodak Co.	U
Quinby Plan for Accumulation of Common Stock of General Electric Co.	U

	Classifications
Quinby Plan for Accumulation of Common Stock of General Motors Corp.	U
Quinby Plan for Accumulation of Common Stock of Standard Oil Co. N. J.	U
* Railway and Utilities Investing Corp.	M-C-N
Real Silk Hosiery Mills, Inc. (Ill.)	M-C-N
Regency Fund, Inc.	M-O-D
Research Investing Corp.	M-C-N
Resource Fund, Inc.	M-O-D
Rittenhouse Fund	M-O-D
St. Louis Midwest Co.	M-C-N
Savings Bank Investment Fund	M-O-D
Science & Nuclear Fund, Inc. (Del.)	M-O-D
Scripps Howard Investment Co.	M-C-N
Scudder Fund of Canada, Ltd.	M-O-D
Scudder Special Fund, Inc.	M-O-D
Scudder, Stevens & Clark Common Stock Fund, Inc.	M-O-D
Scudder, Stevens & Clark Fund, Inc.	M-O-D
Second Investors Corp.	M-C-D
Securities Corporation General	M-C-N
Security Credit Corp.	FA
Security Trust Associates	M-O-D
Selected American Shares, Inc.	M-O-D
Shares in America Inc.	M-O-D
Shareholders Trust of Boston	M-O-D
Edson B. Smith Fund	M-O-D
Southern Indemnity Underwriters, Inc.	FA
Southern Industries Fund, Inc.	M-O-D
Southwestern Investors, Inc.	M-O-D
Sovereign Investors, Inc.	M-O-D
Special Investments and Securities, Inc.	M-C-N
Standard Holding Corp.	M-C-N
Standard Shares, Inc.	M-C-N
Standard System Investment Corp.	FA
State Bond & Mortgage Co.	FA
State Street Investment Corp.	M-O-D
Steadman Investment Fund, Inc.	M-O-N
Stein Roe & Farnham Fund, Inc.	M-O-D
Stein Roe & Farnham Stock Fund Inc.	M-O-D
Sterling Investment Fund, Inc.	M-O-D
Sunrise Fund, Inc.	M-O-D
* Super Corporations of America, Series AA	U
Supervised Shares, Inc.	M-O-D

	Classifications
Tax Exempt Bond Fund, Inc.	M-C-D
Tax Free Income Fund, Inc.	M-C-D
Teachers Association Mutual Fund of California, Inc.	M-O-D
Television Electronics Fund, Inc.	M-O-D
Templeton & Liddell Fund, Inc.	M-O-D
Texas Arkansas Fund	U
Texas Fund, Inc.	M-O-D
Timetrust Certificates	U
Tonopah Mining Co. of Nevada	M-C-N
Townsend U. S. & International Growth Fund, Inc.	M-C-N
Tri-Continental Corp.	M-C-D
Tri-Continental Financial Corp.	M-C-N
Trust Agreements Equitable Trust Co. Trustee	U
Trusteed Income Estates Certificates, Original Series Sovereign Investors	U
Trusteed Income Estates Certificates, Original Series Trusteed American Bank Shares, Series B	U
Trusteed Income Estates Certificates, Original Series Trusteed Industry Shares	U
Trusteed Income Estates Certificates, Series C	U
Trusteed New York Bank Shares	U
Twentieth Century Investors Inc.	M-O-D
Twentieth Century Periodic Investment Plan	U
Unified Funds, Inc.	FA
Union Pacific Investment Corp.	M-O-N
United Corp.	M-C-N
United Fund Accumulative Series T A	M-O-D
United Fund Income Series T I	M-O-D
United Funds Canada, Ltd.	M-O-D
United Funds, Inc.	M-O-D
United Periodic Investment Plans	U
United Power and Transportation Co.	M-C-N
* United States Electric Light & Power Shares, Inc., Trust Certificates, Series A	U
United States & Foreign Securities Corp.	M-C-D
U. S. Railroad Securities Fund, Inc.	M-C-N
* Universal Programs Inc., Programs for the Accumulation of Shares of Philadelphia Fund Inc.	U
Value Line Fund, Inc.	M-O-D
Value Line Income Fund, Inc.	M-O-D
Value Line Special Situations Fund, Inc.	M-O-D
Vanderbilt Mutual Fund, Inc.	M-O-D
Variable Investment Plan for the Accumulation of Shares of Institutional Growth Fund	U
Venture Securities Fund, Inc.	M-O-N

	Classifications
Wade Fund, Inc.	M-O-N
Wall Street Investing Corp.	M-O-D
Wall Street Investment Programs	U
* Wasatch Corp.	M-C-N
Washington Investors Plans Inc.	U
Washington Mutual Investors Fund, Inc.	M-O-D
Webster Investors, Inc.	M-C-N
Wellington Equity Fund Inc.	M-O-D
Wellington Fund, Inc.	M-O-D
Wellington Plan Certificates	U
Western Industrial Shares Inc.	M-C-D
Western Investors Fund, Inc., Oregon	U
Western Investors Fund, Inc., Washington	U
Whitehall Fund, Inc.	M-O-D
Whitney Apollo Corp.	M-C-N
Winfield Growth Industries Fund Inc.	M-O-N
Wisconsin Fund, Inc.	M-O-D
* Woman's Income Fund, Inc.	M-O-D
Worth Fund Inc.	M-C-N

Closed-End Investment Company Securities

COMMON STOCKS

Company	*Where Traded*	*Market Price 12/31/58*	*Net Asset Value 12/31/58*	*Discount (-) or Premium (+)*
Abacus Fund	NYSE	40	39.22	+ 1.99
Adams Express Company	NYSE	29⅜	30.74	- 4.44
American Electric Securities Corp.	O-C	7	13.00	-46.15
American European Securities Co.	NYSE	40	34.77	+15.04
American International Corp.	NYSE	17	18.10	- 6.08
American Research	O-C	37½	50.16	-25.24
Atlas Corp.	NYSE	7½	7.79	- 3.72
Boston Personal Property Trust	Bos. SE	54	67.71	-20.25
Carriers & General Corp.	NYSE	29 11/16	30.53	- 2.76
Central Securities Corp.	ASE	15¼	20.86	-26.89
Consd. Inv. Trust	O-C	18½	22.14	-16.44
Equity Corp.	ASE	3½	6.75	-48.15
General American Investors Co., Inc.	NYSE	33¾	35.16	- 4.01
General Public Service Corp.	NYSE	5⅜	6.03	-10.86
Insuranshares	NYSE	28½	39.21	-27.31
Lehman Corporation, The	NYSE	30⅝	27.67	+11.07
Madison Fund	NYSE	18⅛	21.11	-14.14
National Aviation Corporation	NYSE	25⅞	29.01	-10.81
The Dominick Fund, Inc.	NYSE	17⅝	22.10	-20.25

Niagara Share	NYSE	26⅝	31.75	– 16.14
North American Investment Corp.	Pac. SE	24	29.40	– 18.37
Overseas Securities Co., Inc.	ASE	16⅜	13.71	+ 19.44
Petroleum Corp.	NYSE	18½	19.61	– 5.66
Tri-Continental Corporation	NYSE	40⅜	48.38	– 16.55
United Corp.	NYSE	8½	8.09	+ 5.07
United States & Foreign Securities Corp.	NYSE	32⅜	37.21	– 12.99

PREFERRED STOCKS

* last sale or mean between bid and asked price.
** preceded by prior obligations—bank loans, funded debt, or prior preferred stock.

	*Market Price 12/31/58**	*Yield*	*Approx. Asset Coverage*	*Amount to which Entitled in Liquidation*	*Call Price*
**American Electric Securities Corp. $0.30 Cum. Part. (O-C)	5½	5.5%	$ 8.00	$ 5.00	Non-call
**Atlas Corp. 5% Cum. (NYSE)	16⅜	6.1	128.07	20.00	$ 21.50
**Central Securities Corp. Cum. Conv. $1.50 (ASE)	26½	5.7	132.57	27.50	32.50
**Equity Corp. Cum. Conv. $2.00 (ASE)	40¾	4.9	391.81	50.00	52.50
General American Investors $4.50 Cum. (NYSE)	95½	4.7	1,332.27	100.00	105.00
**North American Investment Corp. 6% Cum. (Pac. SE)	24	6.3	77.30	25.00	Non-call
**North American Investment Corp. 5½% Cum. (Pac. SE)	23½	5.9	77.30	25.00	26.25
**Tri-Continental Corp. $2.70 Cum. (NYSE)	54⅜	5.0	461.30	50.00	55.00

WARRANT ISSUE (Value based on market value of common stock.)

	Where Traded	Market Price 12/31/58	Value if Exercised 12/31/58
Atlas Corp.	ASE	4	$ 1.25
Tri-Continental Corp.	ASE	29	28.72
United States & Foreign Securities Corp.	O-C	⅛ (bid price)	0

BONDS

* not available—market inactive or bonds privately held.

	Market Price 12/31/58	Yield to Maturity
Capital Administration Co. Ltd., 3%, 1960; assumed by Tri-Continental Corp.	*	
Carriers & General Corp., 3%, 1961	98	3.06
General Shareholdings Corp., 3%, 1960; assumed by Tri-Continental Corp.	95	3.16
Selected Industries, Inc., 2⅞%, 1961; assumed by Tri-Continental Corp.	90	3.19
Tri-Continental Corp., 2⅞%, 1961	97	2.96
Wasatch Corp., 6%, 1963; assumed by Atlas Corp.	101	5.94

Facsimile Excerpts from Annual Reports of Four Investment Companies

The Alliance Trust Company Limited

REPORT OF THE DIRECTORS AND STATEMENT OF ACCOUNTS FOR THE YEAR ENDED 31ST JANUARY, 1959

DIRECTORS

ALAN L. BROWN, (*Chairman and Joint Manager*)

T. J. CARLYLE GIFFORD

J. MURRAY PRAIN

SIR GEORGE CUNNINGHAM

CHARLES N. THOMSON

DAVID F. McCURRACH (*Joint Manager*)

The Alliance Trust Company Limited is the largest investment trust company in the United Kingdom and, typical of the great majority of British trusts, does not publish its holdings of securities except in briefly summarized form.

REVENU

For Year ende

1958				
		EXPENSES OF MANAGEMENT AT HEAD OFFICE		
£35,318		Salaries, Pensions, Auditor's Fees, and Miscellaneous Expenses		£37,3
		Directors' Remuneration		
18,000		For services as Directors	£18,000	
12,438		For other services in connection with Management	12,466	
				30,4
£65,756				£67,8
10,304		**FOREIGN EXPENSES AND TAXES**		£11,4
		UNITED KINGDOM TAXES IN RESPECT OF THE YEAR'S REVENUE		
	£712,105	Income Tax	£738,156	
	137,890	Profits Tax	88,592	
	£849,995		£826,748	
	306,139	Less: Estimated Double Taxation Relief	349,777	
543,856				£476,9
3,252		**EXPENSES OF DEBENTURES**		1,7
		INTEREST ON BORROWED MONEY		
229,238		Debenture Interest (gross)	£241,198	
36,404		Interest on Bank Advances and Short Loans (gross)	39,114	
				280,3
876,183		**AMOUNT CARRIED DOWN**		961,4
£1,764,993				£1,799,7

APPROPRIATIO

1958		
£269,459	Interim Dividends paid 15th October, 1958 (less Tax)	£269,4
390,210	Proposed further Dividends (less Tax)	462,6
205,000	Transferred to General Reserve Fund	200,0
152,271	Balance carried forward	181,5
£1,016,940		£1,113,6

CCOUNT

lst January, 1959

1958		
	REVENUE FOR THE YEAR (before deduction of United Kingdom and Foreign Taxes)	
1,656,109	From Investments - - - - - - - - - - -	£1,717,830
6,334	„ Mortgages and Real Estate - - - - - - -	6,538
50,223	„ Mineral Royalties - - - - - - - -	21,924
	TAX RECOVERED in respect of previous years (including repayments under	
51,988	Double Taxation Agreements) - - - - - - - - -	53,127
339	**TRANSFER FEES** - - - - - - - - - - -	324
1,764,993		£1,799,743

CCOUNT

1958		
£876,183	Amount brought down - - - - - - - - - - -	£961,424
140,757	Balance brought forward from previous year - - - - - -	152,271
1,016,940		£1,113,695

BALANCE SHEET as

Liabilities

1958			
	CAPITAL		
£6,400,000	Authorised		£6,400,000
	Issued—		
£700,000	Preference Stock, 4¼% Cumulative		£700,000
650,000	Preference Stock, 4% Cumulative		650,000
750,000	Preference Stock, 5% Cumulative		750,000
100,000	Preference Stock 4% "A" Cumulative		100,000
4,200,000	Ordinary Stock		4,200,000
£6,400,000			£6,400,000
	REVENUE RESERVE		
	General Reserve Fund, at 31st January, 1958	£500,000	
	Add: Transferred from Revenue Appropriation Account	200,000	
500,000			700,000
152,271	**REVENUE APPROPRIATION ACCOUNT**		181,576
£7,052,271			£7,281,576
	DEBENTURE DEBT		
1,648,600	4½% Debenture Stock, 1956 or after	£1,648,600	
500,000	4½% Debenture Stock, 1965	500,000	
500,000	5% Debenture Stock 1971/76	500,000	
675,000	3½% Debenture Stock, 1975/85	675,000	
		£3,323,600	
2,580,935	Terminable Debentures and Short Loans	2,520,540	
			5,844,140
204,528	**SECURED LOANS AND BANK ADVANCES**		177,976
	CURRENT LIABILITIES		
220,215	Purchases for subsequent settlement	£360,970	
29,837	Provision for Taxation	21,143	
44,746	Sundry Creditors and Interest Accrued	35,383	
390,210	Proposed Final Dividends	462,660	
			880,156
	PROVISIONS		
172,327	Provision for Future Taxation	£123,201	
12,036	Provision for Staff Pensions	12,036	
			135,237
£14,030,705			£14,319,085

at 31st January, 1959

Assets

1958			
	FIXED ASSETS		
	Investments, at or under cost—		
£7,120,551	Quoted on a recognised Stock Exchange in Great Britain		£6,887,621
5,334,753	Quoted on Stock Exchanges of repute outside Great Britain		6,175,493
24,512	Unquoted		17,503
£12,479,816			£13,080,617
	Note— Valuation of Investments—		
	£28,710,155 Quoted, at Market Value	£38,320,363	
	39,882 Unquoted, as valued by the Directors	25,757	
	£28,750,037	£38,346,120	
35,086	(*$97,825*) Mortgages and Real Estate (cost $78,489)		28,519
10,200	Office Premises and Furniture at book value		10,200
£12,525,102			£13,119,336
	CURRENT ASSETS		
275,947	Sales for subsequent settlement	£201,062	
567,841	Balances due by Bankers and remittances in transit	373,495	
411,789	Sundry Debtors	375,123	
250,000	Temporary Loans	250,000	
26	Cash on Hand	69	
			1,199,749
£14,030,705			£14,319,085

ALAN L. BROWN, *Director*

C. N. THOMSON, *Director*

DISTRIBUTION OF INVESTMENTS BASED ON VALUATION
(Percentages)

	United Kingdom	British Common-wealth	United States of America	Other Countries	Total	(19 Tot
Governments – – –	—	—	—	—	—	(4·
Insurance – – – – –	3·0	—	1·0	—	4·0	(2·
Banks, Trusts, Finance and Land	6·5	0·9	6·4	0·2	14·0	(14·
Public Utilities – – –	—	0·5	14·7	0·1	15·3	(10·
Railways – – – – –	—	—	1·1	—	1·1	(1·
Brewers and Distillers – –	4·0	0·5	—	—	4·5	(3·
Tobacco – – – – – –	2·2	0·2	2·2	—	4·6	(3·
Food Manufacturing – –	5·1	—	3·4	0·2	8·7	(6·
Retail Trade – – – –	3·8	0·1	1·4	—	5·3	(4·
Textiles – – – – –	1·1	—	—	—	1·1	(1·
Paper, Printing and Periodicals	3·2	0·3	0·3	—	3·8	(4·
Chemicals and Drugs – –	1·8	—	0·9	—	2·7	(3·
Electrical Manufacturing – –	2·0	—	1·2	0·3	3·5	(4·
Motors, Aircraft & Allied Trades	1·8	—	0·6	—	2·4	(3·
Rubber Manufacturing – –	0·4	—	—	—	0·4	(1·
General Engineering – –	3·2	0·2	1·6	—	5·0	(5·
Iron and Steel – – – –	1·5	—	2·4	—	3·9	(4·
Building and Construction – –	2·3	—	2·5	—	4·8	(5·
Miscellaneous Manufacturing –	2·0	—	1·2	—	3·2	(3·
Shipping – – – – –	0·3	—	—	—	0·3	(0·
Gold and Diamonds – –	—	1·5	—	—	1·5	(1·
Base Metals – – –	—	1·1	—	—	1·1	(2·
Oils (Incl. International Cos.)	1·8	—	3·4	—	5·2	(6·
Others – – – – –	2·4	0·5	0·7	—	3·6	(3·
	48·4	5·8	45·0	0·8	100·0	
	(49·0)	(6·0)	(44·2)	(0·8)		

Fixed Interest	6·1	(12·1)
Ordinary	93·9	(87·9)
	100·0	

Massachusetts Investors Trust

34TH ANNUAL REPORT TO SHAREHOLDERS

FOR THE YEAR ENDED DECEMBER 31, 1958

Massachusetts Investors Trust is the oldest, largest, and best known of the mutual funds in the United States.

INVESTMENTS

December 31, 1958
COMMON STOCKS

Number of Shares		Market Per Share	Market Total	Per Cent at Market
AGRICULTURAL EQUIPMENT — 0.7%				
105,000	Deere & Company	48⅝	$ 5,105,625	0.4
110,000	International Harvester Co.	41¾	4,592,500	0.3
AUTOMOTIVE — 3.4%				
90,000	Ford Motor Co.	50⅜	4,533,750	0.3
700,000	General Motors Corp.	49½	34,650,000	2.5
90,000	Libbey-Owens-Ford Glass Co.	97	8,730,000	0.6
AVIATION — 1.3%				
200,312	Boeing Airplane Company	46½	9,314,508	0.7
150,000	United Aircraft Corp.	60⅜	9,056,250	0.6
BANKS AND CREDIT COMPANIES — 1.4%				
160,000	C.I.T. Financial Corporation	56½	9,040,000	0.6
30,000	First Nat'l Bank of Boston	81¾	2,452,500	0.2
147,000	Household Finance Corporation	37½	5,512,500	0.4
17,150	Mellon Nat'l Bank & Trust Co.	154	2,641,100	0.2
BUSINESS MACHINES — 5.1%				
120,192	International Business Mach. Corp.	535	64,302,452	4.6
94,500	National Cash Register Co.	79	7,465,500	0.5
CHEMICALS — 4.8%				
85,000	Allied Chemical Corp.	93⅝	7,958,125	0.6
90,000	Dow Chemical Co.	76½	6,885,000	0.5
112,000	duPont de Nemours & Co.	213¾	23,940,000	1.7
111,000	Hercules Powder Co.	56½	6,271,500	0.4
150,000	Monsanto Chemical Co.	39⅜	5,906,250	0.4
15,300	Rohm & Haas Co.	487	7,451,100	0.5
80,000	Union Carbide Corp.	126⅛	10,090,000	0.7
CONSTRUCTION MATERIALS AND MAINTENANCE — 4.9%				
93,900	American-Marietta Co.	40	3,756,000	0.3
120,000	Caterpillar Tractor Co.	89	10,680,000	0.7
110,000	Johns-Manville Corp.	52½	5,775,000	0.4
149,200	Lone Star Cement Corp.	35¼	5,259,300	0.4
127,500	National Lead Co.	111¾	14,248,125	1.0
50,000	Sherwin-Williams Co.	207¾	10,387,500	0.7
200,000	U. S. Gypsum Co.	98	19,600,000	1.4

DRUGS AND MEDICAL — 3.2%

100,000	American Home Products Corp.	129	$12,900,000	0.9
85,500	Lilly (Eli) & Company "B"	83¾	7,160,625	0.5
125,000	Merck & Co., Inc.	77	9,625,000	0.7
150,000	Parke, Davis & Co.	38⅞	5,831,250	0.4
90,000	Pfizer (Chas.) & Co., Inc.	103⅝	9,326,250	0.7

ELECTRICAL AND ELECTRONICS — 3.0%

164,132	Columbia Broadcasting System, Inc.	37¾	6,195,965	0.4
350,000	General Electric Co.	78⅜	27,431,250	2.0
49,300	McGraw-Edison Co.	38⅜	1,891,887	0.1
100,000	Westinghouse Electric Corp.	73⅛	7,312,500	0.5

METALS AND MINING — 5.8%

423,000	Aluminium Ltd.	33	13,959,000	1.0
155,000	Aluminum Co. of America	93⅜	14,473,125	1.0
155,000	American Smelting & Refining	48¼	7,478,750	0.5
116,800	International Nickel Co., Canada	88¼	10,307,600	0.7
100,000	Kennecott Copper Corp.	98½	9,850,000	0.7
74,000	New Jersey Zinc Co.	27	1,998,000	0.1
68,300	Newmont Mining Corp.	104½	7,137,350	0.5
250,000	Phelps Dodge Corp.	60⅜	15,093,750	1.1
49,000	St. Joseph Lead Co.	31½	1,543,500	0.1
20,600	U. S. Smelt. Ref. & Min. Co.	37	762,200	0.1

NATURAL GAS — 3.4%

85,000	American Natural Gas Co.	65½	5,567,500	0.4
290,000	Consolidated Natural Gas Co.	50¾	14,717,500	1.0
140,000	Lone Star Gas Co.	42	5,880,000	0.4
210,000	Northern Natural Gas Co.	32	6,720,000	0.5
80,000	Republic Natural Gas Co.	32⅛	2,570,000	0.2
137,250	Shamrock Oil & Gas Co.	43¾	6,004,687	0.4
160,000	United Gas Corp.	40⅛	6,420,000	0.5

PAPER — 3.6%

165,000	Champion Paper & Fibre Co.	42½	7,012,500	0.5
150,000	Crown Zellerbach Corp.	57⅞	8,681,250	0.6
227,570	International Paper Co.	117⅝	26,767,940	1.9
118,800	Kimberly-Clark Corp.	65	7,722,000	0.6

PETROLEUM — 20.8%				
200,000	Amerada Petroleum Corp.	103⅛	$ 20,625,000	1.5
110,000	Atlantic Refining Co.	44⅝	4,908,750	0.3
370,000	Continental Oil Co.	63⅛	23,356,250	1.7
208,000	Gulf Oil Corp.	126	26,208,000	1.9
158,000	Honolulu Oil Corp.	66½	10,507,000	0.7
180,000	Mission Corporation	42	7,560,000	0.5
130,000	Ohio Oil Company	39⅞	5,183,750	0.4
140,000	Phillips Petroleum Co.	48¼	6,755,000	0.5
275,000	Royal Dutch Petroleum Co.	47⅞	13,165,625	0.9
222,000	Shell Oil Company	85¼	18,925,500	1.3
125,000	Sinclair Oil Corporation	65¾	8,218,750	0.6
71,000	Skelly Oil Company	66¾	4,739,250	0.3
520,000	Standard Oil Co. of Calif.	59¾	31,070,000	2.2
254,000	Standard Oil Co. (Indiana)	47¼	12,001,500	0.8
791,269	Standard Oil Co. (N.J.)	57⅝	45,596,876	3.2
180,000	Sunray Mid-Continent Oil Co.	27⅝	4,972,500	0.4
527,100	Texas Company	85¾	45,198,825	3.2
134,400	Texas Pacific Coal & Oil Co.	38¾	5,208,000	0.4
RAILROAD EQUIPMENT — 0.4%				
105,000	Pullman, Incorporated	58	6,090,000	0.4
RAILROADS — 6.0%				
715,000	Atch. Top. & Santa Fe Rwy. Co.	28¼	20,198,750	1.4
150,000	Illinois Central R.R. Co.	50⅞	7,631,250	0.5
145,000	Norfolk & Western Rwy. Co.	87	12,615,000	0.9
143,900	Seaboard Air Line R.R. Co.	37⅛	5,342,287	0.4
275,000	Southern Pacific Co.	65⅝	18,046,875	1.3
144,500	Southern Railway Co.	55¼	7,983,625	0.6
360,000	Union Pacific Railroad Co.	35⅝	12,825,000	0.9
STEEL — 10.2%				
330,000	Armco Steel Corp.	66¼	21,862,500	1.5
700,000	Bethlehem Steel Corp.	52⅜	36,662,500	2.6
140,000	National Steel Corp.	75¾	10,605,000	0.8
120,000	Republic Steel Corporation	75	9,000,000	0.6
545,000	U. S. Steel Corp.	96¼	52,456,250	3.7
120,000	Youngstown Sheet & Tube Co.	117	14,040,000	1.0
STORES — 1.7%				
60,000	Federated Department Stores, Inc.	55½	3,330,000	0.2
64,000	Penney (J. C.) Co.	108½	6,944,000	0.5
351,935	Sears, Roebuck & Co.	39¾	13,989,416	1.0

TIRE AND RUBBER — 5.9%

224,400	Firestone Tire & Rubber Co.	132	$ 29,620,800	2.1
175,000	Goodrich (B. F.) Co.	81	14,175,000	1.0
321,300	Goodyear Tire & Rubber Co.	121	38,877,300	2.8

UTILITIES — 10.6%

247,784	American Electric Power Co.	54⅛	13,411,309	0.9
240,000	Central & South West Corp.	58¾	14,100,000	1.0
80,000	Cleveland Electric Ill. Co.	54⅜	4,350,000	0.3
121,770	Commonwealth Edison Co.	56⅞	6,925,668	0.5
90,000	Dayton Power & Light Co.	56½	5,085,000	0.4
219,000	Florida Power Corp.	29⅞	6,542,625	0.5
117,000	Florida Power & Light Co.	90¼	10,559,250	0.7
270,000	General Public Utilities Corp.	49⅞	13,466,250	0.9
190,000	Illinois Power Co.	38¾	7,362,500	0.5
70,000	Kansas City Power & Light Co.	50	3,500,000	0.2
75,000	Kansas Power & Light Co.	28	2,100,000	0.1
125,000	Middle South Utilities, Inc.	46	5,750,000	0.4
121,000	N. Y. State Elec. & Gas Corp.	56⅝	6,851,625	0.5
115,000	Niagara Mohawk Power Corp.	38⅝	4,441,875	0.3
90,000	Ohio Edison Company	60	5,400,000	0.4
127,200	Oklahoma Gas & Electric Co.	29⅞	3,800,100	0.3
126,000	Pacific Gas & Electric Co.	63½	8,001,000	0.6
90,000	Southern Calif. Edison Co.	58¾	5,287,500	0.4
400,000	Southern Company	37⅜	14,950,000	1.1
131,000	Texas Utilities Company	65¼	8,547,750	0.6

MISCELLANEOUS — 3.8%

100,000	American Can Co.	50¼	5,025,000	0.4
22,000	American Research & Devel. Corp.	37	814,000	0.1
25,000	Coca Cola Company	130½	3,262,500	0.2
111,000	Eastman Kodak Co.	144¼	16,011,750	1.1
210,000	Gillette Company	46⅞	9,843,750	0.7
1,100	High Voltage Engineering Corp.	48⅛	53,075	0.0
130,000	Minnesota Mining & Mfg. Co.	114⅛	14,836,250	1.0
78,000	Newport News S. & D. D. Co.	46¼	3,607,500	0.3
	Total Common Stocks		$1,414,328,370	100.0

ASSETS AND LIABILITIES

DECEMBER 31, 1958

ASSETS

Investments at market quotations, including $2,200,278 dividends declared on stocks selling ex-dividend (Average cost per books $598,183,044; cost for federal income tax purposes $598,790,707)		$1,416,528,648
Corporate short-term notes, at cost plus discount earned		2,993,792
U. S. Treasury bills, at cost plus discount earned		13,485,562
Cash in banks, demand deposits		12,013,234
Receivable for shares sold		2,245,676
Receivable for investments sold		53,268
		1,447,320,180
LIABILITIES		
Capital gain distribution payable February 16, 1959	$12,875,511	
Payable for shares repurchased	788,282	
Payable for investments purchased	830,547	
Other payables and accrued expenses	9,629	14,503,969
NET ASSETS at market for 107,295,924 shares		$1,432,816,211
Net asset value per share	$ 13.35	

INCOME AND EXPENSE

YEAR ENDED DECEMBER 31, 1958

INCOME

Cash dividends received		$42,377,528
Dividends in stocks of other than paying companies		144,787
Discount earned on short-term bills and notes		416,107
		42,938,422
EXPENSE		
Compensation of Trustees and Advisory Board including amounts for retired Trustees	$1,082,162	
Research department and general office	571,738	
Fees paid Second Bank-State Street Trust Co.		
As custodian and agent	54,000	
As transfer and dividend paying agent	493,467	
Legal and auditing services	28,550	
Issue tax on Trust's shares and other taxes	24,504	
Securities Act registration fees	6,421	
Printing and postage	126,245	
Miscellaneous	91,465	2,478,552
NET INCOME		$40,459,870

CHANGES IN NET ASSETS

YEAR ENDED DECEMBER 31, 1958

NET ASSETS December 31, 1957:		
Principal	$ 975,139,610	
Undistributed net income	968,484	$ 976,108,094
INCOME:		
Net income for the year as per statement	40,459,870	
Add—net amount for participation in distributed net income included in the price of shares issued and repurchased	383,258	
	40,843,128	
Deduct—cash dividends ($.39 per share)	41,034,978	
Decrease in undistributed income		(191,850)
PRINCIPAL:		
Gains and losses on investments—based on average cost:		
Realized net gain (on federal income tax basis $12,849,312)	12,910,412	
Deduct—special distribution ($.12 per share) from realized net gain, payable February 16, 1959 to shareholders of record December 31, 1958	12,875,630	
	34,782	
Increase in unrealized appreciation to $818,345,604	383,147,282	383,182,064
TRUST SHARES ISSUED AND REPURCHASED—exclusive of amounts allocated to income above:		
Receipts for 8,561,422 shares sold	95,346,185	
Asset value of 1,288,958 shares issued in payment of capital gain distribution to shareholders of record December 31, 1957	12,747,791	
Deduct—cost of 3,024,416 shares repurchased and retired	(34,376,073)	73,717,903
NET ASSETS December 31, 1958:		
Principal	1,432,039,577	
Undistributed net income	776,634	$1,432,816,211

NOTE TO FINANCIAL STATEMENTS

No provision is believed necessary for federal income tax, since it is the policy of the Trustees to comply with the provisions of the Internal Revenue Code available to investment companies and to distribute all of the taxable income from dividends and interest and to distribute from principal realized net taxable gains, if any.

Tri-Continental Corporation

29TH ANNUAL REPORT 1958

Board of Directors

Tri-Continental Corporation is the largest closed-end investment company.

SUMMARY OF ASSETS

Based on market or fair value.

	December 31, 1957	December 31, 1958
Gross assets	$313,268,752	$397,304,221
Current liabilities	9,855,610	5,249,651
Investment assets	$303,413,142	$392,054,570
Debentures, at principal amount	$ 18,060,000	$ 18,060,000
$2.70 Preferred Stock, at par value	$ 40,537,000	$ 40,537,000
Assets for Common Stock	$244,816,142	$333,457,570
Common Shares outstanding	6,721,200	6,891,983
Assets per Common Share	$36.42	$48.38
Warrants outstanding	1,265,660	1,131,185
Shares reserved for Warrants	1,607,388	1,436,605
Assets per Common Share, assuming exercise of all Warrants	$32.82	$43.10

Assets at December 31, 1958, are stated after deducting $2,929,093 payable on behalf of Common stockholders as Federal income tax on undistributed long-term gains realized during 1958.

ASSETS

Cash in banks		$ 1,785,933
Receivable for dividends, interest, etc.		1,454,329
Receivable for securities sold		1,161,148
Investments in U. S. Government securities—at cost (note 1)		4,341,830
Investments in other securities—at cost (note 1):		
Securities of wholly owned subsidiary	$ 2,000,000	
Other securities	203,927,658	
		205,927,658
		$214,670,898

BALANCE SHEET NOTES

(1) Investments in securities at market or fair value as at December 31, 1958, amounted to $392,902,811, or $182,633,323 more than corporate cost. Cost for Federal income tax purposes was $202,672,467.

Investment assets (gross assets less current liabilities) at market or fair value at December 31, 1958, aggregated $392,054,570, represented by (1) funded debt $18,060,000; (2) capital stock $47,428,983; (3) surplus $143,932,264, which includes undistributed net investment income of $229,634, accumulated net gain on sales of investments of $40,709,292, and historical capital surplus since organization January 1, 1930, of $102,993,338, remaining after distributions from capital sources of $1,125,019; and (4) net unrealized appreciation of investments $182,633,323.

(2) Funded debt of $18,060,000 is represented by:

(a) $1,150,000 Capital Administration Company, Ltd. Debenture 3%, due August 1, 1960—assumed;

(b) $2,650,000 General Shareholdings Corporation Debenture 3%, due December 1, 1960—assumed;

(c) $7,360,000 Tri-Continental Corporation Debenture 2⅞%, due March 1, 1961; and

(d) $6,900,000 Selected Industries Incorporated Debenture 2⅞%, due April 1, 1961—assumed.

Such Debenture issues are redeemable as follows: (a) at a premium of ¼ of 1% to August 1, 1959, and thereafter at principal amount to

LIABILITIES, COMMON STOCK AND SURPLUS

Interest accrued and dividends payable			$ 742,448
Federal income tax payable on behalf of Common stockholders			2,929,093
Payable for securities purchased			1,062,993
Payable for securities loaned for cash			175,500
Accrued expenses and taxes			339,617
Funded debt (note 2)			18,060,000
Capital Stock and Surplus (notes 1 and 3):			
Capital Stock:			
$2.70 Cumulative Preferred Stock, $50 par value (note 4):			
Shares authorized	1,000,000		
Shares issued	810,740	$ 40,537,000	
Common Stock, $1 par value (note 5):			
Shares authorized	14,000,000		
Shares issued	6,891,983	6,891,983	
		$ 47,428,983	
Surplus		143,932,264	191,361,247
			$214,670,898

maturity; (b) at a premium of ½ of 1% to December 1, 1959, which thereafter is reduced by ¼ of 1% annually from that date to maturity; and (c) and (d) at a premium of ¾ of 1%, (c) to March 1, 1959 and (d) to April 1, 1959, which thereafter is reduced by ¼ of 1% annually from such dates to maturity.

(3) Debenture indentures prohibit declaration of any dividend, except a stock dividend, unless the Debentures and any other outstanding funded debt have an asset coverage, after deducting such dividend, of at least 200% in the case of dividends on the Preferred Stock, and of at least 400% in the case of dividends on the Common Stock, except that dividends may be declared in any year out of current net investment income.

The Corporation's charter prohibits declaration of a dividend on the Common Stock unless net assets, after deducting the amount of such dividend and after full provision for dividends on the Preferred Stock, shall be at least equal to $100 per share of Preferred Stock outstanding.

(4) The Preferred Stock is subject to redemption at the Corporation's option at $55 per share and accrued dividends, and is entitled in liquidation to $50 per share and accrued dividends.

(5) At December 31, 1958, 1,436,605 shares of Common Stock were reserved for issuance upon exercise of 1,131,185 Warrants, each of which entitles the holder to purchase 1.27 shares of Common Stock at any time at $17.76 per share. During the year 1958, 170,783 shares of Common Stock were issued upon exercise of 134,475 Warrants.

STATEMENT OF INCOME

For the Period January 1 to December 31, 1958

Income:		
Dividends		$11,140,831
Interest		2,424,864
Other income		27,772
		$13,593,467
Expense:		
General expenses:		
Investment and administrative*	$480,135	
Officers' compensation	1,707	
Transfer agent, registrar and trustee	58,037	
Reports and other publications	54,906	
Custody of securities	39,776	
Paying dividends and interest	38,158	
Legal and auditing fees	27,157	
Stockholders' meeting	25,961	
Directors' fees	25,500	
Pension plan	5,490	
Miscellaneous	4,330	
	$921,157	
Taxes†	106,044	
		1,027,201
Net investment income before interest on debentures		$12,566,266
Interest on Debentures		523,975
Net investment income		$12,042,291

* This is the Corporation's portion of expenses of Union Service Corporation, which are shared by the companies served by it on the basis of the relative value of investment assets. Officers and directors of Union Service are chosen from officers and directors of companies served.

† No provision has been made for Federal income tax because the Corporation has elected to be taxed as a regulated investment company. It is relieved of tax on net investment income distributed to stockholders in dividends, and on realized net long-term gain distributed to stockholders as capital gain dividends. It also is relieved, in effect, of tax on net long-term gain retained and designated to Common stockholders in accordance with the Internal Revenue Code. The Corporation has adopted the policy of paying out in dividends in each yeai, when permitted by its Charter, substantially all its net investment income, and of retaining and designating substantially all its net long-term gain.

STATEMENT OF SURPLUS

For the Period January 1 to December 31, 1958

Capital Surplus:			
Balance, December 31, 1957		$73,129,286	
From issuance of Common Stock upon exercise of Warrants		2,851,083	
Long-term gain designated and retained*		8,787,278	$ 84,767,647
Income and Profit and Loss Account, from January 1, 1936:			
Balance, December 31, 1957		$58,631,730	
Refund of Federal income tax for prior year		74,386	$ 58,706,116
Net investment income		$12,042,291	
Special distribution from Tri-Continental Financial Corp.		269,000	
		$12,311,291	
Dividends on:			
Preferred Stock—$2.70 per share	$ 2,188,998		
Common Stock—$1.47 per share	10,082,703	12,271,701	39,590
Net gain on sales of investments†		$12,179,380	
Capital gain dividend from Tri-Continental Financial Corp.		85,000	
		$12,264,380	
Taxes and expenses applicable thereto*		129,098	
		$12,135,282	
Designated gain retained and transferred to Capital Surplus—$1.275 per share	$8,787,278		
Income tax payable to U.S. Treasury for account of Common stockholders—$.425 per share	2,929,093	11,716,371	418,911
			$ 59,164,617
Surplus, December 31, 1958 (note 1 to balance sheet)			$143,932,264

* See note † on page 27.

† The "average cost" method was used in determining net gain on sales of investments. For Federal income tax purposes, net gain was determined on the basis of cost of specific certificates delivered, and amounted to $11,827,669. Such amount included net long-term gain of $11,761,363.

Net unrealized appreciation of investments on December 31, 1958, was $182,633,323, or $76,299,397 more than on December 31, 1957.

PORTFOLIO OF INVESTMENTS

December 31, 1958

U. S. GOVERNMENT SECURITIES

	Principal amount	Market value *
Federal Home Loan Banks Notes 3½%, 4/15/59	$1,500,000	$ 1,501,406
Federal Nat'l. Mortgage Assn. Deb. 3%, 2/10/59	2,000,000	1,999,375
U. S. A. Treasury Bonds 2⅝, 2/15/65	900,000	834,469
Total		$ 4,335,250

CORPORATE BONDS

First mortgage, unless otherwise indicated

	Principal amount	Market value *
INDUSTRIAL		
Am. Investment of Ill. Unsecured Notes 4¼%, 1971	400,000	$ 381,000 (1)
Burlington Ind. Conv. Sub. Deb. 5.4%, 1975 W.I.	300,000	289,500
Commercial Credit Sub. Notes 5½%, 1972	1,000,000	1,050,000 (1)
General Acceptance Senior Deb. 4¾%, 1971	500,000	485,000
Homestake-Sapin Partners Note 5½%, 1961	947,368	947,368 (1)
I-T-E Circuit Breaker Conv. Sub. Deb. 4¼%, 1982	330,000	381,150
Kaiser (H. J.)—Kaiser Industries Conv. Sub. Coll. Trust 5¾%, 1969	800,000	800,000 (1)
Kerr-McGee Oil Industries 4½%, 1971	1,300,000	1,274,000 (1)
Lockheed Aircraft Deb. 4½%, 1976	800,000	738,000
Lowenstein & Sons Conv. Sub. Deb. 4⅜%, 1981	500,000	395,000
Manati Sugar Coll. Trust 6%, 1965	800,000	772,000
Monitor Investing Secured Notes 5¼%, 1986	484,660	465,274 (1)
National Cash Register Conv. Sub. Deb. 4½%, 1981	135,000	206,550
Northspan Uranium Mines Gen. Mtge. 5¾%, 1963	2,377,000	1,806,520
Olin Mathieson Chemical Conv. Sub. Deb. 5½%, 1982	1,000,000	1,170,000
Peabody Coal Deb. 5¼%, 1976	700,000	717,500
Phillips Petroleum Conv. Sub. Deb. 4¼%, 1987	400,000	464,000
Pittston Sub. Notes 6¼%, 1976	500,000	500,000 (1)
Purex Conv. Sub. Notes 5%, 1973	500,000	615,000
Rohr Aircraft Conv. Sub. Deb. 5¼%, 1977	800,000	968,000
Shamrock Oil & Gas Conv. Sub. Deb. 5¼%, 1982	300,000	372,000
Stanrock Uranium Mines 5¾%, 1963	3,623,000	2,862,170
State Loan & Finance Unsecured Notes 4¾%, 1971	500,000	487,500 (1)
		$ 18,147,532
PUBLIC UTILITY		
American & Foreign Power Junior Deb. 4.80%, 1987	2,500,000	$ 1,912,500
Central Hudson Gas & Electric 4⅛%, 1988	225,000	211,500
Gas Service Deb. 3⅞%, 1975	462,000	405,405 (1)
Michigan Consolidated Gas 6¼%, 1982	492,000	533,820
Michigan Wisconsin Pipe Line 6¼%, 1977	980,000	1,073,100
National Fuel Gas Deb. 5½%, 1982	1,000,000	1,070,000
Pacific Power & Light 5¾%, 1987	1,000,000	1,037,500
Pioneer Natural Gas Deb. 5½%, 1977	1,190,000	1,225,700
Tennessee Gas Transmission Deb. 4¼%, 1974	176,000	154,880
Tennessee Gas Transmission Deb. 6%, 1977	489,000	503,670
Transcontinental Gas Pipe Line 5%, 1977	500,000	493,750
Washington Natural Gas 5½%, 1977	1,000,000	1,040,000 (1)
Westcoast Transmission Sub. Deb. 5½%, 1988	500,000	390,000 (1)
		$ 10,051,825

	Principal amount	Market value *
RAILROAD		
Central of Georgia 4%, 1995	$ 400,000	$ 302,000
Central of Georgia Gen. Mtge. Income 4½%, 2020	680,000	440,300
Missouri Pacific 4¼%, 1990	1,680,000	1,260,000
Missouri Pacific 4¼%, 2005	1,595,000	1,188,275
N. Y., Chicago & St. Louis Income Deb. 4½%, 1989	900,000	751,500
St. Louis-San Francisco 4%, 1997	580,000	436,450
St. Louis-San Fran. Conv. 2nd Mtge. Inc. 4½%, 2022	270,000	189,000
Southern Pacific Unsecured 4½%, 1981	97,000	90,210
Southern Pacific (Oregon Lines) 4½%, 1977	400,000	382,500
Western Maryland Deb. 5½%, 1982	294,000	308,700
Western Pacific Income Deb. 5%, 1984	472,000	447,613
		$ 5,796,548
Total Corporate Bonds		$ 33,995,905

PREFERRED STOCKS

Cumulative, unless otherwise indicated

	Shares	
INDUSTRIAL		
Colorado Oil & Gas $1.25 Conv.	40,000	$ 1,065,000
Continental Baking $5.50	4,500	465,750
Grand Union 4½% ($50 par)	10,000	430,000
Great Western Sugar 7%	3,800	515,375
Maytag $3	20,000	1,125,000
Schering 5% Conv. ($30 par)	20,000	855,000
Tidewater Oil $1.20	15,000	335,625
United States Borax & Chemical 4½%	1,000	83,250
United States Rubber 8% Non-Cum.	9,000	1,320,750
United Stores $6 Conv.	2,500	212,500
		$ 6,408,250
PUBLIC UTILITY		
California Oregon Power 5.10%	2,000	$ 193,000
Colorado Interstate Gas 5%	4,000	368,000
Columbus & Southern Ohio Electric 4.65%	1,000	93,000
El Paso Electric $5.40	1,500	157,500
El Paso Natural Gas 5.50%	1,500	150,000
El Paso Natural Gas 5.65%	2,300	232,300
General Telephone 5.28% Conv. ($50 par)	3,500	236,250
Gulf Power 4.64%	500	46,000
Interstate Power 4.36% ($50 par)	10,000	420,000
Long Island Lighting 4.40% Conv.	5,000	642,500
Monongahela Power 4.50%	1,800	163,800
Montana-Dakota Utilities 4.50%	2,000	171,000
Montana-Dakota Utilities 4.70%	2,500	223,750
New England Power 4.60%	2,000	183,000
New Orleans Public Service 4.36%	2,000	172,000
Northern Indiana Public Service 4.40% Conv. ($40 par)	8,000	404,000
Northern Natural Gas 5½%	7,500	789,375
Pacific Lighting $4.50	8,500	752,250
Pacific Lighting $4.75 Conv.	3,000	419,625
Pacific Power & Light 5%	5,600	557,200
Pacific Power & Light 6.16%	5,000	540,000
Rochester Gas & Electric 4.95%	3,900	378,300
Southwestern Electric Power 4.65%	2,000	180,500
Tennessee Gas Transmission 4.90%	1,400	129,500

	Shares	Market value *
Tennessee Gas Transmission 5.10%	1,500	$ 146,625
Texas Eastern Transmission 5%	1,000	87,750
Texas Eastern Transmission First 5.50%	2,500	248,125
Texas Electric Service $4.56	2,000	184,000
		$ 8,269,350
RAILROAD		
Atchison, Topeka & Santa Fe 5% Non-Cum. ($10 par)	70,000	$ 717,500
Southern Railway 5% Non-Cum. ($20 par)	20,000	370,000
		$ 1,087,500
Total Preferred Stocks		$ 15,765,100

COMMON STOCKS

	Shares	Market value *
AGRICULTURAL EQUIPMENT		
Deere & Company	25,000	$ 1,215,625
AIRCRAFT MANUFACTURING		
Boeing Airplane Company	43,600	$ 2,027,400
Lockheed Aircraft Corporation	65,900	4,217,600
United Aircraft Corporation	28,900	1,744,838
		$ 7,989,838
ALUMINUM		
Aluminum Company of America	41,000	$ 3,828,375
AUTOMOBILE AND ACCESSORIES		
General Motors Corporation	100,000	$ 4,950,000
Libbey-Owens-Ford Glass Company	10,000	970,000
		$ 5,920,000
BANKING		
Guaranty Trust Company of New York	12,000	$ 1,102,500
BUILDING		
United States Gypsum Company	44,000	$ 4,312,000
CHEMICAL		
Allied Chemical Corporation	20,000	$ 1,872,500
Christiana Securities Company	305	4,376,750
E. I. du Pont de Nemours & Company	25,500	5,450,625
Hooker Chemical Corporation	100,000	3,875,000
Union Carbide Corporation	28,000	3,531,500
		$ 19,106,375
CONTAINER		
American Can Company	29,000	$ 1,457,250
Continental Can Company, Inc.	70,000	4,051,250
Owens-Illinois Glass Company	25,000	2,193,750
		$ 7,702,250

	Shares	Market value *
DRUG		
American Home Products Corporation	20,000	$ 2,580,000
Avon Products, Inc.	40,600	3,390,100
Bristol-Myers Company	14,000	1,039,500
Parke, Davis & Company	90,000	3,498,750
Pfizer & Co., Inc. (Chas.)	20,000	2,072,500
Schering Corporation	34,000	1,908,250
Warner-Lambert Pharmaceutical Company	11,700	1,079,325
		$ 15,568,425
ELECTRICAL AND ELECTRONICS		
General Electric Company	40,000	$ 3,135,000
I-T-E Circuit Breaker Company	20,400	747,150
Maytag Company	65,000	2,965,625
McGraw-Edison Company	40,000	1,535,000
Minneapolis-Honeywell Regulator Company	125,500	15,154,125
Sunbeam Corporation	39,000	2,583,750
Westinghouse Electric Corporation	50,000	3,656,250
		$ 29,776,900
FOOD		
Continental Baking Company	75,000	$ 3,721,875
General Foods Corporation	24,000	1,806,000
		$ 5,527,875
INSURANCE		
American Re-Insurance Company	58,000	$ 2,595,500
MISCELLANEOUS		
American Chicle Company	26,000	$ 1,189,500
Dresser Industries, Inc.	40,000	1,685,000
National Lead Company	45,000	5,028,750
Peabody Coal Company	57,000	862,125
		$ 8,765,375
NATURAL GAS		
American Natural Gas Company	34,000	$ 2,227,000
Arkansas Louisiana Gas Company	60,000	2,887,500
Mississippi River Fuel Corporation	20,000	752,500
Pioneer Natural Gas Company	30,000	982,524
United Gas Corporation	38,000	1,524,750
		$ 8,374,274
NON-FERROUS METAL		
Anaconda Company	25,000	$ 1,509,375
Kennecott Copper Corporation	15,000	1,477,500
Phelps Dodge Corporation	30,000	1,811,250
Stanrock Uranium Mines, Limited	140,000	262,500
		$ 5,060,625
OFFICE EQUIPMENT		
International Business Machines Corporation	14,700	$ 7,864,500
National Cash Register Company	34,600	2,733,400
		$ 10,597,900

	Shares	Market value *
OIL		
Amerada Petroleum Corporation	36,000	$ 3,712,500
Continental Oil Company	23,000	1,451,875
Gulf Oil Corporation	46,000	5,796,000
Ohio Oil Company	80,000	3,190,000
Phillips Petroleum Company	30,000	1,447,500
Shamrock Oil & Gas Corporation	90,000	3,937,500
Shell Oil Company	20,000	1,705,000
Skelly Oil Company	65,000	4,338,750
Socony Mobil Oil Company, Incorporated	60,000	2,902,500
Standard Oil Company of California	110,000	6,572,500
Standard Oil Company (New Jersey)	93,000	5,359,125
Texas Company	73,400	6,294,050
Texas Pacific Coal & Oil Company	60,000	2,325,000
		$ 49,032,300
PAPER		
International Paper Company	27,500	$ 3,234,688
Scott Paper Company	25,000	1,834,375
Union Bag-Camp Paper Corporation	45,000	1,963,125
		$ 7,032,188
PUBLIC UTILITY		
American Electric Power Company	172,200	$ 9,320,325
American & Foreign Power Company, Inc.	104,000	1,820,000
Atlantic City Electric Company	50,000	1,981,250
Brooklyn Union Gas Company	50,000	2,487,500
Carolina Power & Light Company	55,000	2,055,625
Central & South West Corporation	20,000	1,175,000
Delaware Power & Light Company	17,000	1,034,875
Florida Power Corporation	27,000	806,625
Florida Power & Light Company	125,000	11,281,250
Gulf States Utilities Company	7,000	390,250
Houston Lighting & Power Company	20,000	1,450,000
Illinois Power Company	70,000	2,712,500
Iowa-Illinois Gas & Electric Company	25,000	918,750
Kansas Gas & Electric Company	74,000	3,126,500
Middle South Utilities, Inc.	90,000	4,140,000
Montana Power Company	79,000	5,312,750
Northern Indiana Public Service Company	30,000	1,515,000
Oklahoma Gas & Electric Company	140,000	4,182,500
San Diego Gas & Electric Company	30,000	787,500
Southern Company	165,000	6,166,875
Southwestern Public Service Company	29,000	1,174,500
Texas Utilities Company	85,000	5,546,250
Virginia Electric & Power Company	130,000	4,956,250
		$ 74,342,075
RAILROAD		
Chesapeake & Ohio Railway Company	12,000	$ 796,500
Seaboard Air Line Railroad Company	29,000	1,076,625
Union Pacific Railroad Company	20,000	712,500
		$ 2,585,625
RAILROAD EQUIPMENT		
General American Transportation Corporation	11,000	$ 1,270,500

	Shares	Market value *
RETAIL TRADE		
American Stores Company	35,000	$ 3,675,000
Federated Department Stores, Inc.	20,000	1,110,000
Grand Union Company	50,000	2,475,000
Kroger Co.	50,000	4,681,250
Winn-Dixie Stores, Inc.	33,400	1,494,650
		$ 13,435,900
SHIPBUILDING		
Newport News Shipbuilding & Dry Dock Company	25,000	$ 1,156,250
STEEL		
Armco Steel Corporation	30,000	$ 1,987,500
Bethlehem Steel Corporation	132,000	6,913,500
Granite City Steel Company	50,000	3,050,000
National Steel Corporation	30,000	2,272,500
Republic Steel Corporation	100,000	7,500,000
United States Pipe & Foundry Company	46,200	1,247,400
United States Steel Corporation	100,000	9,625,000
		$ 32,595,900
TIRE AND RUBBER		
Goodyear Tire & Rubber Company	21,200	$ 2,565,200
FINANCIAL		
Tri-Continental Financial Corporation	20,000	$ 17,038,656(1)
Tri-Continental Warrants (reserved for employees)	10,625	308,125
		$ 17,346,781
Total Common Stocks		$338,806,556
Total Investments		$392,902,811

* Unless otherwise indicated, these securities are traded on national securities exchanges or in over-the-counter markets. Values were based on last recorded sales on December 31, 1958, or, in their absence, the mean between closing bid and asked prices.

(1) Fair value in the opinion of the Corporation.

Canadian Investment Fund, Ltd.

26TH ANNUAL REPORT 1958

DIRECTORS

GRAHAM F. TOWERS, C.M.G., *Chairman*

C. T. BALLANTYNE, Q.C.

HENRY BORDEN, C.M.G.

THE HON. F. PHILIPPE BRAIS, C.B.E.

HUGH BULLOCK, K.B.E.

ALAN CHIPPINDALE

NORRIS R. CRUMP

NORMAN J. DAWES

G. BLAIR GORDON

THE RT. HON. C. D. HOWE, P.C.

GEORGE W. HUGGETT

Canadian Investment Fund, Ltd., is Canada's pioneer and best known mutual fund.

Investments

AT DECEMBER 31, 1958

Common Stocks

	SHARES	MARKET VALUE†	APPROX. PERCENT*
AUTOMOTIVE			
General Motors Corp.	66,000	$ 3,148,571.25	2.62%
BANKS			
Bank of Montreal	27,000	$ 1,505,250.00	1.25%
Bank of Nova Scotia	14,000	931,000.00	.77
Banque Canadienne Nationale	8,000	456,000.00	.38
Canadian Bank of Commerce	25,000	1,368,750.00	1.14
Royal Bank of Canada	22,000	1,655,500.00	1.38
Toronto-Dominion Bank	16,000	830,000.00	.69
		$ 6,746,500.00	5.61%
BASE METALS			
Aluminium Limited	10,000	$ 316,250.00	.26%
Consol. Min. & Smelt. Co. of Can. Ltd.	62,000	1,271,000.00	1.06
Hudson Bay Min. & Smelt. Co. Ltd.	40,000	2,320,000.00	1.93
International Nickel Co. of Can. Ltd.	49,500	4,207,500.00	3.50
Noranda Mines Ltd.	43,000	2,246,750.00	1.87
		$10,361,500.00	8.62%
BUILDING INDUSTRIES			
Building Products Ltd.	22,000	$ 858,000.00	.71%
Dominion Bridge Co. Ltd.	46,000	994,750.00	.83
Dominion Oilcloth & Lin. Co. Ltd.	20,000	925,000.00	.77
Johns-Manville Corp.	5,600	283,342.50	.24
		$ 3,061,092.50	2.55%

	SHARES	MARKET VALUE†	APPROX. PERCENT*
CHEMICALS			
Canadian Industries Limited......	15,000	$ 245,625.00	..20%
Du Pont of Canada Limited.......	9,000	182,250.00	.15
E.I. du Pont de Nemours & Co....	4,000	824,006.25	.69
		$ 1,251,881.25	1.04%
FOODS AND BEVERAGES			
Canada Packers Ltd. "A"........	17,000	$ 911,625.00	.76%
Distillers Corp.-Seagrams Ltd......	52,000	1,716,000.00	1.43
John Labatt Limited.............	5,000	142,500.00	.12
Ogilvie Flour Mills Co. Ltd........	13,000	578,500.00	.48
Hiram Walker-Gooderham & W., Ltd.	150,000	5,137,500.00	4.26
George Weston Limited "A"......	12,000	423,000.00	.35
George Weston Limited "B"......	21,000	724,500.00	.60
		$ 9,633,625.00	8.00%
GOLD MINING			
Dome Mines Ltd.................	20,000	$ 372,500.00	.31%
Hollinger Cons. Gold Mines Ltd...	6,000	187,500.00	.16
Kerr-Addison Gold Mines Ltd.....	28,000	574,000.00	.48
Lake Shore Mines Ltd............	22,000	112,200.00	.09
McIntyre Porcupine Mines Ltd....	11,000	1,038,125.00	.86
Wright-Hargreaves Mines Ltd.....	14,000	19,040.00	.02
		$ 2,303,365.00	1.92%
HEAVY INDUSTRIES			
Canadian Bronze Co. Ltd.........	9,000	$ 220,500.00	.18%
General Electric Company........	10,000	755,339.06	.63
Page-Hersey Tubes Ltd...........	65,000	2,015,000.00	1.68
Steel Company of Canada Ltd.....	53,000	3,617,250.00	3.01
		$ 6,608,089.06	5.50%
PAPER AND NEWSPRINT			
Consolidated Paper Corp. Ltd.....	110,000	$ 4,620,000.00	3.84%
Crown Zellerbach Corp...........	9,000	501,993.28	.42
International Paper Co...........	25,900	2,936,052.33	2.44
Powell River Company Ltd.......	75,000	2,728,125.00	2.27
Price Bros. & Co. Ltd...........	43,000	1,978,000.00	1.65
		$12,764,170.61	10.62%
PETROLEUM			
British American Oil Co. Ltd......	65,000	$ 2,567,500.00	2.14%
Continental Oil Company (Del.)...	10,000	608,367.19	.51
Imperial Oil Ltd.................	50,000	2,250,000.00	1.87
Interprovincial Pipe Line Company	30,000	1,496,250.00	1.24
McColl-Frontenac Oil Co. Ltd.....	13,000	819,000.00	.68
Standard Oil of California........	25,000	1,439,601.56	1.20
Standard Oil Company (N.J.).....	35,000	1,943,763.29	1.62
The Texas Company............	6,000	495,849.37	.41
		$11,620,331.41	9.67%

	SHARES	MARKET VALUE†	APPROX. PERCENT*
PUBLIC UTILITIES			
Bell Telephone Co. of Canada.....	90,000	$ 3,712,500.00	3.09%
The Consumers Gas Company.....	25,000	875,000.00	.73
Shawinigan Water & Power Co.....	112,000	3,752,000.00	3.12
		$ 8,339,500.00	6.94%
RETAIL TRADE			
Loblaw Companies Ltd. "A"......	6,000	$ 205,500.00	.17%
Loblaw Companies Ltd. "B"......	43,000	1,494,250.00	1.24
		$ 1,699,750.00	1.41%
TEXTILES			
Canadian Celanese Ltd...........	20,000	$ 395,000.00	.33%
Dominion Textile Co. Ltd..........	80,000	780,000.00	.65
		$ 1,175,000.00	.98%
MISCELLANEOUS			
Asbestos Corporation Ltd.........	30,000	$ 1,042,500.00	.87%
Canadian Pacific Railway Co......	69,000	1,932,000.00	1.61
Consumers Glass Company Ltd....	4,000	132,000.00	.11
Dominion Glass Company Ltd.....	11,000	968,000.00	.81
Famous Players Canadian Corp. Ltd.	25,000	587,500.00	.49
Imperial Tobacco Co. of Can. Ltd..	85,000	1,179,375.00	.98
Industrial Acceptance Corp. Ltd...	65,000	2,567,500.00	2.14
Moore Corporation Ltd...........	15,000	1,361,250.00	1.13
		$ 9,770,125.00	8.14%
TOTAL COMMON STOCKS....		$88,483,501.08	73.62%

Preferred Stocks

	SHARES	MARKET VALUE†	APPROX. PERCENT*
Abitibi Power & Paper Co. Ltd., 4½%	2,500	$ 58,125.00	.05%
Aluminum Co. of Canada Ltd., 4%..	7,000	152,250.00	.13
Aluminum Co. of Canada Ltd., 4½%	5,000	217,500.00	.18
Canadian Celanese Ltd., $1.75 Series	8,200	243,950.00	.20
Canadian Industries Limited, 7½%..	1,600	126,400.00	.11
Dominion Glass Company Ltd., 7%	20,000	280,000.00	.23
Dominion Textile Co. Ltd., 7%.....	1,200	156,000.00	.13
Du Pont of Canada Limited, 7½%..	2,000	161,000.00	.13
Gatineau Power Co., 5%..........	3,000	303,000.00	.25
Goodyear T. & R. Co. of Can. Ltd., 4%	5,140	244,792.50	.20
Howard Smith Paper Mills Ltd., $2.00	2,000	85,000.00	.07
Ind. Accept. Corp. Ltd., 4½% $100 par	4,000	371,500.00	.31
Ind. Accept. Corp. Ltd., 4½% $ 50 par	1,200	53,700.00	.05

	SHARES	MARKET VALUE†	APPROX. PERCENT*
Ind. Accept. Corp. Ltd., 5½% $ 50 par	10,000	$ 493,750.00	.41%
Lake of the Woods Mlg. Co. Ltd., 7%	485	61,231.25	.05
Henry Morgan and Co. Ltd., 4¾%. .	1,200	115,200.00	.10
McColl-Frontenac Oil Co. Ltd., 4%.	738	66,051.00	.05
Ogilvie Flour Mills Co. Ltd., 7%. . . .	1,700	246,500.00	.20
Shawinigan Water & Power Co., 4%.	8,000	348,000.00	.29
Shawinigan Water & Power Co., 4½%	4,000	182,000.00	.15
George Weston Limited, 4½%.	3,000	261,000.00	.22
Zeller's Limited, 4½%.	5,000	236,875.00	.20
TOTAL PREFERRED STOCKS. . .		$ 4,463,824.75	3.71%

Bonds

	PRINCIPAL AMOUNT	MARKET VALUE†	APPROX. PERCENT*
Gov't of Canada, 3% Dec. 1/61	$2,000,000	$ 1,910,000.00	1.59%
Gov't of Canada, 3¾% Sept. 1/65	3,000,000	2,831,250.00	2.36
Gov't of Canada, 4¼% Sept. 1/72	5,000,000	4,787,500.00	3.98
Gov't of Canada, 3¾% Jan. 15/78	2,000,000	1,750,000.00	1.46
Gov't of Canada, 4½% Sept. 1/83	5,000,000	4,787,500.00	3.98
Cdn. Industries Ltd., 5¾%, 1977	135,000	140,400.00	.12
Cdn. Nat. Rlwy. Co., 4%, 1981	5,000,000	4,412,500.00	3.67
Hydro-Electric Power Comm. of Ont., 4%, 1966.	1,000,000	935,000.00	.78
Industrial Accept. Corp. Ltd., 5¾%, 1977 W.W.	500,000	615,000.00	.51
Loblaw Groceterias Co. Ltd., 6%, 1977.	168,000	172,620.00	.14
Shawinigan Water & Power Co., 5½%, 1972.	250,000	320,000.00	.27
U.S. Treas. Notes, 4% Aug 1/61	1,500,000	1,458,274.22	1.21
TOTAL BONDS.		$ 24,120,044.22	20.07%
TOTAL INVESTMENTS. . .		$117,067,370.05	97.40%
CASH, ETC., NET.		3,127,926.54	2.60
TOTAL NET ASSETS		$120,195,296.59	100.00%

* Approximate percentage of total net assets with investments valued at market quotations.
† Investments valued at market quotations.
Market values of United States securities are expressed in Canadian funds at the rate of exchange prevailing on December 31, 1958, 3⅜% discount on U.S. funds.

Balance Sheet, December 31, 1958

ASSETS

INVESTMENTS AT AVERAGE COST (see footnote):		
Bonds	$25,291,983.66	
Stocks of Canadian companies	52,484,761.36	
Stocks of United States companies	5,412,873.11	$83,189,618.13
CURRENT ASSETS:		
Cash on deposit, demand —		
The Royal Trust Company, Montreal	$ 3,086,921.76	
Interest accrued and dividends receivable	875,745.76	
Due by subscriber to capital stock	157,224.67	
Prepaid expenses	5,261.51	4,125,153.70
TOTAL ASSETS		$87,314,771.83

LIABILITIES

CURRENT LIABILITIES:		
Payable in respect of securities purchased	$ 801,298.09	
Payable for special shares of capital stock purchased for cancellation	509.60	
Accrued expenses and sundry accounts payable	16,311.73	
Management and directors' compensation payable	116,225.00	
United States withholding tax	2,203.95	
Canadian taxes on income	60,678.79	
TOTAL LIABILITIES		$ 997,227.16

CAPITAL STOCK AND SURPLUS

Capital Stock:			
Special shares of $1.00 each (redeemable on demand by the holders at liquidating value as provided in the Letters Patent of the Company):			
25,000,000 shares — Authorized		$25,000,000.00	
1,843,828 shares — Redeemed or purchased for cancellation from inception to December 31, 1958		1,843,828.00	
23,156,172 shares		$23,156,172.00	
Issued and outstanding—			
10,804,284 shares outstanding at December 31, 1957		$10,804,284.00	
2,265,651 shares issued and subscribed for during the year ending Dec. 31, 1958 for a consideration of $19,163,976.61 of which $16,898,325.61 has been credited to surplus		2,265,651.00	
13,069,935 shares		$13,069,935.00	
58,952 shares redeemed or purchased for cancellation during the year ending December 31, 1958		58,952.00	
13,010,983 shares outstanding at December 31, 1958		$13,010,983.00	
Ordinary shares:			
Authorized and issued—			
1,000 shares of $1.00 each		1,000.00	
Total Capital Stock			$13,011,983.00
Surplus, as per statements annexed:			
Paid-in surplus	$65,848,073.39		
Paid-in surplus to equalize the accumulated earnings subject to distribution	29,324.90	$65,877,398.29	
Earned surplus		7,428,163.38	73,305,561.67
Total Capital Stock and Surplus			$86,317,544.67
Total Liabilities, Capital Stock and Surplus			$87,314,771.83

***Note:* The aggregate quoted market value of investments at December 31, 1958 was $117,067,370.05 resulting in unrealized appreciation of $33,877,751.92**

Signed on behalf of the Board:

G. F. TOWERS, *Director*
NORMAN J. DAWES, *Director*

Statement of Income Account

FOR THE YEAR ENDING DECEMBER 31, 1958

INCOME:		
Cash dividends	$3,248,877.80	
Bond interest	821,331.76	
Interest on cash deposits	106,037.01	
Stock dividends and subscription rights received, sold	328,188.28	$4,504,434.85
EXPENSES:		
Management	$ 340,280.73	
Transfer, dividend paying agent's and custodian's fees	49,073.77	
General expenses and auditors' fees	37,042.17	
Taxes, other than income taxes	1,949.97	
Legal fees and expenses	7,597.02	
Directors' compensation	81,250.00	517,193.66
Net income before providing for the items shown below		$3,987,241.19
United States withholding and Canadian income taxes paid and provided for		157,542.04
Net income, exclusive of profit or loss from sales of securities		$3,829,699.15

Statement of Distribution Account

FOR THE YEAR ENDING DECEMBER 31, 1958

Balance of income account, as annexed		$3,829,699.15	
Balance of distribution account at beginning of year		1,345,414.29	
Received on subscriptions to capital stock to equalize the per share amount available for distribution on the then outstanding shares (dividends declared are first chargeable against this amount) as provided by resolutions of the Board of Directors		199,963.14	
Transferred from profits on sales of securities an amount equal to management and directors' compensation charged to income		421,530.73	
Adjustment of prior year's taxes		143.37	$5,796,750.68
Deduct:			
Dividends paid—			
Special shares	$4,019,335.55		
Ordinary shares	340.00	$4,019,675.55	
Amounts included in prices of special shares redeemed or purchased for cancellation, equal to the per share portion of income and distribution accounts		3,731.93	4,023,407.48
Balance of distribution account at end of year			$1,773,343.20
Included in paid-in surplus, annexed			$ 29,324.90
Included in earned surplus, annexed			1,744,018.30
			$1,773,343.20

Statement of Surplus Account

FOR THE YEAR ENDING DECEMBER 31, 1958

PAID-IN SURPLUS:			
Balance at beginning of year		$49,635,933.73	
Less: Included in beginning balance of distribution account, annexed		23,810.21	$49,612,123.52
Excess over par value of capital stock subscribed for, not including portion of subscription price credited to distribution account, annexed			16,698,362.47
			$66,310,485.99
Deduct:			
Consideration paid on redemption or purchase for cancellation of special shares during the year, not including amount charged to distribution account, annexed		$ 521,364.60	
Less: Par value thereof		58,952.00	462,412.60
			$65,848,073.39
Portion of subscription price included in balance of distribution account, annexed			29,324.90
Balance of paid-in surplus at end of year			$65,877,398.29
EARNED SURPLUS:			
Net realized profits from sales of securities:			
Balance at beginning of year	$5,162,492.10		
Net realized profits during year	943,183.71	$ 6,105,675.81	
Less: Amount transferred to distribution account		421,530.73	
Balance at end of year		$ 5,684,145.08	
Portion of balance of distribution account at end of year, annexed		1,744,018.30	
Balance of earned surplus at end of year			7,428,163.38
Total surplus at end of year			$73,305,561.67

Index